MY HUSBAND, MY ENEMY

Thalia Courtney

The Book Guild Ltd
Sussex, England

First published in Great Britain in 2006 by
The Book Guild Ltd
25 High Street
Lewes, East Sussex
BN7 2LU

Typesetting in Times by
Acorn Bookwork, Salisbury, Wiltshire

Printed in Great Britain by
Antony Rowe Ltd. Chippenham, Wiltshire

A catalogue record for this book is available from
The British Library.

ISBN 1 84624 038 7

Foreword

I started writing these memoirs in the mid-1980s. At that time I was still having psychotherapy and counselling under the care of Professor Sims, a consultant psychiatrist at St James's Hospital. I was being treated because I was still suffering from the effects of the abuse – physical, mental and emotional – that I had endured for years during my marriage.

These took the form of chronic insomnia, nervous exhaustion, panic attacks and anxiety. I have since been told that it was PTSS, Post-Traumatic Stress Syndrome.

I discussed my writings with my counsellor, Errol, on several occasions during that time and he eventually told me that he thought that I was holding myself back from recovery because of my writing. He explained that I was reliving the past when I should be putting it all behind me, and forgetting about it. Because of this he advised me to stop writing about my past problems. I took his advice and put all my work together with all my notes and records into storage.

On 11th November 1998, my ex-husband passed away from cancer.

At that time, my eldest daughter, Anne and her fiancé, Louis, were looking forward to getting married. This was temporarily postponed. Then, three months later, Anne came to me and told me that she and Louis had now started planning their marriage. It was to be at the end of November that year.

A few weeks after that, Anne told me that she did not want me to take my place at the ceremony under the *chuppah*. The *chuppah* is the canopy under which traditionally all Jewish wedding ceremonies take place. I was to come to the wedding, not as the bride's mother, but as an ordinary guest. She then told me why. I was a bad mother! I had told lies about her father. She went on to tell me that when her father was dying he told my daughters that he had never touched me. He had never hit me or done anything to hurt me. It was all lies, and the abuse had never happened. I had made up all the abuse. I was the one who had lied.

'Dying men don't lie,' she insisted.

v

Well, this one had most certainly lied, but nothing I said had any effect. My three daughters all believed their father's lies.

I told Anne that unless I was treated with respect as the bride's mother and took my rightful place under the *chuppah*, and at the top table, then I would not be at the wedding. Anne refused to listen and Pamela and Ruth sided with their sister.

I heard no more from my daughters and Ruth stopped me from seeing my grandchildren. I was eventually persuaded by my brother to attend the wedding, if only to see my grandchildren. That was the last time I saw them. Six whole, long, heartbroken years have passed since then.

I have always loved my daughters so very much. No mother could love her children more strongly or more deeply. I had protected and cared for my daughters so lovingly, especially through all the traumatic times of my marriage. We had all endured so much. And now they had turned against me, becoming victims again of their late father's deceit and manipulation.

All efforts to see my grandchildren came to nothing, including going to court to get an access order. During the court proceedings, my three daughters and son-in-law produced statements in which they again made allegations against me that I had wrongly accused their father of violent and abusive behaviour towards me. They added other false accusations against me.

I was so heartbroken and sickened that my offspring could make such accusations against me that I stopped the case. This was in spite of the fact that the lies could be proved to be just that, all lies.

After the court case, I realised that it was time that I put the record straight. I had to tell the truth about my marriage. I decided to write the book. My notes and records came out of storage. The law on hospital records had changed and I was now able to obtain my hospital records from St. James's Hospital in which is recorded some of the violence my then husband had committed against me, and which put me in hospital. These memoirs are exactly that. The truth.

Everything that is described in the book is fact. Everything that happened is the truth and exactly as it is described. Nothing is embellished. Nothing is exaggerated. Whatever is written in the book did happen as it was written.

It has taken me four years to write down those events that resulted in my divorce in 1972. I only hope that this book will make my children realise the terrible mistake and suffering that has been caused by listening to their father's lies.

To those women who are still suffering abuse and putting up with violence in their own home, I appeal to you.

Do not put up with it! You are not only suffering now. No one should have to endure torment and fear. But as happened to me, although I believe it is a rarity, there is also some possibility of suffering repercussions many years after the violence has ended.

Thalia Courtney
21 July 2005

Prologue

The phone was ringing!

The phone was constantly ringing in our house. Whenever Harold was at home, he would get business calls. If he was at the office, he rang me at every available opportunity.

'What are you doing? I love you.'

'Where are you going? I love you.'

'Where have you been? I love you.'

More frequently it was,

'When are you coming down?'

I don't think he could have survived without the telephone, even in those days.

The phone was ringing!

I was deliriously happy. We had been married for ten glorious years and I knew this was going to be another blissful day. It was a Thursday, and ever since Harold had joined the company, we had always met for lunch on Tuesdays and Thursdays.

The phone was ringing!

I took a quick glance around my now gleaming kitchen, feeling greatly pleased with myself. My morning's work was done and I was highly satisfied, excitedly looking forward to my regular lunchtime date with my beloved husband. Ruthie played on the floor with her toys.

I glanced at the clock in eager anticipation. It was just after eleven o'clock. Time I was getting the two of us ready to go and meet my darling husband at his office. I bent down and gathered Ruthie up in my arms, intending to put her coat on.

'Come on sweetheart. Time to go and meet Daddy.'

The phone rang.

It stood on the kitchen worktop, so I grabbed the handset still holding Ruthie in my arms.

I knew it would be Harold telling me he was waiting for me. I immediately recognised my husband's deep, rich velvety voice.

'I'm not going to be able to meet you this lunchtime. Something's come up.'

I gasped, put Ruthie back on the floor.

'Oh!' My disappointment must have been very obvious.

'Eddie's here beside me,' he continued. 'Why don't you come down anyway, have lunch with him? He'd be only too pleased.'

I thought I detected a hint of a sneer as he spoke those words, but I was too dumbfounded to reply immediately. I froze. I felt glued to the floor.

He repeated, 'Why don't you come and have lunch with Eddie?'

I stood as though paralysed. I felt rooted to the spot for several moments, with the phone still in my hand, staring at it. This was not my husband speaking. This could not be the man to whom I was married, had been married to for ten years. My husband would not, could not be making such a suggestion. And yet he had.

It was not the change in the arrangements that had shaken me. It was the idea that he could suggest that I should meet another man, alone. Even worse, that I should have a meal with him.

No! This was not the behaviour of my obsessively jealous and extremely possessive husband. To have even proposed the idea would have been preposterous, outrageous, unthinkable.

'No! No!' I managed to stutter back.

'Why not?' He's here waiting for you.' Harold insisted.

Now I was even more perplexed. My mind was quaking in turmoil. That he should be so insistent as well. How could I tell him that the man sitting beside him in his office was the office Casanova, a Don Juan, who seemed to revel in harassing and embarrassing the ladies in the office, with his sexual innuendoes and wandering, groping hands, be they staff, wives or girlfriends of the representatives. It seemed to me no woman escaped his attentions, myself included.

'No!' I insisted more strongly this time. 'I'll tell you about it when you come home tonight.'

I must have stood quaking, as though in a trance, for several seconds. Then I felt Ruthie trying to grab my legs. She was sitting on the floor at my feet. I replaced the phone on its stand, bent down to pick her up, and gathered her close in my arms, cuddling and kissing her.

No way did I want to be alone with that over-sexed associate of my husband's, but more to the point, I could not understand my husband's attitude. What could he have been thinking of to make such a suggestion, that I should have dinner alone with another man? He seemed to have undergone a complete change in his character. To even

2

suggest I be alone with some other man went against the grain, as far as my husband was concerned.

Little did I know then that from that moment on, my life was to change forever. And yet, somewhere in the deeper recesses of my mind, I knew that something was very wrong.

A complete reversal in my way of life, in my whole life itself, was happening, and not for the good. The blissful happiness that I had enjoyed up till then and had expected to last forever was about to end and be replaced by an almost non-stop round of misery, nightmares and terror.

My whole world was being turned upside down for no explicable reason, or so it seemed then. It was to be four long years before all the pieces of the jigsaw were to fall into place, and in my naivety, it was to be the cause for what appeared to be a catastrophic change in my husband's character, in the state of our marriage, and perhaps more importantly, in the state of my health.

Chapter 1

Once upon a time there was a lovely, young princess who used to often think and wonder if she would ever find her handsome, dashing prince. Would he come bursting into her life on his magnificent white charger and whisk her away to live happily ever after?

Many fairy tales start like that. My story started something like that. It seemed like a fairy tale in the beginning. I would never say I was beautiful, but I know I was considered attractive. I did meet my dashing, handsome, young prince, and he did come bursting into my life. He did not need a white charger to whisk me away. The only thing is that this tale does not have a 'happily ever after' ending.

New Year's Eve, 31st December 1953, is a date that was deeply etched into my heart and into my soul. A date I could never forget for ten glorious years.

In those days, there were two main events of the annual calendar held at the Social Club at the Jubilee Hall, Leeds. One was the Christmas Dance, the other was the Whist Drive and Dance held on New Year's Eve. This latter dance was always admirably supported by people of all ages, possibly because of the Whist Drive.

I went to the dance with several of my friends, all around twenty years old. Mum and Dad, together with my brother Monty and his lady friend, had also gone along to join in the fun and festivities, particularly to enjoy the Whist Drive. My parents loved a game of cards.

My friends and I, Thalia Kleiman, were stood in a group at the edge of the dance floor, listening to the band playing. We were particularly watching the dancers, enjoying themselves.

As I glanced across the ballroom, eyeing up the possibilities for a suitable dance partner, I was suddenly bowled over. I was looking at a most gorgeous specimen of manhood. Very tall, just over six foot, with a grand mop of fair wavy hair, he was just so handsome. He was wearing a dark blue suit with a double-breasted jacket. I was captivated, hypnotised. And yet he was talking to some friends. He could not have possibly noticed me.

Barely seconds later, I felt a tap on my shoulder.

Those were still the days when traditional values were upheld. No decent respectable lady would ask a gentleman to dance with her, no matter how strong the urge. At least, that was the way I had been brought up.

'May I have this dance?'

I turned around and stared in astonishment. I was gazing into the intense, deep brown eyes of the very guy I had just been admiring. I was ecstatic, shocked with disbelief. Suddenly I felt as though my feet had become glued to the floor. I was floored literally. Did I show my feelings so blatantly? I just could not believe my luck, that this so very handsome man should answer my prayers, and so soon.

He took my hand and led me onto the dance floor. He introduced himself as Harold Cohen. As he spoke I immediately became aware of his rich, deep velvety voice. I was hooked, and as he told me later, so was he.

At his invitation we went downstairs to the canteen for a cup of tea. He sat me at a table and went to the bar to get our teas.

'I'm going to marry you.'

I looked up, very bemused, in the direction of the strange voice.

'I'm going to marry you!' the guy repeated.

In front of me, at the table, stood an impish looking character with a cheeky grin. Very thin and not too tall, he was sucking the third and fourth fingers of his right hand, these being supported by his left hand.

'That's what Harold says,' he continued. 'He says he is going to marry you.'

He then introduced himself as Cyril, Harold's best friend. He explained that the two of them had come to the dance together, and he sat himself down at our table. Cyril became a full-time personal friend, who played a very large and loving part in all our lives. But he always had his fingers in his mouth whenever I saw him.

Harold soon returned with our teas and Cyril politely left us to ourselves. By the time we had finished our teas, we had become totally wrapped up in each other.

It was getting quite late when we went back to the ballroom. Mam and Dad and the other members of our family there had finished their game of whist and were now enjoying the dancing. I introduced Harold to them all.

The midnight hour was still some minutes away but Harold asked to take me home, there and then. We went to say goodnight to all the family. As Harold did not have a car, Dad offered to let me use his.

He told us they could all go home with Uncle Gershie, Dad's youngest brother, who with his wife Auntie Doris was also at the dance. I had been driving Dad's car on a regular daily basis since passing my driving test three years earlier.

And so it was that Harold and I saw in the New Year, 1954, in my Dad's car on the way to my home in Moorland Drive, Moortown. The next couple of hours were spent in my parents' lounge holding each other and exchanging some of our life histories.

I had already told him that I was twenty-one years old, and had trained as a schoolteacher, that I taught music and singing, my favourite subjects, at Rowland Road School in Dewsbury Road, in South Leeds. I had been playing the piano since I was seven years old, and playing the piano was my passion.

For background, I told him that my father had his own tailoring business, with a small workshop in town. My younger brother, Monty, worked for him on the business side. Harvey, my youngest brother, was still at school.

Harold explained that he had recently finished his National Service in the RAF. He had been a batman and had been stationed mainly in Scotland, at Cambuslang, just outside of Glasgow. He had left school at 13 and then had several jobs with local tailors, mostly as an errand boy, supposedly as part of his apprenticeship to become a tailor. He was now working at M. Brown & Co., a large clothing factory not far from his home.

Harold then plunged into a full and lengthy discourse on his exceptional talents as a salesman. It was to be the first of countless renditions of self-praise about his brilliant ability to 'sell coals to Newcastle', to 'sell ice to Eskimos', and to make people believe that 'black was white and vice versa'.

Nevertheless, I had become deeply besotted by him. I had succumbed to his charisma. For charisma he certainly had. He had great ambitions as a salesman, though in what field he had no idea. He stressed that it had to be with a large sophisticated organisation because he could sell anything to anyone and his talents were priceless. That he certainly sold himself to me, is one way of describing what happened in those early hours of New Year's Day 1954.

In the meantime, he continued, he was gaining experience by working in the company's clothier shop in Hunslet Road, on the southern side of town, then known as 'Neville Reed', as an occasional Saturday salesman.

7

At about two-thirty in the morning, Harold proudly announced that he wanted to introduce me to his parents, there and then.

'What! Now,' I exclaimed, emphasising that it was the middle of the night. 'Why not?' This was my first introduction to the impetuous, headstrong side of his nature.

His parents lived over a tiny shop on Camp Road, near the centre of Leeds and about two miles from my home. It had until recently been a sweet shop, I was informed. Having agreed to what seemed like an absolutely crazy idea, and in spite of my apprehensions about Harold taking a complete stranger to his home at such an absurdly late hour, we drove to his parents' home, again using Dad's car.

After much banging on the front door, a grey-haired, extremely thin, toothless and wizened-looking man answered our calls. Having been woken up at such an unearthly hour, the aspect of anger on Harold's father's face should not have been unexpected. We walked into the one living room whilst his father exploded.

'Dad! Dad!' Harold shouted back, trying to make his voice heard.

'I want you to meet the woman I am going to spend the rest of my life with,' he continued.

I do not know who was more shocked, his father or me. It certainly silenced the 'old man'. Harold then called up to his mother, who was still in bed, to come down.

'What's going on? It's three o'clock in the morning,' Harold's mother managed to voice, when she emerged downstairs, very more than half asleep.

'I want you to meet the woman I'm going to spend the rest of my life with,' Harold repeated.

'Is that all?' his father retorted. 'And for that you get us up in the middle of the night. Couldn't it have waited till tomorrow? Come on Fanny. Let's go back to bed.' And so they did.

It was nearly five in the morning by the time we got back to my home. I queried how he was going to get back to his own home and I said I would drive him there.

'I'm not having you driving around on your own at this time of night,' he declared.

He said he preferred to walk. In spite of my protesting at the distance, he steadfastly refused to let me take him home. Whilst so obviously headstrong and impetuous, he seemed so gallant, kind and generous. I had fallen for his charm so madly, deeply, I just could not fault him.

Chapter 2

Barely two weeks later, Harold asked me formally to marry him. During that time, we had seen each other every day, meeting after work during the week. On the Saturday afternoon, I went to Neville Reed's at Harold's request, and waited for him whilst he finished his day's work, selling gentlemen's clothing. Our first date was to see a film at the Odeon Cinema in town, accompanied by a packet of Butterkist, my favourite popcorn then. This was the first of numerous visits to the cinema, and I learned early on in our relationship that film-going was one of Harold's favourite interests.

Neither of us wanted to be away from the other more than necessary, so my Saturday visits to Harold's workplace became a ritual during the coming months up to our wedding.

I had been helping Dad on Saturdays for sometime, driving for him on his Saturday rounds, around the Castleford and Airedale mining areas, but this now took second place. Dad did not seem to mind. Later in the year, Harold was asked to work the occasional Saturday, selling in the company's shops at Huddersfield and Halifax, so I went to see him wherever he was working. Having asked me to marry him, and having ecstatically accepted, we broke the news to Mam and Dad. They told us they were not in the least surprised, but they felt that we were rushing things, particularly as Harold wanted us to get married as soon as possible. I did explain to him that we would have to get married during the school holidays in any case. I could not take time off from teaching, much to Harold's disappointment. Reluctantly he agreed.

Mam promised us an engagement party to beat all engagement parties. She insisted it would take at least six weeks to arrange, so a date during the middle of March was arranged. I think it was Sunday the fifteenth, as far as I can remember.

We introduced Harold's parents, Sam and Fay. Sammy called her Fanny, to Mam and Dad. Sometime during this period I met Harold's younger sister, Doreen.

Sam, although a cabinet-maker by trade, worked as what was known as a 'Clapper'. That is, he bought antiques at the doorstep,

9

travelling around villages in the Yorkshire area, and selling them on to antique dealers, many of whom had become his close friends. It was through these connections that Sammy obtained a beautiful diamond stone, which he then advised us to take to one of his colleagues, Bruce, who would manufacture a setting, and would make us a diamond ring to our own design. This ring, a one-carat solitaire was made up in time for our engagement party.

We were both very much on a high the whole time; we were so very much in love. Life was one long moment of continual paradise. At the same time we grew very close to some of Harold's friends, Cyril and Solly, who were around us much of the time. But I did not realise then that in some distant way Harold did not seem to like my friends; at least, he kept making up excuses to stop me seeing them. It was not until some time later that many of my friends made it obvious that they did not approve of Harold either, and they gradually drifted away. His jealousy and possessiveness had begun to show itself, albeit it in little ways, but I failed to notice it, so besotted was I with him.

The engagement party was a wonderful affair initially, or it should have been. Mam baked for what seemed like weeks and weeks ahead, making sponge flans by the dozen. I remember the kitchen table being covered by masses of these sponge flans, which she filled with an assortment of jellies and fruits. These were then decorated with swirls of whipped cream, cherries and 'hundreds and thousands'. Mam was a fabulous baker and she certainly did herself proud for this special occasion.

About sixty relatives and friends from both families were invited. The party was held in our home in Moorland Drive and everyone appeared to enjoy Mam's sumptuous tea.

We were all delighting in the celebrations, when we were suddenly invaded by a mob of a dozen or so rowdy, roguish-looking men. My father-in-law to be had taken it upon himself to invite a group of his cronies, unknown to Mam and Dad. They intruded at the table, avidly devouring all the food they could grasp, whilst Mam and Dad and all our other guests looked on with a mixture of horror, anger and disbelief, yet managing to maintain their composure at seeing the party turned into some kind of menagerie, and at this disgusting display of ignorance and exceedingly bad manners by our future in-laws and their uninvited guests.

This was an introduction to the type of ignorant behaviour that we were to experience many times from Harold's parents during our future lives together.

And yet I was so enamoured with my fiancé that nothing else mattered, although I do not think my parents ever forgot that incident at our engagement party.

It was about this time that Harold took me to meet his very elderly grandma, Bobby Cohen, his father's mother, who had not been well enough to attend the party. Harold obviously thought the world of her and he had told me that she had brought him up for most of his young life. On reflection, she was the only first-generation relative I ever met from either his mother's or his father's family. Apart from the fact that his father was born in Whitley Bay on Tyneside and that there were a few long-lost cousins living there, I was never able to learn anything more about both parents' ancestry. That always remained a mystery.

I had now learned that the Cohens were forever screaming and arguing. They were in a perpetual state of mêlée. Dad had persuaded the in-laws to move from the slum they called home and they bought a modern semi in Stainburn Drive not far from my parents' home.

Within a very short time of them moving in, neighbours were complaining about the noise, the screaming and shouting from the new occupants. Rev. Rothschild lived two doors away, and knowing my father, the Reverend went to see my father to ask him to speak to the Cohens, in the hope that Dad could influence our future in-laws to stop their nuisance. Dad was asked on several more occasions over the next few years to intervene on behalf of the neighbours, but without much success.

Not long after the party, Harold told me he could no longer stand the constant fighting and bickering of his parents, so he moved into our house. Mam gave him the small boxroom. He was so happy to live with us until our wedding.

Chapter 3

With our engagement party now behind us, we were eager to get on with the wedding arrangements and to start planning for our future. We had already agreed that the wedding would have to be during school holidays, so 23rd August was chosen to give Mam and Dad sufficient time to arrange everything to their utmost satisfaction.

Harold had frequently been spelling out his ambitions as a salesman, so Dad put it to him that he would give him a job working for Dad's business but that he, Harold, needed to gain some experience of the credit trade from outside sources initially. Harold soon got himself a position with S & U Warehouses.

This involved going from door to door in a particular area collecting payments each week, at the same time selling more goods, mostly of a domestic nature as well as clothing, to try and increase the financial commitment of the customer. In those days, that would be about a shilling a week.

At the end of the second week, Harold came home with the news that he had been dismissed. This was the first in a series of similar episodes that occurred throughout the next two years. Harold could certainly sell himself, but keeping the job was another matter. It emerged that Harold was unable to deal with figures, or keep records of any kind.

He had told me that he had left school at13, and he now admitted that he had hardly been at school at all during that time, playing truant for much of the time. His father had been in the Army throughout the war and had served abroad for most of the time, throughout the North African and Italian campaigns. His mother found other interests and sometimes kept him off school for her own purposes. His grandma, Bobby Cohen, had brought him up for much of his school years. This left him with a huge void in his education. He found he had much difficulty with understanding manuals and numbers, particularly at a business level.

He went back to tailoring at Brown & Co. Dad offered him work in his workshop in the evenings to supplement the very poor wages he earned at Brown's. Dad was no longer interested in giving Harold a full-time position, at least for the time being.

I, too, had been doing the occasional sewing for Dad. When at school in the sixth form, Dad had shown me how to fell a jacket, that is, hand sewing in the base lining seam and sewing in the sleeve lining to the main body lining. I was also taught how to sew in the lining of a waistcoat. This was one way I earned some pocket money, intermittently, until I left school to go to college. Dad usually brought the work home for me so that my homework and my piano practice did not suffer. I was devoted to my piano playing, it was my lifetime's love. By then, I had achieved a considerable local reputation as a pianist.

After qualifying as a schoolteacher at the Nottinghamshire County Training College, I occasionally helped Dad again. Whenever Harold was working at Dad's in the evenings, then I would join him there if Dad needed me. Dad always preferred to work in the evenings after all his employees had gone home, so that he got no interruptions.

It was getting nearer to our wedding day and Harold was working his Saturday jobs, when he put it to me that he wanted to change his surname. He felt that his name 'Cohen' was a handicap, as he had lost several sales when he had given his surname. It seemed to him to identify his Jewishness. He told me he wanted a name that was different. I agreed, and after much thought and after making various suggestions, I came up with the name 'Courtney'. It had, to our knowledge, never been used in this way and it seemed to have an aristocratic sound to it. This appealed to Harold. Thus he had his surname changed to 'Courtney' by deed poll by Uncle Charlie, my father's solicitor brother.

Harold then found himself a position with another credit company. We realised that he really needed a car, so I took upon myself the task of teaching him to drive, at his own request. I did say that I would teach him to drive, initially, but he would eventually have to have professional lessons in order to pass his driving test.

With the £100 I had in the bank and £70 engagement present money, we were able to buy an old Wolsley, I recall. It was certainly a great age, but it had four wheels, an engine of sorts, and it went! Its first reasonable test came when we were invited to the engagement party of a friend of Harold's, Wally Stein. They had met when both were in the R.A.F. and remained close friends for some time. Wally lived in North London, so we drove down. There was no motorway then. The road, the A1 was merely a narrow two-lane struggle for the most part, so Harold took the wheel for the occasional few yards, but he had tremendous difficulty dealing with the traffic in those conditions. His enthusiasm was frequently dampened through frustration, a quality which showed itself at the slightest problem and something that I had to learn to cope with.

We stayed the first night after the party at Wally's home, and then went into London. We had booked into the Regent Palace Hotel in Piccadilly for the one night. The following morning, having collected the car from the garage, Harold insisted on driving. The traffic around Piccadilly Circus was quite heavy as was to be expected, even in those days, but this was one challenge that Harold was determined to master. Outside the hotel's entrance he insisted on taking the wheel. He drove us out into the mainstream of traffic circling Eros. He had travelled about 10 yards when he abruptly stopped the car, right in the middle of the road.

He yelled at me, 'This is too much! I can't cope with this!'

Before I could say a word, he had opened the driver's door, jumped out of the car on to the road in the midst of all the moving traffic, and ran round the back of the car to the front passenger door. As he pulled the passenger door open, he again yelled at me to move over into the driving seat and take the wheel. Once he had so rapidly ensconced himself into the front passenger seat, I drove off. It was to be several weeks before Harold decided to continue with driving lessons.

Our plans for the future included buying our own home. After having looked at several possibilities without success, we learned that small, semi-detached three-bedroomed houses were being built in the Allerton Granges by Messrs Fish & Co., close to my parents' home. We chose one that had already been built to ground level, so we were able to watch it being built stage by stage. We were promised that it would be completed and ready for us to move in by our wedding day. We wanted to spend our first night in our own home.

Mam and Dad put a £200 deposit down for the house and garage. They also bought us a bleached burr-walnut bedroom suite as a wedding present. It consisted of a his and hers wardrobe, a dressing table and the bed. They also gave us the bedroom curtains. At the time of our wedding that was the total amount of furniture in our new home.

We were soon able to buy a three-piece grey moquette lounge suite from our wedding present money, but it was to be some time before we would be able to furnish the rest of the house. Nevertheless we were so very happy, and time was on our side.

Now that I was wholeheartedly besotted with my fiancé and our preparations for our life together, much of my own personal previous commitments and involvements with community interests fell by the wayside.

From being ten years old, I had been involved with one youth organisation or another. Starting with the Girl Guides, I had become the Leader of the Scarlet Pimpernel Patrol. I was also very actively involved with 'Habonim', a youth group, for several years until I went to college. I had made many friends through these activities.

On leaving college, I was approached by the late Gertie Rosenthall and Mrs Henry Hyams and asked if I would be interested in forming a 'Wizo' Group. These groups were established throughout the world's Jewish communities to raise funds for ladies' and children's causes in Israel. The ladies explained to me that there was no group in Leeds for young ladies around my age, and asked if I would consider forming such a group with my friends. I and certain of my friends agreed, and following a meeting in my home, the 'Sharonah Wizo Group' was formed. I was nominated as the Founder Chairman by my friends Nita Lurie, née Galinsky, the late Maureen Port, Myra Solk, the late Ethel Gollem and several others whose names escape me now.

It is interesting to relate that as I write these memoirs, fifty years later, the 'Sharonah Group' is still going strong with many of those early members still with the group, having raised many thousands of pounds. The group has just celebrated 'Fifty Golden Years' with a dinner and celebratory cabaret, at which I had the very delightful pleasure of being present.

A year after forming the group, I met Harold. He refused to have any interest in any of my community activities. But I had fallen so deeply under his spell and wanted to be with him as much as possible. We spent as much of our spare time together preparing for our future lives together, that I, now much to my shame, was very easily persuaded to abandon my other interests.

It was now more obvious that Harold was preventing me from having any contact with my own personal friends, but his jealousy and possessiveness failed to register on my mind. We were just two very happy sweethearts and very much in love.

Chapter 4

August 23rd 1954 was a truly magical day. Mam and Dad did us all proud with the wedding arrangements. Everything went to plan, although the whole day seemed very unreal to me. I felt as though I was floating throughout the ceremony. Under the *chuppah*, in the Beth Hamedrash Synagogue, in its old building in Newton Road, Leeds 7, no one could have been happier than me, with my very handsome groom by my side. Rabbi Dr H. Medalie performed the wedding service, although his words floated above my head. He was assisted by the beautiful tenor voice of the Chazen, Cantor Rev. Copperman who sang the blessings and some of the prayers.

Harold's closest friend, Cyril, was best man. My friend from Nottingham, Valerie, and Harold's sister Doreen were bridesmaids. Alison Sinclair-Morris, Harold's toddler cousin, was our flower girl. Alison's mother, Harold's father's youngest sister, had only recently passed away, yet Alison looked so pretty.

I knew how lovely I looked in my bridal outfit. Gertie Lane, Mam's friend, and an exquisite dressmaker, made my gown from my own design, and it was absolutely gorgeous. The bodice was of white guipure lace, with a linen taffeta shoulder collar, which Gertie had beaded in a scroll design with diamanté and pearl bugle beads. The front panel of the skirt was pencil-slim and beaded to match the collar, whilst the back was very full, pleated from the V-shaped waist with a huge bow at the waist. It fell to the floor with a short flowing train. On my head, I wore a diamanté tiara that held in place a shoulder-length veil. A pearl and diamanté choker around my neck completed the whole effect. My bouquet was totally white, carnations and roses with trailing gypsophilia.

After an hour-long cocktail reception, almost two hundred guests sat down to a seven-course dinner in the same hall, the Jubilee Hall, where Harold and I had met. The catering, by Ansell Addleman, the Leeds community's leading caterer, was superb. The reception and bar were provided by J. Silver of the 'Palestine Wine & Trading Company' of Leeds. We were serenaded by the music of Charlie Marcus and his band during the meal, which continued to play for the dancing after the speeches. It was a very lively and enjoyable affair. Full details of my wedding including costs, receipts, wedding lists and presents given etc. were contained in records kept by my mother, and which I found after she passed away. These are now in my possession.

Many of Dad's relatives had come up from London. Dad was originally from London's Whitechapel, in the East End. His family evacuated to Leeds during the First World War and had stayed in Leeds, but he still had his Auntie Becky and Uncle Alec, with their family, Renee, Hymie and Wolfe and several cousins, Ronnie, Dinah and another sister living in London.

I had visited my London family frequently during school holidays, staying with them and had become very close to them all, so woe betide anyone who had even the slightest thought of missing my wedding.

Dad's other cousins, Alf and Miriam, who had previously moved to Manchester with their daughter Joan, were also at my wedding.

Most of Harold's family came. Noticeably absent were his Auntie Eva, his father's sister, and her husband Joe and their family, who were unable to make the journey from their home in Los Angeles, in the United States.

These and all our other guests had made our wedding such a wonderfully enjoyable and memorable event that Harold and I felt compelled to stay till the very end, after midnight.

When we eventually retired to our new home on the first evening – really early morning – of our new life together, we were both so exhausted, or so I believed, I took no notice of how very intoxicated my new husband was. We threw ourselves onto the bed and immediately fell fast asleep. We did not wake up until eleven o'clock the next morning. Harold was very upset and extremely apologetic at falling asleep so quickly and blamed his heavy drinking. He seemed to find it hard to accept that I had not noticed that he was drunk, as I was so exhausted myself.

I soon forgot what I considered to be a silly matter, and nothing more was said until many years later, when Harold brought up the subject that our 'first night' had been an abysmal failure, according to him. 'Without even a cuddle,' he complained. He still firmly believed that I had held it against him for all those years. The actual truth was that, from the very first, I had totally forgotten the matter and it would have stayed buried but for his own reasons he chose to bring it up again.

However, that was to be in the future, although unnecessary guilt had embedded itself into his subconscious. But back to the start of the first full day of our marriage.

We piled our luggage and ourselves into our 'old banger', with L-plates attached, and after a light lunch of tea and toast we set off on our honeymoon. We had made no definite plans other than that we would make our way down to Devon and Cornwall, stopping whenever and where ever our fancy took us.

We trudged down the Great North Road, which was still a narrow meandering byway passing through every town and village south-wards. We crossed country to the Midlands and found ourselves at Broadway, a wonderfully oldy-worldy but gloriously beautiful village. The Lygon Arms was the only available hostelry in the area, but it was a very old, historic, baronial hall, now a hotel in the grand manner.

Built of stone, with stone flooring, the hall must have been an ancient courtyard, festooned with numerous heraldic arms around the walls which had been passed down for generations. We felt steeped in its history, and loved the ambience.

The hotel epitomised the highest standard of luxury that I had ever experienced. We were both bowled over with the cost when we enquired about the tariff. But then we both considered that this was the first real night of the rest of our lives together.

'What the heck!' we both thought aloud!

So what if it did make a huge hole in our budget. We would work it out, a promise to ourselves, which when we made it, was going to be a belief we were to maintain forever after. Or so we believed at the time

And so we enjoyed the four-poster bed and all the luxuries of that fabulous bedroom, followed by an abundant and scrumptious break-fast the following morning.

Goodness knows what the management and guests thought about our old banger when the porter loaded our luggage into it, but we were too happy for it even to pass through our minds at the time.

We continued our journey south, wandering through the fruit-picking lanes of the Vale of Evesham. The fruit was then in full season with many stalls at the side of the road, selling the just-picked apples, plums and other produce of the season. We lived on the fruit we bought for the next couple of days, and we slept in the car for those two nights to conserve our money after the lavish spree we had indulged in at Broadway.

18

On that third night, we slept in the car in a parking area outside the coastal village of Lynmouth, North Devon. Again, I had driven most of the way south, with the occasional short stretch driven by my new husband. As I drove through Lynmouth, I saw the devastation caused by the floods of two years earlier, and which still remained. I was now aware of the problem which lay ahead of us. I was very apprehensive of Harold taking the wheel again until we were clear of the area. However, he insisted that it was his turn to drive.

I warned him of the very well-known extremely steep incline, one in three, and with hairpin bends, which took one up to the top of the hill where stood the sister village of Lynton. I also advised him that he had to use bottom gear with great clutch control, and that I felt that the drive would be too difficult for him. Nevertheless, he still insisted, telling me that he was as expert as any driver could be in this situation, in spite of the fact that he had not yet passed his driving test. This was Harold once again displaying a persistent feature in his character, his arrogance and overestimated belief in his ability. His insistence and determination meant that I had no choice but to go along with him.

He took the wheel, put the car into the correct gear and started us off, rounding the first bend that took us out of the village. He was then confronted by the sight that I had warned him about. The challenge that he had taken upon himself really struck home. He became filled with a mixture of determination and panic. He could only creep up the first few yards, whilst I was urging him to have more clutch control and go back into first gear. I pleaded with him to use the clutch more, to keep on using it more. And then, after struggling some 20 feet up the hill, the car juddered to an abrupt stop.

Harold tried to inject more life into the engine. The car immediately started to roll backwards, as my stomach and Harold's too, I suspected, rolled in all directions. As the car slipped slowly backwards down the hill, I tried desperately to persuade the driver to use the brake, but he just froze. I grabbed the wheel and managed to guide the car into the wall at the side of the road, so ending that part of our ordeal.

Fortunately, the damage to the bodywork was limited to a few scratches at the rear, but when I tried to restart the car myself, I found that the clutch had gone, kaput!

Leaving the car, we walked back down the hill to the village to find a garage. Fortunately, we were able to find one whose owner was willing to help us out, when we told him we were on our honeymoon.

He agreed to collect and repair the car for us straight away. It still took the whole of the day. Not only had we to wait around for it, but another large dent was made into our remaining finances.

When we were eventually able to leave the village, I took the car up the hill and made for Ilfracombe. We took a look at the Woolacombe Hall Hotel on the way, and sadly drove on. We eventually settled for a very small bed and breakfast, very cheap and not at all satisfactory, but now it was all we could afford.

Nevertheless we were determined to make the most of our stay, and we spent four delightful days scouring the rocky beaches and the sights of the coast, and having fun. Then we realised we could no longer afford to stay on. With only enough money left for petrol and a couple of sandwiches for the journey, we returned to our home.

Chapter 5

Once back home, we knew had to dispose of our old banger. It was no longer safe to drive, so Dad put it into a car saleroom for us. It meant we had to use public transport again, but we had the future and Harold's ambitions to look forward to. I returned to my teaching, and Harold resumed work at Brown's, tailoring.

Two weeks after our return home from our honeymoon, we enjoyed the first of many religious festivals with my family. It was Rosh Hashonah, the Jewish New Year, followed a week later by Yom Kippur, a solemn fast day, and the most serious and important of all the Jewish religious holy days, when we are supposed to atone for our sins of the past year.

Mam, as always, exhibited her self-same talents and generous hospitality, as all the family sat down to a scrumptious meal after the synagogue's morning service. Chicken was always the main course, with all the accompaniments, a variety of vegetables, and *szimmas*, a slightly sweet kind of meat casserole, being the one of the festival's traditional dishes. Chopped liver was the usual starter, followed by chicken soup. The meal was finished off with some highly calorific pudding, and a hefty selection of cakes and biscuits. *Lekach*, the traditional honey and ginger cake, representing the hoped-for sweetness for the coming year, was always served with a cup of tea. Meals seemed to last all day.

We did visit Harold's parents very briefly during the festivals, but never did we ever sit down to, nor were we ever asked to a family meal round the dining table throughout the whole period of our marriage. His parents never made any attempt to celebrate and enjoy the festivals. I never ever felt comfortable in their home. On the odd occasion, Harold's mum would produce a snack of sorts. This was usually a small can of salmon between us with a tomato, some bread and a cup of tea. This we had to eat in their tiny kitchenette at a small folding table which barely had room for two people, amid regular complaints from my mother-in-law that her husband never gave her enough housekeeping.

Harold continually declared his determination to pursue a career in

21

sales. During the next two years he had a total of six very short-term jobs as a salesman. He obviously had a very glib tongue, about which he frequently boasted, and with his charm and charisma he was able to talk his way into just about any position he chose, but he was never able to maintain them. The longest period he lasted was three weeks. After that, each time, he spent varying periods out of work, looking for a job.

When nothing became available, he very reluctantly returned to his tailoring job at Brown's. To my amazement, they always took him back. They even gave him a raise in wages from £5 to £7 a week on the last occasion he went back.

During this time, Harold also made efforts at working the markets. His Uncle Abe, a trousers manufacturer, supplied us with an assortment of his stock on 'sale or return'. We went to several outlying towns, Scunthorpe, Thorne and Doncaster, on Saturdays for a few weeks. All this time I was still teaching. My husband proved that he was a determined worker, but within this time, sales never materialised.

Being too impatient for success, Harold returned the goods to his uncle. He then decided he would have a go at selling jewellery on the markets. Uncle Abe very generously recommended us to a friend, a wholesale jeweller. Again we were very kindly supplied with sufficient stock on 'sale or return', to set up another stall.

We spent several more Saturdays and some Wednesdays working the reputedly 'good markets' of Knaresborough and occasionally Selby as well as those we had previously tried. Yet again, we did not get the immediate success my impatient husband would have liked.

I tried to point out to him that it took time to establish oneself in that kind of business, but as before, his impatience got the better of him. Harold decided to pack the markets in for good, stating that it was not his cup of tea.

Sadly, Harold's Uncle Abe died shortly afterwards.

At the end of February 1955 I knew I was pregnant. In those days, once pregnant, schoolteachers were no longer allowed to work, nor were they able to return to work after having a baby. So I had to hand in my notice, thus ending my teaching career.

We were both deliriously happy and eagerly looking forward to our new baby, Unfortunately, I had a very difficult time towards the latter end of my pregnancy. Due to complications, I had put on a huge amount of weight and developed very high blood pressure. I had to rest in bed. This I did staying with my mother. Lying in bed, I spent most of the time knitting baby clothes and making a Readicut rug for the bedroom.

Harold suffered intermittent outbreaks of psoriasis. He told me that this had first occurred when he was doing his National Service. The irritation and discomfort in his armpits, elbows and groin lasted usually for only short periods as he was treated with certain ointments prescribed by his doctor which for the most part were very effective. Whilst I was pregnant, however, he did suffer a severe outbreak which put him in hospital. He spent six painful weeks in the Leeds General Infirmary.

This gave us severe problems, particularly financially, as we had no money whatsoever coming in, and it was going to be some time before Harold could get back to work. I used to think that it was the stress at the disappointments he had at not being able to secure the type of job he wanted that brought on his skin problems. He was constantly promising me that one day things would change. He was always full of confidence and optimism that the right job would eventually turn up, and we would be able to enjoy the kind of lifestyle with all the luxuries that he wanted for both of us.

In spite of all these problems, they never affected our happiness. If anything, it grew even greater. It seemed as though we could never be more happy. Certainly the approaching birth of our baby gave me more happiness than I could have ever imagined.

I developed acute toxaemia towards the end of my pregnancy and so I was admitted to the Leeds Maternity Hospital at Hyde Terrace two weeks before the due date. I was induced, but our baby did not seem to be in any hurry to venture into the world. After a week of on-off labour, eventually on the 6th October 1955, at 8.20 a.m., Anne Denise Michelle made her debut into the world, a very welcome sight. At that time, fathers were not allowed to be present at the birth. As there had been several false alarms during the week, at the time of the birth Harold was nowhere around. He arrived considerably late and somewhat dishevelled and bewildered. He never told me where he had been other than he had spent the night drinking with friends.

Anne was the most beautiful baby, with a covering of fine black down on her head, which gradually changed into a mop of fair curly hair.

Mam presented us with a high coach-built Hubcar pram, as well as the cot. She and Dad helped us out with many of the accessories, cot bedding, nappies and a selection of essentials for baby caring.

The greatest surprise of all was the washing machine that Mam and Dad bought us. It actually had electrically-operated rollers in the place of the wringing-machine, a really modern piece of equipment in those days. Yes, a very much state-of-the-art for the 1950s and very welcome it was with dozens of nappies that had to be washed every day. The days of the disposable nappy had not yet arrived, at least not for me.

I enjoyed motherhood immensely. Nobody had a more beautiful baby and I enjoyed parading her in our beautiful pram to the shops, and more especially to Mam's, who lived only a couple of hundred yards up the road. Mam was such a proud and happy grandma.

Money became even tighter with having a young baby to care for. Harold was not at all happy at not being able to find his lifetime's career. And so I took to doing knitting for friends to earn an extra few pennies.

I remember on several occasions knitting all day and much of the night, sewing up a cardigan or jumper so that I could deliver it the same day and so collect the £1 I earned in order to be able to buy food for our evening meal. Such was the diabolical state of our finances at that time.

Chapter 6

By February 1956, we both recognised the need for drastic action to improve our financial position. Harold decided he would try developing his own business whilst he continued working at M. Brown & Co.

Taking advice from Dad, each Friday evening, after a full day's work at the factory, he travelled to Huddersfield to the Sheepridge estate. Dad took me to one of his wholesalers and I bought a selection of goods that Harold would be able to sell using Dad's credit system. Carrying a suitcase, he went from door to door selling towels, tea towels and other kitchen goods, and opened up accounts with weekly payments of one shilling. On his first night, he opened up about ten accounts.

During the next few weeks, Harold worked every Friday evening, building up existing accounts and making new ones, so increasing the business. He returned home on the last bus, getting back not long before midnight.

Harold seemed to enjoy the work in spite of the tiring hours. The venture developed very satisfactorily. It was the first time we had both experienced success in any business enterprise so far, and it greatly boosted Harold's confidence. Every penny was poured back into the business. My beloved left the business and financial side to me, by mutual agreement, so I kept the books and did any paperwork that arose. At the same time, I continued to buy stock and service the orders that Harold made on his rounds.

Within a few weeks, we realised that the business had increased so much that Harold would have to work on Saturday mornings, at first for an hour or so. Then for longer, until he was working the whole morning. We had come to a crossroads!

With the increasing numbers of customers, and their need for more goods, a very large injection of capital had become necessary to keep the business viable. There was an obvious need for transport, as Harold was now travelling twice a week, there and back, with a very heavy suitcase. A car had become a necessity if the business was to continue expanding. A big decision was now inevitable.

We had no capital, and to borrow sufficient capital meant that Harold would have to put much more time into the business. Time he did not have whilst he worked at Brown's.

After much deliberation, we had to acknowledge that even with a large injection of cash and a car, there would still not be sufficient business to make it a full-time concern, at least for some considerable time to come. This did not justify Harold leaving his tailoring job.

Harold also stated that in actual fact he had not envisaged this kind of business, the credit business, as the means of spending the rest of his working life. He still had dreams of becoming a super salesman with a large sophisticated organisation.

One major problem still stood in the way if Harold was to apply for any situation of distinction. We still had no car, or means of buying one.

Again, we turned to my father as mentor and advisor and discussed the whole situation. He thought our ideas were very stable and offered to buy our credit round. He proposed that Monty should take it over. Monty had become engaged to Leila and the credit round would contribute towards building up Monty's side of the business. We agreed on the sum of £200. This was sufficient to enable us to buy our first brand new car, a baby Ford.

Harold had now to decide how he was going to go about finding the type of sales position he really wanted. I suggested placing an advert in the local paper, in the 'Jobs Wanted' column. I worded the advert on the lines of: 'Ambitious salesman seeks position with worldwide company.'

It appeared in the *Yorkshire Evening Post* for four nights. We received a total of six replies of which four went straight into the rubbish bin. The fifth seemed more satisfactory. I rang the number given in the reply. The gentleman would not identify himself or the company he represented so I handed the handset to Harold. He made an appointment for the next day. He was to meet the gentleman in the car park of the Broadway pub on Dewsbury Road, on the south side of Leeds, at three-thirty the following afternoon. Harold insisted on me going with him. Again, it was a case of him never doing anything without me. It seemed to me at that point in time that, ultimately, it was up to me to make all the final decisions.

We met the gentleman as arranged. We were not able to understand the type of business this person represented or the commodity that was to be sold. Everything was very vague. The stranger then produced a wad of notes from his pocket and pushed it under our noses.

'This is fifty pounds. This is what you will be earning every week!'

£50! Every week!

Harold and I looked at each other, our mouths gawping wide open. To someone who was earning and living on £7 a week, it seemed too unbelievable. And yet this could be the opportunity that my darling had long been waiting for.

We insisted on knowing the kind of work that Harold would be expected to do. The reply was that it would all be explained at a later date, and a second interview was proposed. We told our interviewer that we would like to think it over, and would be in touch.

There was something very shabby and unsavoury about the whole proceedings. £50 a week was beyond our wildest dreams and was an extremely tempting proposition, yet the fact that the whole interview was conducted outside, standing in a car park and not in an office or some more official place, together with the fact that the meeting was so tenuously mysterious, meant that we felt very dubious about the whole situation and decided not to pursue it.

The sixth and final reply had come from a Mr Routledge. On phoning him, Harold was told that Mr Routledge represented the Sun Life Assurance Company of Canada. This certainly sounded a much more feasible possibility.

Chapter 7

Arrangements were made for Mr Routledge to visit our home a couple of days later for an initial interview.

I pulled out all the stops to put on a show that would hopefully create a positive impression. Out came our best china tea service, a wedding present, and I served Appledorn biscuits, my favourite chocolate-filled wafers. The evening turned out not only to be very enjoyable but also a great success.

At about five feet ten, and of sturdy build, Mr Routledge was an affable, laid-back, amiable, homely person. His persona, to me, was not that of a successful life assurance saleman. We must have impressed Mr Routledge considerably, or at least Harold did. Harold insisted I stay and sit through the interview with him. Midway through the evening, we were asked to call Mr Routledge by his first name, Paul. By getting onto first-name terms, the meeting became much more relaxed and comfortable. Mr Routledge told Harold that he would recommend that he meet the branch manager in the company's offices which, at that time, were then located in the Leeds Permanent Building Society building in the centre of Leeds. Mr Routledge then explained that should Harold be appointed as a life assurance salesman with the company, he would join Mr Routledge's 'unit', with Mr Routledge his supervisor. By this stage, Harold was in no doubt that this was the kind of position that he had been seeking for so long.

The phone call from the branch manager came the very next day, to arrange a further interview. At this meeting, the branch manager, who introduced himself as Laurence Murgatroyd, told Harold that at twenty-two years of age, he was considerably younger than the minimum age for employing sales staff; however, both he and Mr Routledge had been so impressed by Harold that they were willing to make an exception in his case. They offered my darling husband a position with the company as a sales representative. This, however, was subject to two weeks' successful sales training.

Harold was overjoyed. He came home floating on cloud nine. I had insisted that on this occasion he should attend the interview on his own. At last he had found the type of work he had been seeking. His

28

ambitions were about to be realised, and if he was happy, then I was equally happy.

We had both struggled for so long, to make ends meet and bring up our baby daughter Anne, who was by then almost a year old. When he got home, Harold was so excited by his success that he immediately promised me an end to all our problems. Everything was about to change and I would have everything I had ever dreamed about.

Harold gave in his resignation to Brown's. They immediately tried to talk him out of it. He was offered an instant raise in his wages to £15 a week, double what he had been earning. The position at Sun Life of Canada was on commission only. It seemed a very daunting situation to decide between a regular guaranteed £15 a week, which in 1956 seemed a huge amount after what we had been living on, as opposed to a commission-only job with no basic salary.

Ultimately, confidence and a steadfast belief in his own ability as a salesman motivated Harold to take the plunge and follow his ambition to become the type of sophisticated sales representative he had always wanted to be. Feelings which I whole-heartedly endorsed.

At the end of August, Harold began his two weeks' training. It was not to go as he or I expected.

The training was made up of two five-day weeks' study. He was given a manual with a chapter for each day. Towards the end of each day he had to complete a written examination on the material he had studied that day.

On the third day, the Wednesday, he came home very despondent. He told me he could not go on and was giving in his notice. I was thoroughly shocked. When I asked him why, he said that he could not understand a word he had read, let alone learn the contents. It seemed that Harold's earlier problem of not being able to handle figures and statistics had reared its ugly head again. Each day's chapter explained the different types of policies and their varying benefits. Harold found these difficult to understand, but he was completely lost when it came to deciphering insurance tables.

I was very upset for him. Just when he was about to achieve his lifelong ambition, he was so easily prepared to give in to his problem and throw his whole future away. This was the man who so frequently and so vociferously had proclaimed that he could 'sell coals to Newcastle', 'sell ice to Eskimos', and 'make anyone believe that black was white and vice versa'.

I repeated my concerns that he was throwing the opportunity of a lifetime away, but he was adamant that he was unable to do the work. After much thought I came up with what I believed to be the solution. I decided to call in my teaching talents, of which I had always been very proud. Questioning him on his sales ability, I challenged him, 'If you knew the material, could you sell it?'

'Of course,' came the reply. He repeated that he could sell anything to anyone.

I then suggested, 'If I were to do your training for you, do the exams for you, would you let me teach you the different policies?'

Harold agreed. The training system at that time was very flexible and unrestricted. The manuals could be brought home. I proposed that after I had completed the training exams and passed the course, then I could teach him one policy at a time. He would go out and sell that until he had mastered it, and then we could go on to the next one, and so on. In theory, it seemed a sound proposition, but as to how it would turn out in practice, was anyone's guess.

As agreed, I sat down and studied the manuals at home. The first two days' chapters were concerned with the history and structure of the company, which was centred in Canada. The remaining chapters explained each type of policy, endowment, whole life, and their additional benefits, family income and accidental death benefit, all of which were the required type of policies to be sold by trainees. Each day I completed the exam paper according to the training schedule and Harold took it into the office.

Successfully passing the training schedule, I did try to explain the first policy to my husband. Paul Routledge, as Harold's supervisor, took him out on his first week in the field. Paul was to become another close family friend, together with his wife Marjorie and their family.

Success in the field became immediate. Paul and Harold were to work together many times in the future, but it was clear from the very beginning that Harold's sales ability was outstandingly superior. Once on his own, Harold was very happy being in front of prospective clients, but he was having extreme difficulty with the more mundane side of these operations. His lack of ability in dealing with figures, as has already been detailed, could have been a stumbling block to his career. He was faced with the dilemma of form filling and record keeping. He obtained the signatures of his clients on the forms, but as he was unable to understand the life assurance tables, he waffled his way through the sales presentations. Nevertheless, his extraordinary

30

charm and charisma together with his gift for selling brought him immediate success.

Having acquired the client's signature, he brought the incomplete form back to me to fill in, having made a note of the personal details of the client, together with the monthly premium paid. He left it to me to work out the financial details, which would be verified by the company and written into the policy. These details he would then read to his client when he delivered the policy.

Harold constantly expressed his wish to spend as much time as possible in front of his prospects. He did not want to be burdened with what he called time-wasting paper work. So from the beginning of his career with Sun Life of Canada, it was a case of joint teamwork between the two of us, with the friendly support of the office staff. We soon became on friendly terms with the office staff, especially Rose Hardy. She was then only an office clerk, but she helped me in particular, showing me how to keep records and check the salary sheets and to cope with any of the paperwork that was required before Harold took his application forms into the office.

Soon after joining the company, I was introduced to the branch manager, who immediately invited Harold and myself to his home for dinner and to meet his wife. Laurence and Florence were a very delightful couple. We had an excellent rapport from the start. We visited each other's homes many times for dinner, or on other family or social occasions.

In the early months, Harold spent much time cold calling, door to door, in selected areas, which were usually chosen through our joint decision. His success rate was phenomenal, and from there he was able to build up referrals. I also scoured the local papers and journals, for possible leads, which he could then phone, hopefully for an appointment.

By the end of his first month in the field, my husband had produced the highest amount of business of any rep in the branch. The following month he reached the company's target of £12,000 of business, achieving the award of SHR, Senior Honour Roll, for which he won a prize.

For the rest of his sales career with the company, over five years, every month Harold produced never less than Senior Honour Roll. Frequently, he vastly exceeded this figure. On a few occasions he found himself struggling to meet the target, but he was constantly determined never to go below it. Then he would turn to members of the family, or to his friends, usually Cyril, to whom he was able to sell that extra small policy to achieve his target.

As his career prospered, and his reputation developed, his business continued to expand. He would say regularly from then onwards that he was not interested in how much money he was making. As long as he was producing the figures, he knew that the money was coming in.

Harold was stereotypically motivated by money in his quest for success, but this motivation was substantially reinforced within the first few months of his career by an unfortunate incident that demonstrated the value of life assurance.

A 21-year-old local butcher purchased a policy. It contained a family income benefit clause. That is, should the policyholder die within the specified period of the additional benefit, the deceased's family would receive a monthly income, the amount determined by the additional premium. This was in addition to the main lump sum life assurance paid out on death.

The butcher married two weeks after taking out the policy. Six months later, tragically, the butcher took ill and died. His young widow was very pregnant.

Harold requested that he personally deliver the death benefit cheque. He told me at the time that he found the whole experience shattering, devastatingly emotional, coming so early in his career. It became a symbolic point. He learned his first lesson in the value of life assurance, which was a motivation in its own right, and also it became a useful tool to use in his sales presentation.

By the end of his first year not only had he become the branch's top salesman, but he had also become the company's top salesman for the whole of the United Kingdom. For his success, he was awarded the James Porter Cup for the whole year. He also received a silver tankard, engraved accordingly for the year 1957–58, for his personal use. Small prizes had already been won, the first being a Wedgwood table cigarette lighter. Numerous other prizes were to follow, from cut glass vases, to silver cutlery, a silver candelabra and other mainly silver items, during the ensuing five years, to mark his success. These were all displayed in our home with great pride.

With the expansion of his policyholder clientele, Harold found that he was being asked to deal with other general types of insurance, household and motor especially. As it was in his contract that he could not accept other forms of insurance with other companies, and not wishing to turn down this other form of business, although he found it the least profitable side of his business and time-consuming, he asked me to deal with this sideline, as he called it. To this end we set up an agency in my name and I dealt with the clerical aspects. He delivered the policies himself. This all added to the goodwill and service Harold provided his clients, and often produced more referrals.

It was a company rule that any mistakes on an application form had not only to be corrected but also countersigned by the client or prospective policyholder. This only happened very occasionally. I usually completed the application forms for Harold at home, as I have previously mentioned, but sometimes mistakes were made. My husband soon came to realise early on in his career, that returning to the client for their signature could be very time-consuming and costly. Time was money to Harold. He often said that he could sell another policy in the time it took to return to the client for his signature on the corrected document. And so he took to copying the clients' own signature. Forging signatures became one of Harold's areas of expertise in the field of selling life assurance.

I often queried if anyone in the office knew about this, but his reply was always the same, that it was common practice amongst the reps. I never heard of anyone complaining so I just accepted it.

Those were very heady and exciting times for us both. As the business grew and the money came in, so our life style improved.

Chapter 8

Much of Harold's selling was done in the evenings. He did find he was able to call on certain prospective policyholders at their places of work during the day, but most people preferred to be seen in their homes during the evening, after work. I was frequently asked why I allowed my husband to work in the evenings. Was this not putting temptation in his way? My reply was always that I trusted him implicitly. In any case, I always added that I was very happy with this situation, especially as on most nights he came home with at least one policy application form, sometimes two and even three forms on occasions. This proved that he was working. The excitement and enthusiasm he displayed on arriving home with the 'loot', as he called it, left me in no doubt as to how and where he was spending his evenings. There were also the evenings when I escorted Harold on his travels.

His daytime calling was generally to nursing homes, old people's homes, children's homes and the like, selling policies to the staff. I spent many hours sitting in the car outside these establishments waiting for Harold to return with yet another application form for me to complete, or waiting whilst he delivered the policies. Anne frequently came with me when she was still young.

It was around this time that I realised how demanding my husband really was. He had shown this side of his nature all through our marriage, and from that day we had first met. Now his possessiveness was being truly expressed, all the more with his success. I was very happy with the situation most of the time. I was just contented to be close to him, but there were the odd occasions when I felt I should be doing something else, particularly at home. Harold kept insisting that he came first and he needed me to accompany him on his calls at every available opportunity, so Mam came to the rescue sometimes and looked after Anne.

Harold called me his 'Lucky mascot'. He repeated often that he was sure to make a sale if I was in the car waiting for him. Being very superstitious, he also believed in the 'lucky black cat'. He did frequently make a sale after having seen such an animal, but with such a successful sales record, could he really consider the cat to be responsible? On the other hand, on that rare instance when he had failed to make a sale after seeing a black cat, his optimism was never dampened.

Although I myself was never really superstitious, at least not to the extent that my beloved was, I was so engulfed in the web of devotion encompassing us that I supported him to the hilt. He could do nothing wrong now.

Chapter 9

His first year with Sun Life of Canada was so successful that Harold's earlier self-laudatory declarations that he could 'sell coals to Newcastle', could 'sell ice to Eskimos', and convince anyone that 'black was white and vice versa' were proving to be justified.

With this success, we were now able to start providing ourselves with some of the comforts that we had hitherto been unable to afford, and which we dearly needed to turn our sparsely furnished house into a home.

I had always believed in having sufficient money to pay outright for whatever I wished to buy, and I had lived accordingly. My husband had other ideas on this subject, but because of our impoverished predicament hitherto, he had had to curb his more generous inclinations. Now, he started to strain at the leash. Thankfully, he respected my more restrained attitude to money.

The very first item we considered buying when he had been with the company for three months was a television set. We still had insufficient savings to pay outright, so Harold demanded that we pay by monthly instalments. I wished to wait until we had saved the full amount. Eventually, I agreed to compromise and suggested that I would agree to nine monthly payments on the condition that, if at all possible, we would pay off the full remaining amount as soon as possible. We paid off the outstanding debt after only three months. My husband's desire to please me set the pattern for all our financial dealings for the rest of our marriage, or so I hoped. Apart from the mortgage on our house, we never again bought anything on credit.

This was the also the time when my husband reassured me most emphatically that whatever I wanted, however much it cost, I could have it. He would go out and earn the money immediately. He had now proved that he could do this and it was a promise that he always kept throughout his sales career with the company.

Harold's good taste in design of both dresses for myself and of furniture was now able to express itself. Maples, a top-class furniture store, provided us with some of our smaller items of furniture. He also demanded that he had a say in choosing my clothes. Because I was

36

aware of his good dress sense this was no problem for me, and since it resulted sometimes in him buying two and occasionally three garments at a time, it did not trouble me unduly for some years.

Some few months into his career, I happened to be looking in the window of a jewellery shop on Commercial Street, in the town. There on full display was a large but especially beautiful topaz ring. The stone was set high on a gold filigree shank. I expressed my admiration for it, and Harold took my hand and pulled me into the shop. Within moments I became the delighted possessor of the first piece of many items of jewellery that would be given to me by my beloved husband.

I did learn a lesson from that experience. I realised that I only had to admire anything in a shop window and it would be bought for me, whether I wanted it or not. So I had to resist showing my admiration when window shopping, or Harold would be straight into the shop to buy it for me. Such was his carefree attitude to money, and the high degree of his generosity.

Chapter 10

When Harold joined Sun Life of Canada, it was explained to him that the training course was divided into three parts spread over two years.

Part 1, the introductory section, as previously explained, was completed by myself.

Part 2 had to be completed at the end of the first year. Part 3 had to be completed at the end of the second year. Until all three parts were completed, sales agents were regarded as trainees.

In spite of his tremendous success in the field, Harold still failed to master the use of his manuals, figures and the use of figures in general. This situation continued throughout his years with the company. So again, I came to Harold's rescue and repeated our earlier arrangement, completing all his exams successfully. Failure to pass the whole course would have resulted in him having to leave the company, regardless of his outstanding sales record.

Part 2 dealt with the taxation system with regard to life assurance premiums. The tax relief on premiums, which was the rule at that time, confused my husband. Rose Hardy, in the office, was a solid rock of support and thought the world of him in spite of his difficulties. She helped him to deal with them by trying to clarify the taxation system to him, but also realised his shortcomings.

Mortgage endowments were also a constituent of Part 2. These Harold seemed more able to absorb and understand. He was then more successful in being able to add them to his sales repertoire.

Pension schemes formed the main substance of Part 3. I found it quite difficult initially to understand the many and varied and what seemed at first complicated clauses that made up a pension scheme. So I had no doubts that Harold would find it even more arduous for him to take in all the details.

In the late 1950s, the main purchasers of pension schemes were business executives and the professional classes. This type of prospect always needed to have every clause explained explicitly from the start. Negotiations were usually long, requiring several interviews to complete a sale.

Harold soon learned that he could not waffle his way through a sales presentation. Having failed to make a sale with his first two prospects, he realised his limitations and decided to concentrate on selling the more straightforward forms of life assurance. He never ever sold a pension plan during the whole time he was with the company.

Working together seemed to bring us even closer. Harold showed his appreciation for the contribution I made to his success by constantly singing my praises to the other representatives in the offices, as well as to the office staff. I frequented the office regularly and was always made especially welcome. It was obvious that everyone knew how I helped with my husband's career. It made me feel as though I was one of the staff.

No one could have felt prouder of her husband than me. I was to see him going from strength to strength over the next few years.

Harold kept the three sets of training manuals with the completed exam papers at home. He proudly showed them to family and friends as well as our visitors, constantly boasting about the contribution his wife had made to his success.

Chapter 11

Branch meetings were held once a month throughout the year. There were also the annual celebrations for representatives and their wives held around Christmas time. As Harold wished, I always tried to make a point of calling into the office with Anne after the monthly meetings. This gave me the opportunity to meet and chat with the other salesmen, as well as getting to know the office staff.

By the end of his first full year, Harold had become the idol of the branch, not just because of his tremendous sales record – but also because he had broken several sales targets – already his charismatic charm captivated whoever he met. Everyone fell under his spell, no one more so than Rose Hardy, who had yet to be promoted to office manager. She became Harold's mentor as well as being a close family friend.

Whether it was known to the executives at head office in London of my contribution to Harold's achievements at that stage, I was not sure until some time later.

Sometimes one or other of the reps would commend me for my work and the support I gave my husband. It was then I started to become aware that when ever I was in conversation with any of his colleagues, my husband would be watching me with extreme intensity, his deep, penetrating eyes glaring at me. Then he would come over and, grabbing my elbow, would steer me away. He nevertheless always remained cool and charming.

Later in the year, we started our twice-weekly ritual of going across the road to the Guildford Hotel in the Headrow for lunch. Each Tuesday and Thursday, like clockwork for the remainder of Harold's career as a salesman in Leeds, we would have lunch usually with our children, the exception being when we were away. We had our regular table with the same two waitresses.

Mam and Dad had also been meeting every Tuesday and Thursday, but at teatime, ever since Dad bought his own business in 1946. I used to sometimes meet Mam in town after school. After shopping we then met Dad for tea, initially at Schofield's department store cafe, and then at Matthias Robinson's. This ritual I resumed after leaving

college and starting to teach. Once married, I occasionally met up with my parents in town for tea, time permitting.

When Anne came along, I still managed to join my parents for tea on the odd occasion. It was always Mam's pleasure to buy Anne an ice cream when she was shopping in Leeds market before meeting my father.

Auntie Julia, Mam's sister, and her husband Uncle Ike, also met us regularly for a family teatime gathering.

Of course, Harold usually made a point of joining us, if I went to the café. I did not have a car until Harold had been with the company for a couple of years, so I used mostly public transport, unless Dad let me use his car from time to time. If Dad needed his car then Harold would give Mam and myself a lift home. There was, however, generally a snag! We were advised by Harold that he had to make a call on the way home, to deliver a policy or for some other business purpose.

'It will only take a minute,' we were always promised.

Never did any call ever only take a minute. I spent many an hour waiting in the car on the way home with whomsoever we were giving a lift to, if anyone. This often resulted in getting home way past Anne's bedtime. This waiting was in addition to the daytime waiting I did accompanying Harold on his calls.

Such were the vicissitudes of being the happy, loving wife of a successful life assurance salesman.

Chapter 12

The head office of the Sun Life Assurance Company of Canada was situated in Cockspur Street, London and overlooked Trafalgar Square. The chief executive and chairman at that time was Jack Brindle, a very amiable and charming gentleman. For someone in his position, I always found him to be pleasantly relaxed and easily approachable. His vice-chairman, Alan Kemp, to me seemed to be a more traditionally conservative type of person, with a very sharp wit. He was responsible for the financial affairs of the whole company.

These two gentlemen toured all the branches with regular frequency. I had met them both in the Leeds office a few months previously. Sometime at the beginning of Harold's second year, I had gone into the office as usual and as I was wont to do for Harold, after a branch meeting, and had met up with the two executives once more.

Harold and I had got into conversation with the two visiting executives, who were congratulating my husband on his performance thus far. Alan Kemp then brought up the subject of our accounting system. Mr Brindle wondered whether in view of Harold's continuing success, his increasing income, and he was now starting to accumulate renewal income, which was certain to increase, we had done anything about getting an accountant to sort out our tax affairs.

Up to that point, I had to confess, I had not given the matter any thought, although I had been keeping careful records of the salary sheets. Every commission sheet, which we received monthly, gave full details of every payment.

Alan Kemp suggested to us that we ought to have the very best accountant. This idea was endorsed by Jack Brindle. He then went on to advise us of the company's accountant who, Jack told us, would be only too pleased to help us. They would arrange an introduction for us.

Harold immediately informed them that I was responsible for the bookkeeping and that the decision was up to me. We were then told that the accountant, Bill Smith, lived in Croydon on the south side of London. This would mean a trip to Croydon to discuss the possibilities. The two executives told us that they thought it would be a wise move in spite of the distance.

Having been advised to give the idea some thought, though it did seem to me at the time a sensible and necessary step, we did decide to follow up the suggestion after a little consideration. How much better could we do than to have the company's accountant as our own financial taxation advisor? The only apparent obstacle would be the distance.

We decided to phone Mr Smith and sound him out. He had already been informed about us, so we were pleasantly surprised to be told that our phone call had been awaited.

Harold made the initial call, and as had become something of a habit, he told Mr Smith that I, his wife, dealt with the records and bookkeeping. We were then invited to go down to Croydon and made arrangements to do so the following week.

Ten days later saw us driving down the old A1 route to London, once again. It took us several hours, allowing for meal breaks and hygiene purposes. We still had to drive through central London to get to the southern town of Croydon, so it was late afternoon when we finally arrived at our destination. Mr Smith suggested we stay at the inn in the High Street.

We invited Mr Smith to join us for dinner at our hotel. We got on very well from the start, and had a very enjoyable meal. We were invited to call our new friend by his first name. Bill explained that once he had shown us the bookkeeping system he wanted us to use, all our affairs could be transacted either by post or via the phone. It would only be on very rare occasions, a crisis or suchlike, that we would be expected to go down to Croydon.

Everything seemed to be satisfactory at that stage, and we accepted Bill's invitation to go to his home the following morning so that he could explain the bookkeeping system he wished us to use.

When at Bill's home, Harold once more made it clear that he had no wish to be concerned with this aspect of his work. Bill had already prepared some books for me and he carefully explained them to me, going through the various columns and describing their use. He made it seem so easy and straightforward.

We then made an arrangement that had been well advised and was to prove beneficial to us all over the next few years. Jack Brindle and Alan Kemp had spoken very highly of Harold and his work. My husband and I were to be deeply grateful to them both for recommending Bill Smith as our accountant.

Chapter 13

Laurence Murgatroyd was manager at the Leeds branch for only a short time after Harold joined the company. He and his wife Florence retired to live down south in Bournemouth. Despite the short time we had known them, we knew that we would miss them.

Their successors, Jimmy Johnson and his wife Maxie, were entirely different personalities. Both were very tall with imposing appearances and were considerably younger than their predecessors, somewhere in their mid-forties. Jimmy was over 6 feet tall, slim and with a mop of grey, almost white hair. Maxie was almost as tall. With jet-black hair, she was very attractive, and very bubbly and effervescent. She constantly kept us amused with her antics, certainly when she was in our company. They were an extremely charismatic couple.

They bought a large residence at Bond End, at Knaresborough, just north of Leeds, to which we and other representatives with their wives were frequently invited. They were avid partygoers.

Whenever we had been invited to the previous manager's home, it was always on a formal basis, for dinner. Their style was typically conservative.

Jimmy and Maxie were a very much more laid-back couple. But in spite of their apparently casual attitude, Jimmy soon commanded great respect with much love. He developed a good rapport with both the representatives and the office staff, and particularly with Harold. Sales production increased significantly under the new management.

Harold had become an avid student of Frank Betger and Dale Carnegie. Both Americans, they had achieved tremendous success selling life assurance. They had written books on self-motivation, sales techniques and means of achieving happiness through successful sales.

These writings inspired Harold. He was now giving the occasional talk at the monthly branch meetings. I prepared these for him from the material he gave me, and which were often based on these books. It was becoming more noticeable that Jimmy Johnson was looking to Harold as his right-hand man.

The more successful Harold became, the more he relied on me for active help, such as writing his speeches, something that I was always happy to do. It seemed to bring us even closer.

Those were very happy and fulfilling times for both of us.

Chapter 14

On 4th March 1957, my brother Monty married his sweetheart Leila. This celebration was an event which added to our and all the family's happiness.

The *chuppah* ceremony was held at the same synagogue as our wedding, and brought back happy memories. The festivities were held at Addleman's Hotel in Brunswick Street near the centre of Leeds. The hotel was owned by the same people who had so successfully catered our wedding.

I always remember Anne almost carrying the day. She was only seventeen months old, too young to take part, but she looked absolutely stunning in a canary-yellow organza dress. It had a very full, quilted skirt, and with her fair shoulder-length hair, she looked an absolute picture.

Almost a year previously, on 26th May 1956, Mam and Dad had held their silver wedding anniversary at the same venue.

Shortly after Monty's wedding, we joined in the celebrations of Harold's best friend, Cyril, on the occasion of his marriage to Chana. When I reminisce at the extent of our social life, I wonder how Harold found the time to work, or how I managed to keep up with him.

My husband now found it practically impossible to stay in on the nights he did not work, unless we had invited company. Entertaining friends at home or elsewhere became to him a means of cultivating more business.

I always enjoyed having friends in my home. On those nights, we usually ended up having supper at one or two o'clock in the morning, with me frying *vorsht*, a type of salami, and eggs with chips. Alternatively, Harold would arrive home in the evening with his mother, telling me to get ready to go out as he had made arrangements for us.

Harold strongly believed that behaving successfully and living successfully, that is, going to the best restaurants and creating the right impression, was necessary to achieve success. It certainly worked for him.

However, as time went by, I came to realise that this idea of Harold entertaining and cultivating friendships was all one-sided. Whilst concentrating on his own friends and making new ones from among his clientele, none of my friends were ever approached for business. Whenever I did suggest someone, he found an excuse not to contact him or her. It was as though they did not exist.

Towards the end of 1957, with Monty now married and only Harvey remaining at home, Mam and Dad decided to move into a smaller house. They had a three-bedroomed detached bungalow built in High Moor Avenue which they were able to move into in the early summer of 1958.

My parents now lived a further half mile or so away, along Street Lane. This meant a slightly longer walk with Anne in the pushchair on occasions, but as I now had my own car, our life style reflected Harold's continuing and increasing success with Sun Life of Canada.

Chapter 15

During 1957, not long after Monty's wedding, my Uncle Sam, my mother's eldest brother, and his wife Auntie Sophie celebrated their golden wedding anniversary. This was held at the prestigious five-star Queen's Hotel in the town.

Prior to the occasion, my parents had received their invitations, but it was only for themselves. Their children, Monty, Harvey and myself, had not been invited. Mam was very upset about this and refused to go without her children.

My mother had had a chip on her shoulder about her brother Uncle Sam for as long as I could remember, and this only reinforced her feelings. She always believed Uncle Sam treated her badly.

My grandfather, Tevya, passed away when Mam was only sixteen years old. She was the youngest child. Her brother Sam was twenty years older, and the eldest of five boys. Auntie Julia, her sister, although always close to my mother, was ten years her senior. Mam was left to look after her mother.

At that time, my grandparents had a grocery shop on Camp Road, near the centre of the town, but in the heart of the Jewish community at that time. Uncle Sam had a very successful clothing business, Alexandre. According to my mother, the family came to an arrangement whereby my mother would look after her mother at home, and Uncle Sam would pay her a weekly income. This continued as far as I know until my parents married. My grandmother continued to live with them until her death some four years later.

My mother often told me this story, complaining that Uncle Sam only paid her a pittance, insufficient considering Uncle Sam's own financial status. My father worked for Uncle Sam as his factory manager until he bought his own business in 1946. He had worked at the factory for some time before meeting his wife-to-be. My mother complained that Dad was treated badly there and was poorly paid. It seemed that Mam was ready to find fault with her brother at the slightest provocation.

Her children not being invited to her brother's celebration fuelled her resentment against him. Mam was a very stubborn and extremely

48

strong-willed woman. She refused to have anything further to do with her brother, so she said, despite our exhortations that none of us really cared that we were not invited.

My husband had always regarded himself as the epitomy of diplomacy and charm, and that he could sweet-talk anyone into doing anything he wanted. He offered to speak to Uncle Sam. Harold told us that he just wanted to make peace in the family.

I accompanied Harold round to Perlevere Court, my relatives' home, and true to his word he sorted the whole matter out to the satisfaction of my mother, who ultimately agreed to go with her family to the celebrations. My uncle's business had by then grown into becoming part of a national enterprise, United Drapery Stores Ltd, and he was well known in Leeds as a leading philanthropist.

The celebrations proved to be as opulent as was to be expected, and were most enjoyable. Harold certainly enjoyed himself. He had endeared himself even more to my mother in view of his success with Uncle Sam, and he found he had a drinking partner in his mother-in-law. Together they really let their hair down. I had never liked alcoholic drink. Harold would inform any company that we were with that I did not need drink to enjoy myself, but it became more and more noticeable with each family event that to Harold, drink was the essence of enjoyment. The occasion was a success for my mother, thanks to her son-in-law, and one that was to be remembered for some time.

Chapter 16

Those years in the second half of the 1950s were indeed blissfully happy ones for both of us. Harold's success, however, seemed to bring out the darker aspects of his character, but I either failed to recognise them as negative ones, or I simply overlooked them, so besotted was I with the man.

Sometimes, I think I preferred to believe his success acted as a whitewash to this other side of his nature. I even thought that this was his way of demonstrating how deeply he loved me.

Harold never carried keys to our home, as I was always expected to be at home if I had not gone out with him. With a job such as his that involved irregular hours, this occasionally presented problems, particularly during the day.

Other than the local shops, the only other place I could visit was my parents' home, or to meet them elsewhere, as when I had tea with them in town. Sometimes it was not always possible to time my return home accurately to be there before my husband, but I always tried to do my best, which I am sure Harold realised, but he insisted in the belief that the number one person in the household was the husband, and the wife was there to serve her husband.

There was one occasion when he actually let me go out without him, albeit reluctantly. Knowing my love of the theatre and especially musical programmes, a love not shared by my husband, Rose Hardy asked if I would like to go with her to see a performance of the ballet *Swan Lake*, at the Grand Theatre. I had anticipated Harold making some excuse to prevent me going. He never actually said outright I was not to go anywhere, but was very good at making vague excuses as to why I could not.

I always assumed, whether correctly or not I never knew, that he felt that as it was Rose Hardy, someone from the office, who had invited me to accompany her, to prevent me going was inappropriate. I happily accepted Rose's invitation. It made a very pleasant change.

That Harold considered himself, the husband, as coming first before anyone else in the family was a very old-fashioned idea, but as I have already recounted, Harold was a very possessive and jealous husband.

I believe that his success caused these traits to exacerbate over the years. Again, I saw these as his way of demonstrating his feelings for me. I did not see any problems there, at least not for a long time.

When I was visiting my mother, he would phone me there frequently as though checking up on me to see if I was where I said I would be. Whenever he found the line engaged, as happened sometimes, when Mam or any other person in the household could be gossiping, he resorted to what became a regular habit.

In those days, the telephone switchboard was manually operated from the town's central telephone exchange. When finding the line engaged, Harold dialled the operator, and then with his usual glib tongue would plead the most dire emergency that made it extremely imperative that he speak to his wife, and would the operator kindly interrupt the line so that he can speak to me at once. The operator always complied with his demands, to his great satisfaction.

The first few times Harold used this ruse it gave whoever was interrupted using the phone a great shock, such was the urgency that was explained by the operator, after having heard Harold's dramatic pleadings. But as this became a regular habit, we got used to it. In fact, whenever I was at Mam's, we were almost always expecting a call of this nature. It became a family joke. Harold's impatience was ably exhibited. He admitted frequently to being an impatient man. This behaviour he denied being impatience. He explained it by announcing that he was saving time. 'Time was money', was a favourite cliché of his.

At that time, it never occurred to me, or possibly to the other members of my family that in truth all Harold's fabrications were just that, lies. He was lying through his teeth, and really enjoying it. And so his charismatic plausibility continued to draw my love and admiring devotion.

Chapter 17

The company held its national sales conference every two years during the summer. It was held at one of the major south coast seaside resorts, taking over three or four of the town's top most prestigious hotels. The conference itself was usually held in the town's conference centre, and was a five-day affair, Monday to Friday.

Attendance at the conference was dependent upon each salesman's performance. The minimum qualification was 12 Honour Rolls during the preceding year. An Honour Roll meant at least £6,000 worth of production per month. A Senior Honour Roll, £12,000 worth of business minimum each month for·the preceding 12 months, entitled a salesman to take his wife with him.

The conference in 1958, to be held in Bournemouth, was the first conference my husband was to attend. As he had completed a non-stop record of Senior Honour Rolls from the second month of his appointment with the company, my presence at the side of my husband at the conference became a foregone conclusion and a matter of great pride. His sales record was an outstanding achievement by company standards, and one that was rarely attained. Harold had promised from the start that no way would he attend the conference without me, so that once we were given the official confirmation, and that he would be taking me, we were overjoyed. Sometimes the excitement seemed too much for us, especially as Harold, as one of the few top producers in the company would have a place of honour.

The excitement was exacerbated when my sweetheart was asked to address the company at one of the sessions, the subject being: 'How I achieved my success in such a short time'. We now had so much to look forward to. The conference, due to be held in the first week of July, gave us about three months to prepare.

We had been advised that the event was always a very glitzy affair, particularly for the wives, with the evening entertainment, and a glamorous ball held on the final night.

I designed myself what I considered to be a special ballgown. The basic dress was simple, it had a deep, square neckline and a straight full-length pencil-slim skirt. The separate very full overskirt had a hemline that extended into a train, a foot longer than the dress. It fastened over the dress at the waist with a belt of the same material. The material I chose was a fairly heavy, deep rich red brocade, embossed with a scroll pattern in the same colour and with a very fine gold thread running through. The overskirt had a deep rich plain red satin lining.

I felt very proud of my design, as I knew it would look sensational made up. Mrs Lane, Mam's friend, who had made my wedding dress, agreed to make it for me.

The next few weeks were quite hectic. I wanted everything to be just right. As always, Harold insisted on accompanying me on our shopping sprees, even when he was supposed to be working.

At the same time, I believed I had another good reason for celebration. Eight weeks before the conference, I thought I could be pregnant again.

There was, in those days, no means of confirming one's pregnancy so early. Contraceptive tests and scans were still a thing of the future, so I had to wait another month, when I was able to have my pregnancy confirmed by the gynaecologist, Mr Agar, under whose care I had been when I was having Anne at the Leeds Maternity Hospital.

This, for me, really was something to celebrate. Harold was engrossed with his preparations for the forthcoming event in Bournemouth, but I believed he was happy at the prospect of increasing our family.

He was thrilled at being asked to address the conference, but he still found it a daunting prospect, nevertheless. The only audiences he had spoken to thus far were his own branch colleagues, and then I had written his speeches for him, putting his own ideas into black and white

I suggested to him that we put the same tactic into practice, bearing in mind that on this occasion the audience would be substantially greater. We really had no idea of the numbers who would be attending the event at that point in time, but there would be 200 or 300 people possibly. Also attending would be several senior company executives including the company chairman from Canada.

During the preceding week that we were to leave for Bournemouth, Harold gave me all his ideas that he had been jotting down. I sorted them out and wrote his speech.

Then, the day before we were due to drive down to Bournemouth, we went to collect my gown from Mrs Lane. I tried it on for the last time to ensure that everything was fine. It was a dream. I felt as though I looked a million dollars. We were so delighted with the result. Then we went in to town for some last minute shopping.

As I came out of one of the shops, I thought I felt some bleeding. I told Harold straight away, and in a panic we went for the car and he drove like crazy to the hospital. After an examination, the doctor informed me that I was having a threatened miscarriage. I remember thinking of the shock I had at hearing this. There was still a chance they could stop the threat. No way did I want to lose my baby, and I thought the intense shock alone would cause me to lose it. They reassured me that everything possible would be done to save the baby, but it did mean that I would have to go to bed immediately in the hospital and have complete rest for the next week. I was in the twelfth week, and if I could get over the third month safely, I should be all right.

I had no choice. I wanted my baby. I told Harold that he had to go to the conference without me. I would still be in the hospital when he returned, if all went well. I was given an immediate injection to stop the bleeding, hopefully, and was told that from there all I could do was to lie as still as possible and pray.

Mam had already agreed to care for Anne for us, so that was a problem already solved. It was a very worrying time for us all and a dreadful disappointment for both Harold and myself, after all the excitement and preparation of the previous weeks. I never got to wear my gorgeous gown. I never got to hear my beloved make his first conference speech. But my baby was saved.

Thankfully, I was still in the hospital bed when Harold got back. He had rushed straight to the hospital as soon as the conference closed. He was able to take me home at the end of the seven days, as the doctors thought I was now well over the danger point. But from then on, I was still determined to be as careful as possible to watch myself, whilst caring for Anne and business continuing as normal.

Chapter 18

We had been living in our home for about three years when we noticed that the dining-room ceiling was undulating a little.

Harold had a determined belief in the strategy of cultivating his policyholders as friends so that he could more subtly obtain referrals. Anything that would lead to increased sales was not only acceptable to him, but absolutely necessary.

I think some of his policyholders saw through him, but there were those who proved useful in other directions as well. One such person was Terry P. He was a young plasterer who lived in Mirfield, on the way to Huddersfield. Harold suggested we ask him to have a look at our problematic ceiling.

Ultimately, Terry was able to correct the fault and level it, amidst much dirt and upheaval. He made a very satisfactory job of it, and we were well pleased. There followed another of our strong friendships. We were invited to Terry's home and met his wife Hilda, and they then came to us, as is usual. Our friendship developed from there.

Harold, some time later, told me that Terry had put it to him that he wished to go into the building trade, having his own business. One snag: he needed help financially.

I knew that Uncle Charlie had interests in the building trade. Always looking for ways to help my husband, I suggested to Harold that a chat with him would do no harm, and could be useful.

An appointment was made for Harold to take Terry to meet Uncle Charlie. Before long, after further negotiations, Uncle Charlie agreed to back Terry. A contract was drawn up and signed. Terry was given some building work as a subcontractor to get him started.

Terry was on the road to success. Harold would handle Terry's insurance business. This also opened the path to bigger and hopefully more business for my husband, as was his intention in the first place.

All went well for some time, then eighteen months later, I was told that Terry had gone bankrupt, and that his wife had left him. I heard no more about that couple after that, but a closer business relationship with Uncle Charlie developed.

Shortly after Harold joined the company, he told me he had had some interesting discussions with his then branch manager, Laurence Murgatroyd, on the subject of the Freemasons. Laurence had recommended my husband to join at some time in the near future. Harold told me that he thought that as a Freemason he would have access to the best contacts possible.

I heard nothing further for some time, but no doubt the matter had remained at the back of his mind, and he had been making enquiries about how he could enter that 'sacred domain'.

He must have broached the subject with Uncle Charlie. One day, he came home quite excited. He told me that having spoken with my uncle, he had been advised that if he wanted to become a Mason, his best procedure was to get into one of the few Jewish lodges in Leeds. He would need to be sponsored by a Mason, but even so, it would take several years before he could be voted in and accepted. Harold was recommended to speak to my cousin, Rudolph.

He did speak to Rudolph, who, I was told, agreed to be a sponsor. Harold was also informed that he would require a second sponsor. Rudolph then repeated Uncle Charlie's warning that there was a several years' waiting list. Harold would just have to be patient! And the process of being voted into a lodge even with sponsors was such that acceptance as a Mason was far from being a foregone conclusion.

Patience was not one of Harold's best assets.

Chapter 19

At twenty past four on the morning of the 17th January 1959, I gave birth to my second baby. A most beautiful little girl, we named our second daughter Pamela Maxine. She weighed in at 9 pounds 4 ounces. To describe her as a bundle of joy was a huge understatement. I had none of the problems I had experienced having Anne. The pregnancy had progressed well after the trauma of the threatened miscarriage at the end of the third month. I had done my best to look after myself whilst continuing to support my husband in his work and take care of Anne.

Husbands were still not yet allowed to be present at their wife's childbirth, and had to adhere to strict visiting rules, so Harold had to wait until later in the day to see his new daughter.

She was a most glorious vision with her round face, chubby cheeks, delicate puckered lips, and a head that was covered with a light down of fine golden-orange hair. It was obvious even at that early stage that our second baby was going to be a glorious redhead.

Once settled back at home and into our new routine with two young children, our thoughts turned to looking for a bigger house. Initially we considered extending the house at the rear, but then decided that perhaps it would be wiser to move altogether.

We decided to look for a four-bedroomed house in our chosen areas of Moortown and Alwoodley. Nothing was suitable. We took a look at some houses being built a little further away in Shadwell. These, being built by West & Co., were very superior style stone residences. But on enquiry, we realised that these were well beyond our reach, even with our much-improved financial status.

We were getting highly despondent, and then Harold happened to mention our predicament to Uncle Charlie, who told us that he owned a plot of land in partnership with a builder, Thorpe & Co., at the end of Primley Park Crescent in Alwoodley. They were planning to build seven or eight properties on it. We could have first refusal.

We looked at the plot, and after further discussions, we agreed to accept Uncle Charlie's offer and build our dream house.

I had built up ideas in my head as to what we wanted: a double-fronted detached house with four large bedrooms and a double garage, a large fitted kitchen with a breakfast bar, and so on and so on. These were passed to my uncle and his architect. Together with the builder, they were able to draw up plans for our dream home well within our budget range. We were now in a position to look forward to moving with great excitement.

Building commenced on our new home, and we were delighted to be able to sell our house in Allerton Grange Gardens at our asking price. Unfortunately we soon hit a snag.

We expected to be able move into our new house towards the end of the year, and so arranged completion of the sale accordingly. We were eventually informed that there was no way the new house could be completed on time. It would be several weeks before the house was habitable, so making it impossible for us to move directly into our new home.

Not wishing to lose the sale of Allerton Grange Gardens, and as we were unable to alter the completion date, it meant that we would have to find alternative accommodation for the intervening period. This proved to be just about impossible, having two young children.

Ultimately we were able to book into Addleman's Hotel in Brunswick Street. This kosher hotel was owned by Mr and Mrs Ansell Addleman, who had catered for our wedding. It had also been the venue for my brother Monty's wedding. Their reputation as caterers for all forms of celebrations and functions could not be excelled.

The food in the hotel was indeed scrumptious, and their hospitality was superb. We were made extremely comfortable and enjoyed the best cuisine. Huge portions of fried fish were our regular breakfast fare, and we were encouraged to partake of their festive fare following a function. It would have been a very enjoyable episode but for the constant running around needed to get our home completed and furnished ready for us to move in.

Having lived in the hotel for six weeks or so, Harold suddenly became ill. We were having a period of bad weather and he succumbed to a bout of 'flu. Dr Ellis, our GP, attended him, but his condition continued to deteriorate. He was desperately ill. I was so terribly worried that I rang the surgery, and Dr Dales, another practice partner, came to us. He diagnosed Harold to be on the verge of pneumonia. It looked as though my darling husband would have to go into hospital. Dr Dales prescribed some strong antibiotics, telling us he would give Harold another day before sending him into hospital.

I do not recall what the antibiotics were, but they certainly worked. Dr Dales came every day for the rest of the week, despite the fact that we were living in the hotel well away from his practice area.

Thankfully, due to Dr Dales's diligent care, Harold eventually made a complete recovery, and after a month or so he was his normal self.

It had been a very gruelling time in spite of all the care and attention we had received from the Addleman family. Our stay at the hotel lasted three months, until our house was habitable, although there was still much to do as far as the décor and furnishings were concerned, but we were now desperate to get into our own home.

I don't think any words could ever describe the excitement and elation the Courtney family felt on the day we moved into 'Pamanda Court'.

Chapter 20

Shortly before we moved out of Allerton Grange Gardens, Harold came home with the news that Jimmy Johnson had called him into the office and offered him promotion to unit supervisor. So far Harold had never made a decision without first consulting me for advice. This was no exception.

He explained that he would have to recruit and train his own team of salesmen, a branch within a branch, so to speak. He would earn a small commission on the business produced by each unit member. He would continue to produce business as he had been doing at the same time. He then went on to add his own codicil that I would continue to help and support him. To me this was a foregone conclusion. Of course: I was so excited and proud of him, and that I would continue to work and support him was never and could never be an issue for me. I reassured him of that.

On accepting the position of unit supervisor, Harold strongly stipulated that he would only take on married men. He believed that family commitments were the finest motivation to success. Something that single people did not have, or so he felt, and told me so frequently.

He wanted to make his own contacts, and pondered the problem of whom he could approach for some time. They had to be proven salesmen. One of the first people to come to mind was our friend and neighbour, Malcolm T., who fitted our criteria. However, Harold soon learned that the biggest stumbling block to recruiting for his unit was that the idea of a commission-only vocation was not acceptable to salesmen who were currently on a basic salary plus commission. Harold found himself in a Catch 22 situation. Married family men were very apprehensive of a commission-only situation. They all, understandably, wanted a fixed regular income. My darling was himself an example of a commission-only salesman with a family, but he found it exceedingly difficult to convert others to the notion.

It was to his credit that as a persistent and determined salesman he was, after a long struggle over several weeks, eventually able to win Malcolm over and to convince him to believe in himself as a successful salesman with Harold's company.

Once Malcolm was recruited, Harold scoured through his records for suitable possibilities. He found Billy B. and then went on to recruit several more representatives. He soon had, with much hard work, a team of eleven men.

He brought each and every one of them home for my opinion before appointing them. Only if I thought he was on to a winner would he engage them, so deeply did my husband have faith and respect in my judgement. I cannot recall turning anyone down up to that point.

A few weeks into getting his unit off the ground, Harold told me that he had signed up a twelfth person without asking my approval. Leonard was Jewish, and met his criteria. My beloved told me he knew I would agree he was doing the right thing.

He now had a team of twelve tried and tested salesmen. He could not fail.

Chapter 21

The first six months of 1960 continued to be the happiest and most successful period of our married life thus far. Being blissfully and hopelessly in love, we both wallowed in the euphoria that Harold's hard work and prosperity afforded us.

We moved into our new home. Harold got his unit together. Anne started school at Moortown Primary School. All this, together with the pleasure that our two young daughters were giving us, was a far cry from the difficulties and hardships we had had to endure during the first two years of our marriage.

Our new house at 40, Primley Park Crescent was truly our dream home. As we had had to spend those three months in a hotel, we could not wait until it was completely furnished and moved in as soon as it was habitable.

We named the house after our two gorgeous daughters. I had resorted to calling our firstborn 'Andy', as I dreaded the possibility that she would become 'Annie', and Denise being her second name, 'Andy' seemed to come naturally. It was used for most of her childhood years. Combining the two girls' names, we came up with 'Pamanda Court'. It seemed such a naturally loving and homely development. We felt so certain that it would continue to bring us luck and total happiness. The gates to the drive were made of wrought iron in a floral, decorative design. The two words were incorporated into the design across the top, 'Pamanda' on one gate, 'Court' across the other. It was our gateway to extreme happiness and bliss.

Being a double-fronted house, the front entrance was placed in the centre, and was made up of three full-length glass panels, the middle one being the actual door. Made of decorative glass, each panel was backed up with a protective wrought iron cover in the same design as the gates. The rail up the central staircase and the protective barrier to the full-length picture window on the landing were all in the same design of wrought iron. A very distinctive feature.

The full-length through lounge to the left of the staircase opened out on to a crazy-paved patio that spread across the full width of the house, and was reached through glass doors which could be folded back flush to the walls. The marble fireplace, in the coolest of pale blues and greys, was one of my lifelong desires, very sleek and chic, but looking totally restful.

The dining room on the opposite side of the staircase was less spacious, but the square bay window held more full-width plate glass, giving it an airy feel. The whole design of our home was meant to give an ambience of warmth and comfort, an expression of our love and devotion for our family.

Behind the dining room was a very large, living kitchen. Again this had a huge, full-width picture window, below which were situated some of the most up-to-date kitchen appliances, including a Bendix automatic washing machine. On the far side was the eating area. A downstairs toilet that complemented the mosaic fitted bathroom was another luxurious feature that we had both desired for so long.

The garden also received our detailed attention, as the one in the Allerton Granges had been completely ignored. Here the services of one of my husband's clientele, who was a landscape gardener, were secured. After clearing all the debris, back and front, we decided to turf both areas and give the children as much play space as possible, turf producing an almost immediate garden.

The crazy-paved terrace across the rear of the house had a low stone wall surrounding it, into which plants could be sown, and gave access to the lawn.

All in all, we were delighted with the outcome, and straight away we bought the girls a swing. I think this gave me as much pleasure seeing the children enjoy it, as much as the girls enjoyed it, for all that Pamela was still a baby.

Furnishing the house was more pleasurable, in its way, although more time-consuming. Another policyholder was brought in to help us.

This gentleman had recently set up his own workshop, manufacturing hand-carved superior fitted furniture. I was taken to meet the gentleman, George Strachan, at his premises in Barrack Road. I was very intrigued to find that his workshop had been established in premises formerly occupied by the Judean Club, a very popular youth club in my teenage years. I had last been in that same building when as a Girl Guide, our troupe had met there briefly before moving to other premises.

But back to our furniture manufacturer: George did build our fitted bedroom furniture, with matching bedhead and chest of drawers. All were exquisitely carved, and embellished with gilt fittings and carvings.

Several other pieces of furniture were made for us including coffee tables and chests of drawers for the girls' bedrooms. The Strachans joined our now quite wide circle of policyholder friends and Harold and I were delighted to watch George's business develop and grow. It eventually became a nationally well-known company, Strachan & Co.

These and the carpets and curtains were another ambition achieved. The thick embossed, pale green carpet had long been a dream we never thought would be fulfilled. It was laid throughout the house.

Although it did take several weeks to turn our house into a home, the sense of achievement and joy in fulfilling so many of our dreams could never be really put into words.

Two other happy events took place during this period. Harold's sister became Mrs Brian Taylor, and my brother Harvey married his sweetheart Eleanor.

Anne was a bridesmaid for Harvey's wedding, which took place on 17th January 1960. Now almost four and a half years old, she looked absolutely gorgeous in her white organza dress. It was trimmed with royal blue ribbon to highlight the lacy borders round the neckline, the short puffed sleeves and the bottom of the knee-length skirt. A small circlet of tiny white flowers adorned her fair wavy hair, and a furry muff on a thin white ribbon round her neck completed the outfit, making her look so absolutely adorable.

Both Anne's dress and mine, a pink quilted, strapless gown, which was all the fashion at the time, had been bought from the top couturier in Leeds, Anne Corbett, and chosen by my darling husband. It gave Harold great pleasure to choose our gowns, and he had such good dress sense, that again I was happy to abide by his choice on this occasion.

We all enjoyed ourselves immensely at these *simchas* (festivities), but what was becoming more noticeable upon each occasion were Harold's drinking sprees.

From our very first meeting, Harold had expressed his admiration for my mother. Always the charmer, he never failed to take the opportunity of repeating his admiration for her whenever my mother's behaviour met with his approval. They appeared to get on very well, and never more so than at our family celebrations, as had already been witnessed at earlier celebrations. Harold now found he had a regular drinking companion in my mother. I never drank other than soft drinks. I had never seen my mother drink except for the odd glass of wine at family get-togethers for the Holy Festivals. Yet now, when

64

Harold persuaded Mam to have a drink with him, he somehow managed to get her to drink quite heavily. She obviously enjoyed herself and no one seemed to mind.

Everything was now going so perfectly and we were so very happy. I believed the future was sure to continue in this way.

Chapter 22

Anne had only been at school a few weeks when my beloved husband decided to drop a huge, huge bombshell. He told me that he wanted the girls to go to boarding school, and he asked 'Wasn't it time we put their names down on the waiting list?' Coming totally out of the blue, I was so stunned that I suppose I must have hesitated for a while before I asked him his reasons.

I have always believed that boarding schools were places where parents sent their children to get them out of the way, so that the parents could pursue their own interests. Harold told me that the children took up too much of my time. Looking after the girls, taking Anne to and from school, when I had a much bigger house to look after, as well as supporting him in his work, meant that I had less time to spend with him. In other words, the girls were in his way.

My belief about boarding schools was strengthened by my husband's attitude, but coming from my own husband, this was beyond belief. My husband's possessiveness was now way over the top. I told him in no uncertain terms that in no way would I ever send my girls away to boarding school. I doubt if he had really considered what was involved, or what school they should go to, but I stressed that the place for girls, and certainly my girls, Jewish children, was at home with their mother in a loving, caring environment.

I was never a religious person, but I was committed to being Jewish. Throughout my childhood, my parents and all my relatives were deeply religious, maintaining the rites of family life. The war years, 1939 to 1945, caused so much devastation to all our lives, together with the food rationing and shortages, that my parents sought to relax their attitudes and behaviour. Nevertheless, my mother continued to cook and bake in our traditional way, with myself watching and often participating, especially when she was preparing for the Sabbath, and all our Holy Festivals. Watching my mother lighting the candles on a Friday night just before our Sabbath meal, when all my family were sat around the dinner table, was the highlight of the week.

I now practised much of what my mother had taught me. I hoped that my daughters would learn from me in the same way as I had done. Where else would they learn the joys of Jewish life?

Who would tell them their bedtime stories, which I frequently made up as I went along, and to which they looked forward each night?

I loved my children so much, and they were so young, that the idea of them being away from me for whatever reason was unthinkable. I also stressed to Harold that I still loved and cared for him as I had always done, and I would continue to support and work with him.

This was our first major disagreement, but one which I was determined to win and felt justified in so doing. In any case, Harold had had no real experience of education, and to want his children out of the way so that he had me to himself seemed so dastardly at the time. Where was his love for his children? This made me wonder. Reluctantly, he agreed to my decision and nothing further was said on the matter, but he made it quite clear that the girls' upbringing as well as all domestic matters were my total responsibility. He was the breadwinner, and his responsibilities were solely in providing for his family financially; anything else was up to me.

All the same, the reality was that I did have much to cope with, and a compromise was suggested. I should have an au pair to help me in the house. I was able to contact a local agency and I arranged for a young Spanish girl to work for us quite quickly. Eighteen years old and very attractive with typical dark, shoulder-length hair and dark Spanish eyes, she was obviously conscious of her good looks, but she came with good references, so the proprietor of the agency told me.

Harold was now working hard with his new unit. I had been given the job of writing his monthly unit bulletin recording the efforts of his team, with the information passed on to me by Harold, and which was included in the branch's monthly bulletin.

He also held monthly unit meetings in our home on a Monday morning. Our au pair had only been with us a few days when Harold was due to have his monthly unit meeting. He held it in the dining room whilst I did my usual Monday morning washing. I had prepared a trolley in the kitchen with the cups and saucers for coffee together with the cakes and biscuits for their mid-morning break. Harold would call me when he wanted me to take the trolley in and serve the coffee.

I had done a load of washing in the washing machine and asked the au pair to empty the machine so that I could hang the washing out. At

67

that point, I was called to serve the coffee. I asked our au pair if she would take the trolley through to the dining room.

She stopped in her tracks and pulling herself to her full 5 foot 5, looked me straight in the eyes and yelled that she only had one pair of hands. She grabbed a tablet of soap from the sink and threw it at me, hitting me full in the face. She then hurried out of the room.

Although my face was stinging from the blow and I was bursting with anger, I served Harold and his colleagues their coffee, but did not say anything until after the men had left and Harold was on his own. We were soon able to laugh about it, but no way could I allow an unwilling and hot-tempered person to remain in my home to help with the children

I rang the agency up and told them about the incident, telling them that I wanted the girl out of the house immediately. The proprietor apologised, and I told myself that was the last time I would engage an au pair to help me in the house.

Chapter 23

The summer of 1960 was conference time again, and we were both determined that this time I would be there. It was to be held in the Grand Hotel at Brighton, once again, a five-day Monday to Friday event. The salesmen and their wives would again be accommodated in the top hotels in the resort.

Harold's successful run as the branch's top salesman had kept up its momentum, and qualifying for both of us to attend was never in doubt. There was, however, for Harold one big difference: he was now a unit supervisor, and through his continued hard work had produced a very successful team. With only one exception, all the team had qualified to attend the conference, and some had also qualified to take their wives.

Sadly, the one exception was the gentleman whom Harold had appointed without me meeting him first. Leonard had been struggling from the beginning, and after six months, days before the conference, he decided to call it a day. Harold was very upset about this, although he had expressed his concern about Leonard's results several times. Harold had no time for defeat: there was no such word as 'No' in his vocabulary. Leonard leaving regrettably spoilt his success record.

It did, however, cause him to review the commission-only structure. He considered a method of funding commissions, small monthly loans set against sales, which he felt would give some basic confidence to future salesmen. He campaigned for this with the company's executives from time to time, but the idea was constantly rejected for a long time.

For us all at the conference, it was a wonderful week. Harold again gave a speech that I had written out for him, about his continued success. He introduced me to the company's managers and their wives. He was constantly boasting to them about my contribution to his success, so that I was repeatedly feted and congratulated. As the wife of one of the top salesman in the company, I was treated to a place of honour at the evening celebrations.

This gave rise to one minor problem, the very heavy drinking that was all around. I did not drink, and I hated seeing people drunk even more. As a child of about nine or ten years old, I had always remembered my mother sending me to Auntie Julia's, who at that time lived a short bus ride away. On the way back, I was walking up to the bus stop when I saw an extremely drunken tramp staggering around the bus stop. He eventually fell down on the spot. I was absolutely terrified, so much so that I was frightened to go near the bus stop. Fortunately the bus, when it did arrive, stopped near enough for me to run on to it in terror. I could not get away quick enough.

That incident has always haunted me, so that for years seeing anyone drunk frightened me and made me feel ill. It also left me with an intense dislike for anything alcoholic. I have never been able to understand how anyone can enjoy beer and spirits. They taste foul to me. Nor can I understand what pleasure anyone gets from drinking oneself silly and being totally out of control of one's own behaviour. The fact that I did not drink had never been a problem for Harold till now. I enjoyed soft drinks, orange juice and tomato juice. All of a sudden, Harold started complaining that I did not drink. He called me antisocial and came up with suggestions to try and persuade me to drink. He put some brandy in my orange juice, 'Only a little drop,' he insisted.

I did not want to upset him, but he kept complaining that I was showing him up, and that for someone in his exalted position, I was letting him down very badly. Not wanting that to happen, I tried sipping the doctored orange juice, but it tasted horrible.

Harold realised I was not enjoying the drink, so that whenever I was asked to have a drink after that and I responded by asking for a fruit juice, he would comment that I did not need a drink to enjoy myself, that I could still be the life and soul of the party on tomato juice. I just laughed off these remarks.

I still found myself being admired by fellow salesmen as well as by their superiors. Alan Kemp told me from time to time that he wished all wives were like me, a comment which when it was occasionally made to me by others caused Harold to drag me away. He still donned his possessive cloak throughout the conference.

All in all, we had a wonderful time. Before leaving, we discussed meeting up with Billy, one of our unit representatives, and his wife Sheila, in London where we planned to spend a couple of days on the way home. We reserved accommodation at our regular hotel, the Regent Palace, and then arranged to go for dinner to the Caprice restaurant in Piccadilly, one of London's reputedly finest restaurants of the time.

The meal at the Caprice was fantastic, living up to its reputation. We all enjoyed the magnificent creamed crab as a starter. Neither Harold nor myself believed in eating strictly kosher, and as the starter came highly recommended it was abundantly well worth eating. Ever since Harold started to become more affluent, he had taken to eating steaks at every opportunity. Steak Diane, with lashings of creamy mushroom sauce drowned in wine and brandy and flambéed at the table by the waiter, was like nothing we had ever eaten before. The dessert was the then fashionable Crinoline Lady, hot ice cream covered with meringue and decorated in the shape of a crinoline lady. I was given the china lady that adorned the confection as a present, and it has always been a treasured souvenir of one of the most, if not the most, amazing and memorable meal any of us had ever had. An enjoyable visit to the Talk of the Town, a popular cabaret nightclub that was on every tourist's schedule in those days, made our stay in London a resounding success.

A stroll through the sidestreets between Piccadilly and Regent Street in the early hours of the morning concluded a wonderful week for the four of us. Now I was only too pleased to be able to get home and see my precious darling daughters who had been tenderly cared for by their Grandma Florrie.

Chapter 24

The last week of August 1960 was spent on holiday in Jersey. It was our first holiday abroad. We had previously always spent our holidays at Blackpool, which had been a favourite holiday destination of my parents during my growing-up years.

The first holiday Harold and I ever had after our honeymoon was with Mam in bed and breakfast accommodation in a back street off the North Front Promenade. We then graduated to the more comfortable Readman's Park House hotel directly on the North Promenade, overlooking the sea, where we had several delightful breaks.

Once we had become more affluent, the exotic Norbreck Castle Hotel became a regular venue as it had more room for the children. On our last main holiday there, it was to be remembered for being the first of quite a number of Anne's wee small peccadilloes which were to cause us considerable consternation.

Our accommodation was en suite. Anne, then only four and a half years old, must have decided to explore the more public facilities of the hotel. When our backs were turned for only a brief moment, out she stepped into the hallway and tried a couple of doors, one of which was a toilet. Whether she actually used the toilet, I doubt, but standing as high as she could she managed to bolt the door. Unfortunately she was unable to unbolt the door and was locked in. She had always been told never to lock toilet doors, not that she was ever allowed to go to the toilet on her own. We found her almost immediately, unable to release the bolt.

We were on the third floor and I had frantic images of her trying to climb up onto the windowsill to try to get out. All our efforts to explain to her how to unbolt the door proved useless. She just could not reach the bolt to reverse it, and I was getting more and more agitated and fearful for her safety, although Anne seemed unconcerned at her predicament. We called the hotel management who were able to force the lock and release her after a short while, very much to our relief.

We decided to take our next holiday abroad soon after the company conference. I had never flown before and was absolutely petrified at the thought, so Jersey being a short flight seemed the best option. By the time we travelled, we knew then that I would be three months pregnant expecting our third baby. I was determined, in view of the problems I had had with my earlier pregnancies, that I would take extra care of myself, at least as much care as two young darlings would allow me.

We booked a room for the four of us at the beautiful Pomme D'Or Hotel in the centre of St Helier. We had four lovely days looking around the sights as well as enjoying the beach. On the fifth day, we decided to go to St Brelades Bay, where the beach was reputed to have the most glorious white sands and be very safe for sunbathing, as the tide went out an extraordinarily long way. The whole bay was dominated by the luxurious L'Horizon hotel, which at that time prohibited children.

We found a spot on the beach immediately in front of the hotel and esconced ourselves in our deckchairs. Pamela sat in her pushchair. Harold then chose to take Anne to the water's edge to paddle. As they walked towards the sea, my eyes followed them for a while but the tide was so far out that eventually I could no longer see them amongst the many bathers. Some half an hour later, Harold returned alone, desperately looking around.

'Where's Anne?' he asked.

'Where is Anne?' I agitatedly threw back the question. I could already feel something was terribly wrong.

He told me Anne had asked to go back to Mummy and she had run off, or so he believed.

'Hasn't she come back?'

I told him I had never seen her since she went with him to paddle.

'Oh my G-d. Where is she?'

She was nowhere to be seen. Harold thought she had come back to me. The last time he had seen her was in the sea. Now my mind was spinning with every terrible thought. We had to report her missing, last seen in the sea.

I could not believe this was happening to us. This sort of thing happened to others but not to my precious family. Harold went to report Anne missing to the coastguard and the police. I stayed with Pamela, hoping against hope that my darling daughter would turn up. There are no words to describe the excruciating pain and anguish I felt, not knowing what had happened to my precious Anne, fearing the worst.

73

Within moments there was a flurry of heated activity, with the coast-guards scouring the beach and the sea closest to the beach. Every lifeguard was involved as well as the police and many holidaymakers, in the search for my daughter. Time went on, first one hour, then another hour. I was feeling more and more helpless, frantic. I tried not to despair, but I did not know what to believe. The search had continued for well over four hours. Teatime had come and gone unnoticed by us.

Then, as if by some miracle, a policeman came and told us a lady had found Anne, wandering lost through the town. She was crying, and the lady, very thankfully, took her to the police station. We were united with our beloved daughter.

For days after, I felt the pangs of worry and agitation at the incident and thoughts of what could have happened. I was so elated at Anne's safe return. It did put a small cloud over the rest of our holiday, but thankfully we were all able to return home to Leeds safe and sound. I was so overcome with worry and desperation at the time that the only thing in my head was seeing my baby alive again.

It was not for a very long time after, many months later, when I was able to review the situation more coolly and practically, that it occurred to me: how come Anne's father allowed her, a four-year-old child, to wander off in the sea to find me on her own, all that way? No wonder she lost her way and was unable to find me. She should never have been allowed to be on her own under those circumstances.

Chapter 25

At the end of September I suffered a heartrending setback that caused me much anguish and distress. I was at home, Harold was working, when for the second time in my married life, I had some of the signs of a threatened miscarriage. I called the ambulance and was rushed to St James's Hospital. I was admitted to the maternity unit. Only this time, my baby could not be saved.

Harold arrived at the hospital only in time to be told the awful news. I was immediately whipped down to surgery to have a 'D & C' to ensure that there was no debris left in my womb and that I was all right. The date was 29th September 1960, and I was in my sixteenth week. The foetus was just four months old. According to Jewish law a foetus over three months old is regarded as a human being. If it passes away after three months it must have a funeral and be buried in accordance with the rites and customs of our law.

I asked to see my baby but was told it would be better not to. I asked Harold if he had seen our baby and if he knew the sex. He only repeated what I had already been told: that the foetus was so badly misshapen that the sex could not be determined. I asked if the baby was a boy, as I had heard that sometimes one could only carry one sex, but I was told this was nonsense. I then queried as to what had caused the miscarriage.

I had had a minor bump in Harold's Rover car the previous week. There was only slight damage and I was unharmed, but I suggested that the shock might have brought it on. The answer was that I was in no way responsible. The foetus was so badly malformed that it could not have possibly survived any longer. As to why the foetus was so badly malformed, no one could say. The doctors told me that it was just a freak of nature that it was abnormal, and so my womb rejected it.

Harold went to bring the Rabbi to the hospital to collect the foetus and I was allowed to see the coffin very briefly. It was such a very tiny coffin. Then Harold went with the Rabbi to the cemetery.

Thankfully this was not my first pregnancy. I had my two beautiful daughters, and I was told that there was no reason why I should not be able to have more children, should I wish to do so.

I must state at this point that Harold and I never, ever discussed having children. I could never get him to discuss the matter. Whenever I tried to broach the subject with him, he either clammed up, as in the early years of our marriage, or he told me in very loving terms that I could always have whatever I wanted and that included having children, as long as I understood that I would be wholly responsible for the domestic side of our marriage, and that included the upbringing of our children. He would always provide for whatever I wanted, but he wanted to be able to concentrate on his work to ensure the money continued to roll in, and that meant that he was always number one in our family.

I always told him that he was the number one in our family, to keep the peace, and that I was with him 100 per cent as I idolised the man, but the children were still always my prime consideration, and I felt that he should have felt the same way.

Consequently, none of our daughters were deliberately planned. If I had never become pregnant, I cannot say what I would have done. I did have two very welcome babies whom I have loved very deeply and who constantly gave me great happiness during their early years.

Contraception was a perpetual nightmare for me. The Pill was not available till the mid-1960s, and when it did go on the market (I believe it was only obtainable initially on prescription), I found I could not tolerate it, so my choice was limited to the diaphragm or the coil, neither of which I was happy with. They caused me frequent infections and pain and I had to stop using them, much to my husband's consternation, as this put the responsibility onto him. Nevertheless, we coped admirably with the problem and still continued to delight in our blissful relationship.

Chapter 26

We were all sat around my mother's dining table in her bungalow, stunned to silence, conforming to her request not to let on to Dad what had happened until after she served him his dinner. It was 13th October 1960, and early that morning, Uncle Charlie had been found passed away in his home, having had a severe heart attack. He had had heart problems for a while, and his wife Auntie Mae had passed away the previous year.

Dad was the eldest of five brothers and they were all extremely close. Dad had told us many times how, as a young boy, he had passed his Eleven-Plus exam to go to grammar school, but had had to give up his place later to go out to work to give his parents money to help Uncle Charlie so that he could pursue his education as a lawyer and become a solicitor.

Dad had been out at work all day and did not get home until seven o'clock. Monty had also been working with Dad, but he arrived home a little earlier, in time to be told the news. So we all, Harold and I, and Monty and Mam, and others in our family sat about in dreaded anticipation as to how Dad would react on hearing about his beloved brother.

Mam knew he would take it very badly, so she asked us to wait and not say a word until he had eaten so as not to spoil his meal. He would perhaps be able to cope more with the news on a full stomach. We all sat there, very agitated, wondering how Mam could restrain herself under such conditions, even though we knew she was a very strong-willed and determined lady and had Dad's sensitivities at heart. The atmosphere was stifling and claustrophobic. I felt choked. No one spoke for fear of blurting out the wrong thing.

When Mam eventually decided to tell Dad, we had all been given a cup of tea. Dad had now sensed the atmosphere, and asked what was wrong. I think we were all relieved in one sense, when she did tell him, as I think we had all reached bursting point not being able to discuss a death in the family.

We were all in awe and deep admiration at the way Mam handled the situation. But I think the person most impressed was my husband.

He had always admired my parents, especially my mother. The way she put her husband's feelings first boosted his own beliefs about the man of the house being number one in his domain. He expressed his strong admiration for my mother about how she had handled the day, very clearly, as soon as we left to go home.

Harold's experience of his parents' family lifestyle was so totally different to mine. My parents held firm beliefs in never showing their feelings in front of my brothers and me. They always kept their arguments away from us. I did from time to time hear them arguing in the bedroom after we had gone to bed; unknown to them, I would presume. By the same rule of thumb, I never saw any displays of affection either. But my mother's behaviour to Dad left us in no doubt that they felt very strongly about each other.

Harold's parents constantly argued and verbally abused each other with no consideration for anyone who could be listening, usually upsetting those who could hear them.

I did nevertheless try to make my husband always believe he was my number one whilst putting my children and their needs first. Not such a problem when I loved them all so much.

Chapter 27

Harold's meteoric success rate continued, both as a salesman and a unit supervisor, throughout 1961, in spite of intense competition from two of his colleagues who were also enjoying supersonic success. I had met both gentlemen at the previous conference. Brian B. was a southerner, but Ken N. and his wife lived much closer to home, at Doncaster, though he was with the Sheffield branch. We enjoyed our friendship with Ken and Hazel, visiting each other from time to time.

Harold had now achieved the highest accolade by becoming the company's top salesman for which he was awarded the McAllister Shield. This shield was held by its winner for that year and was accordingly inscribed with a description of the winner's success. Harold also received a small silver tankard, a souvenir similarly inscribed for his permanent record.

I was extremely proud of this momentous achievement, but I could not help but feel some pride for myself for the huge contribution I had made towards Harold's success, and which he constantly acknowledged.

To me this was an especially great achievement because of the difficulties we had had to endure from my father-in-law during this period.

Chapter 28

My father-in-law never believed in banks. He said he did not trust them. To us this meant that he did not wish to declare his earnings to the Inland Revenue, so he hid his money in his bedroom. Both Harold and myself frequently pleaded with him to put the money in a bank, but he blatantly refused. I believed that being the greedy person I had learned him to be, he just did not wish to part with any of his earnings under any circumstance.

The frequent rows that my in-laws had were usually about money. Fanny constantly complained that her husband kept her uncomfortably short of money, and that she could get by only by working. She had a part-time job two days a week as a saleswoman in a Wallis fashion shop. Sammy always told us that he needed to have cash on him in case he came across a very important item in his work, so he could buy it instantly. He also insisted on doing most of the shopping, so that he could keep his eagle eye on the spending. He refused to leave the house except to work, or for some very special purpose, as he was afraid of being burgled.

This all added to the worry that my husband felt. His father was the only member on either side of our families who refused to purchase any form of life assurance from his son. Nor, to the best of my knowledge, did he have any other kind of insurance.

Over the years, his collection of porcelain and china ornaments, cats, dogs, certainly some of the most beautiful vases I had ever seen, and other antique artefacts grew to an immensely large number, all of which he kept in his home. They stood on all the furniture and the floors and filled both living rooms and eventually the entrance hall. This rendered the front door inaccessible. This made me feel even more uncomfortable visiting my in-laws. One had to tread very delicately through the house for fear of knocking or falling over the precious ornaments and there was hardly anywhere to sit in comfort. We were always asked to take care, especially with the children.

My father-in-law displayed his avid avariciousness particularly with the children. Our girls always found his appearance very intimidating. He would not wear his false teeth in the house, and more often than not, he went out without them. He usually looked unkempt and unshaven. To me he looked like a tramp more often than not, and he did not seem to understand or even care how he looked, particularly in front of the children. So I understood why they always felt intimidated, and cowered and clung to me, when we visited their grandparents.

The Cohens had had a sweet shop prior to my coming on the scene, and now the old man continued to bulk buy sweets and chocolates which he stored in the sideboard in the dining room. It was filled with 7lb jars of sweets of every description and every variety of chocolates.

He would put his hand into one of the jars of sweets and take out just one sweet, and holding it between his thumb and fingers would point it at my girls and tell them they could have it if they gave him a kiss, such was his greed. My girls' reaction to this was as a rule for them to bury their heads against my lap and refuse the sweet. Such was my disgust that I could not bring myself to encourage the girls to accept the sweet. I think my children grew up in the full knowledge that their grandpa was an extremely selfish and greedy person. I never heard of them going to visit their Cohen grandparents alone, only if their father took them.

To some people, I know he came across as a rather bizarre character. I just found him grossly unpleasant and nasty. I could never visit my in-laws on my own, and only tolerated my father-in-law because I loved and adored my husband, who seemed so entirely different from his father. This was a completely different situation to that with my parents, whom my girls always loved dearly.

When Harold's father started to torment us with his tempestuous tantrums over his tortuous (to him) tax troubles, both Harold and myself realised we had something to worry about. The old man had received a letter from the Inland Revenue telling him they were looking into his tax affairs. Whether someone had reported him, as it seemed to be common knowledge amongst his mates that he hid money in his bedroom, or it was just a routine investigation as he refused to send in any tax return, we never found out, but he was told that they, the Inland Revenue, were coming to see him.

He then asked my father if he could put his parcel of money in his safe until the affair had blown over. Harold's father was very confident that he would get away with it. My father agreed, which I certainly felt was foolish of him. But then that was the sort of kindly act my father did.

Harold's father was visited by tax inspectors who, we were told, made a thorough search of the house, but were not able to find what they were looking for. Shortly after, when the old man felt the whole matter had blown over, he retrieved his parcel of money and returned it to its previous hiding place.

My father-in-law often told me that everything he had, the money and all the valuable ornaments and antiques, would eventually pass to my children, his grandchildren. Whether this came to happen when he passed away some years ago, I was never to know, but I doubt it.

The whole incident left a sour taste in my mouth. I know I have made previous references about my father-in-law's unpleasant behaviour, but I have recounted this incident particularly as it was a great example of his character, and the sort of person that I had to contend with throughout my marriage.

Chapter 29

On the 29th September 1961, a couple of minutes before midnight, exactly one year to the day since my miscarriage, I gave birth to my third daughter, Ruth Sandra. Once I was well into my pregnancy, about halfway, and I had been reassured by my consultant gynaecologist, the same Mr Agar who had looked after me when I was having Anne and Pamela, that the pregnancy was all right and that the worst was not likely to occur now, Harold suggested that I should have some help during the first month or so after the birth. I told him that I would only consider a properly qualified nanny, and that her duties were mainly to help with the two older girls.

We advertised, not really knowing where to start looking for a suitably qualified person, and of the few replies we received, one looked particularly promising. The lady, who called herself Barbara, promptly came to see me for an interview and I was pleasantly surprised. She was very tall, almost six foot, and very slim, quite plain-looking, but with a generous smile. She dressed very neatly, as I remember, as I was most impressed with her appearance, and her attitude filled me with the confidence I sought from someone to whom I was going to allow sole care of my children whilst I was in hospital.

She told us that with her previous position she had worked as a nanny and had lived as part of the family for seventeen years. She had had no formal nanny training but she tried to reassure us that from her experience she was completely knowledgeable and competent in all aspects of baby care and child rearing. The children whom she had been caring for were all now too grown up to have a nanny, and although, as she told us, she was dreadfully sad and reluctant to leave the family, she wanted to move on. She really was looking for a family similar to the one she had left, with long-term prospects, but until such a position came along she would be content with short-term employment such as we were offering. I had explained that I required short-term services, for three months from the birth, but requested she would come to us two weeks before the due date so she could get used to our family and the girls and vice versa.

I asked her how she felt about looking after Harold during the period I would be in hospital – which would just mean making an evening meal for him. She pointed out that she expected her duties to finish as soon as the children were in bed. She was no cook, but would put a meal on the table for him at six o'clock. I tried to explain that my husband's work meant that he usually had late meals and at various times, but he would do his best and try to comply with her arrangements. She was obviously willing to help us to the best of her ability, but within the constraints of her position.

She told us she would be happy to work for us, but asked if she could have a little time to think the matter over. As I needed to check her references, which did appear impeccable, the arrangements suited us all. In the eventuality, her references did check out and Harold and I were happy to engage her.

By the thirty-sixth week of my pregnancy I had put on a colossal amount of weight. When I attended the hospital for the eighth monthly check-up, I was told that I had acute toxaemia. It was at a dangerously high level, and I should be admitted to hospital immediately to be induced.

We contacted Barbara to ask her if she could come to us immediately, explaining the situation. She agreed. It meant that she was going to be thrown in at the deep end, but she had appeared to be quite capable of coping, so I wasn't too worried, though I was very upset at having to leave the children so soon and so abruptly.

The very first day I was admitted I was put on a drip, which was meant to induce my labour. I had previously been given an enema. After twenty-four hours nothing happened. I was then prescribed a second round, an enema followed by the drip. Again nothing happened. By the end of the first week, I had had at least four, maybe five sessions of the same treatment to start off labour – but nothing! I was feeling very weak and ill. At some point, it was decided to break my waters, but my baby just refused to be born. It must have been very warm and cosy in there.

The doctors then decided that in spite of the urgency, I should be given a day's rest to recoup my strength. The treatment was resumed about two days later, and again I failed to produce. I was dreadfully weak, and I think I must have collapsed and was in a critical condition. I remember hearing voices, but I was not able to do or say anything. Mr Agar was sent for and he told them that as I was so ill, they would have to wait till I recovered, before proceeding further. I believed that mainly the constant round of enemas that kept weakening me, had brought on my collapse further. What happened to me during that blackout remains a mystery to me, but after that I had no more enemas, and another session on the drip did finally produce results.

Having been in hospital for two weeks, in the thirty-eighth week my gorgeous darling daughter, my third, came into the world, weighing in at 7 pounds. That was the worst labour I had ever had, but Ruth Sandra could not have been loved more.

Harold could not have been more supportive, visiting me almost constantly whilst trying to juggle his work with visiting times and attempting to maintain his supremacy in the company's sales' records. I would have hated him to lose face because of me. Fortunately, we had come up with a gem of the highest quality with Nanny Barbara. Harold was full of praise for her care of the children. After all, she had not only been thrown in at the deep end, but in view of the unexpected turn of events with my labour, she had to work almost non-stop for over two weeks till I was able to go home.

Harold brought the girls to see me at the weekends, which gave Nanny a few hours off, and though she insisted in not actually working once the girls were in bed, it still meant she had to stay with them when my other half visited me in the evenings.

There was only one complaint. Harold did find that Barbara put his evening meal on the table promptly at six o'clock. He also learned that Barbara could only make one pudding, Durban Pudding, It was a jam roly-poly over which some milk is poured and then baked in the oven. And served with cold custard! Harold found it adorning his dinner table every night. Everything was cold by the time he arrived home! And Durban Pudding became a family joke. Actually, Barbara was very proud of her concoction and offered me the recipe when I went home. I obligingly wrote it down in my recipe scrap book, where it can still be found, but to venture to introduce it into my cooking repertoire: never, at my peril!

Ten days after Ruthie was born, I was able to return home happy in the knowledge that Anne and Pamela had been very well looked after and had taken quite well to their carer, although I knew only too well that they had missed me dreadfully, as I had missed them. I had been away from home for three and a half weeks.

Once home, Barbara helped me through the first few days with bathing the children and trying to adjust to my new situation. Mam also came along to help, thoroughly enjoying her enlarged grandparental position. Then it was time for Nanny to have her well-earned rest.

On her first full day off, she disappeared, returning home during the evening. Her arrival at the door was quite a cabaret. She stumbled into the hall, sort of singing and muttering, and wobbling most precariously all over the place. She'd had a good time by all appearances, but her attempts to get up the stairs to her room proved a little complicated for her. I was utterly stunned by her behaviour. She had never shown any indication that she even touched alcohol, and there I was having to guide her to her room. She was absolutely stone drunk.

What came next was an even greater surprise. As I opened the door for her, a picture of absolute disaster greeted me. It was utter chaos. The room was the untidiest scene I have ever witnessed, with clothes of every description carelessly discarded all over the floor as well as on her furniture, the bed, chairs and dressing table. Drawers left open displayed her personal items. Make-up and toiletries were strewn everywhere. I could not believe that a person who I had seen to be always scrupulously clean, neat and immaculately dressed, who always seemed very particular in her appearance and who had cared for my girls in the same way was occupying this room.

As I guided Barbara into her room I felt as though I was helping a complete stranger, someone with a dual personality. Thankfully, the girls were fast asleep, so I assumed they heard nothing. The following day, she resumed her duties as though the events of the previous evening had never happened. I believed that what she did in her own time and in her own room was her own business, so the incident was never referred to. After all, she did deserve to let her hair down now and again. There was never any repetition.

At the end of the third month, by the time she was due to leave us, I had certainly become very fond of her. Apart from that one drunken incident, she had always maintained an attitude of fairly strict decorum, yet she showed that she cared for her charges. I was sad to let her go, but I needed to have my home back, for my family and myself. We never heard from her again.

Chapter 30

Once I had my family to myself, I could get into some sort of routine. We had been to the St Nicholas Hotel in Scarborough a couple of times, and had always found it extremely homely and warm in spite of its luxurious decor and furnishings, so we decided to make a habit of taking a weekend break at the hotel at the end of each month with all the family.

A few days before our monthly break in January 1962, Harold informed me that he had been invited to a meeting with the company's directors at their London head offices on the Friday prior to our weekend break. Realising the importance of such a meeting, he suggested that I take the children and with my mother go to Scarborough, and he would join us there immediately after the meeting, which we did.

As soon as I saw his face, when he joined us, I knew that something very serious had happened. He was so excited. I was surprised he had not phoned us with such great news. He had actually restrained himself until he saw me, as he realised there could be problems. He had been offered promotion to branch manager. It would mean moving to another town, but he would not be told where until he decided to accept the position.

The offer of a promotion in itself was something to celebrate, and being at the St Nicholas Hotel was particularly propitious, we were in the right place at the right time. We decided to leave the decision-making for when we returned home, and have a great celebratory weekend and thoroughly enjoy ourselves.

The decision-making was very difficult. There were initially two major aspects that we had to consider. The prime one to my mind was the change in job description that Harold had to deal with.

The branch manager was responsible for the whole sales team, the hiring, firing and motivating, and, as Harold was to learn, dealing with the personal problems of those under him. Ultimately, as far as the company was concerned, it meant reaching national sales targets. It was mainly a desk job. There would be little, if any, time for personal production. Harold's lifelong ambition had been to be a successful salesman. That he had achieved, but promotion involved him forsaking his sales career. The question he really had to consider was, would he be happy behind a desk for the most part? And would he be happy not being in front of perspective policyholders? He would be assisting his representatives with their sales presentations, if required. But that was not the same as making one's own sales. I knew, from when he started being a life assurance salesman, that seeing his client put their signature to the page of an application form to close the sale gave him a tremendous buzz of satisfaction.

Another factor to consider was the move itself. We had put so much of our joint lives into building our dream home from virtually nothing, and now after having lived there so happily for only two years, did we want to give it up? Could we give it up? We had also to consider that we would both be leaving our families behind. If he chose to move to another town, then so be it. I promised Harold that the decision was really his, and that whatever it was to be, I was right behind him.

He was given a month to decide. It must have been one of the hardest decisions we had ever had to make.

During that month, my dearest husband renewed his previous proposal that he thought the girls should go to boarding school. He repeated that having three young girls now taking up so much of my time did not leave me with sufficient time to give to my husband, and if he were to become a branch manager it would be even more important that I have as much time as possible to help him.

Never at any time since our children had been born had he given me any help at all with the children, neither by changing a nappy, nor by feeding the baby with its bottle – except one very rare occasion. Mam was in our house helping me with Ruth, who was an exceptionally slow bottle feeder, and she must have decided to call Harold's bluff. She suggested to him that he have a turn feeding Ruth. He accepted, showing some enthusiasm, which I always thought was feigned for Mam's benefit. He sat down to feed her, struggled for a few minutes, then impatiently threw in the towel. He commented on his lack of patience, or words to that effect, and asked my mother to take over what he regarded as women's duties.

It was clear to us all that my husband had no interest in his children's upbringing from the practical side. Again, he was demonstrating that his first interest was his work, providing for his family was the be-all and end-all of his paternal responsibilities, and he had to have my total and full-time support and cooperation, particularly if he was to take up the offer of promotion.

I was extremely upset at his attitude as I thought I had made it quite clear that no way could I allow my girls to be sent away to school, and I repeated my refusal to reconsider the suggestion. It was even more important, if we were to go to a new and unfamiliar place that the girls should have a full home life, and I would cope with the situation. I had given him more than loyalty and support. There was no way he could have got to this stage in his career with the company without me, and nothing was going to change that if he decided to accept promotion. Again, I was determined that no way was he going to persuade me to change my mind, and I told him so whilst trying not let him feel put out. My children would not be and would never be sent away from home. He reluctantly accepted my response. We had other important matters to think about.

During the succeeding week, he received further information about the post, which we were happy to discuss. He had been offered the promotion not especially on account of his sales ability, but more for the way he had shown his leadership abilities. He had successfully led a unit for almost two years, making it one of the top units in the country. He still retained the eleven men that he had appointed, all being successful in their own right. Two of his unit team, Malcolm and Bob, had themselves been promoted to unit supervisors. His ability to show diplomacy and tact in handling and manipulating his men were exemplary, and the company felt that Harold was the right man to build up and develop a successful branch.

His salary as a manager would be at least commensurate with the income he was currently earning. He would continue to receive the commissions he had already earned in the field. He would then earn production commission on the results of his branch salesmen, so expanding the numbers of representatives would have to be one of his prime objects. Harold was also reassured that he was free to make his own sales, but in his own time and as long as it did not interfere with his managerial position and responsibilities. He would be totally responsible for the sales side of the branch activities. The financial and administrative side of the office including the office staff were the sole responsibility of the branch cashier, who worked side by side with the branch manager. This meant that Harold would not have to worry about the running of the office or the accountancy department. He was further advised that he would have to have three months' training as an assistant branch manager at Reading branch. We both found it an attractive package, but we still had to resolve our quandary about leaving our wonderful new home and our families. Would it all be worth it?

Mam and Dad had already expressed their delight at Harold being offered promotion. When we asked for their opinions on moving away from home, their response was no less than I would have expected from them, having old-fashioned traditionalist views. A wife's duty is to go with her husband wherever his work takes him. They added that of course they would miss us, and particularly the children, but it was not for them to offer advice or to interfere with any decision we would make. In any case, we would always visit as often as we could.

Eventually, Harold came to the conclusion that having been given more or less carte blanche with his proposed new situation, he would actually enjoy being in a position of authority. Before confirming his acceptance, he did insist that he be told of the new location.

Newcastle-upon-Tyne!

The company's directors explained that the Newcastle branch was just about at the bottom of the company's national branch table. With over twenty branches in the United Kingdom, it was at the bottom of the table in England, even though the city was in a heavy industrialised area, added to which, territorially, the Newcastle branch covered the largest area of any branch in the country. The executives believed that Harold was the man to take it out of the doldrums, that the branch should be much nearer to the top of the list. It was a challenge that Harold could not refuse.

In addition, Harold's father came from Tyneside, so the family connection added to my husband's enthusiasm.

Harold was now eager to accept the position, which of course was subject to his successfully completing the three months' training at Reading. I could not help but be as excited for him as he was. He would start his training at Reading at the end of March through to the end of June, so there was so much to be done.

Chapter 31

The Thames Valley is renowned for its sites of exciting historical interest as well as for its picturesque scenery and pretty towns, one of which is Reading. When Harold told me that he wanted me and the children to join him for at least some of the time, I was only too pleased, not just because I hated the idea of being separated from my beloved, but because it was a part of the country that I had never visited, although I knew that with its reputation, there would be much to interest us all.

The company had booked Harold into an old coaching house hotel in the centre of the town and he ensured that he would have a family room to accommodate us all for his 'all expenses paid' training period. The hotel was only a few yards down the road from his new temporary office, within easy walking distance. I could not spend the whole three months with him in Reading. I did not want to keep Anne off school any more than necessary, and I realised that I would have to start preparing for the move to Newcastle. I had no doubts that Harold would succeed with his training. He had very little paperwork to worry about, so I started planning our move in my mind.

He went down on his own for the first two weeks to feel his way around. He then suggested to me during one of his numerous phone calls that I should take the children down on the train. The girls had never been on a train, and he thought that being the first time for them, it would be an adventure. He explained that he hardly ever used his car, being in the office most of the time, so I could have it to take the children out during the day.

At that time there was one train a day in the mornings, from Leeds to Bournemouth, with a stop at Reading, so I was able to let the girls have their adventure, though Ruthie was only six months old. I sometimes reflect on the fact that it was something of an adventure for myself, trudging onto a train with two young girls, a baby in a pushchair, and our entire luggage, but I managed.

I arranged to spend the whole of the second month, four weeks, with him. The family room was very large and comfortable and the whole month turned into a wonderful holiday for us all. I took the children to many of the various lovely towns – Pangbourne and Cookham, amongst others – and we enjoyed walks along the riverside, the girls playing in the playgrounds. Henley-on-Thames was one of the big attractions with all the boats. It was spring and the weather was amenable for almost the whole time.

On one of our afternoon jaunts, I took the children to Marlow. At the side of the bridge, on the riverbank, and facing the Compleat Angler, a nationally reputed restaurant, I found a baker-cum-café which made the most wonderful pastries. Taking the children to cafés for tea had almost become a hobby, as we all loved our food. Harold frequently took us to his favourite Betty's, either to their Leeds café, or to the one in Harrogate, for afternoon tea.

In those days, a three-tiered cake stand fully laden with chocolate eclairs, meringues of varying description, sometimes filled with fruit, *palmiers* and other assorted pastries, all filled with luscious whipped cream, was placed on the table. In this way, one could have as many as one wanted, there was no need to worry about the bill. I found that the café in Marlow served the same luscious type of cream cakes. We, Anne and Pamela and myself, had two cakes each with cold drinks for the girls and tea for myself. The bill came to 18 shillings! It was unbelievable! And all freshly baked on the premises. That was a really sumptuous and happy afternoon

Being with Harold throughout that month, sometimes meeting him for lunch, was another one of those happiest periods in our marriage, and we both firmly believed it was the stepping stone to our new future in Newcastle to which we were all looking forward.

Chapter 32

The company's biennial conference for 1962 was held at the beginning of July, almost immediately after Harold completed his training as assistant branch manager. That year it was held at Torquay. The conference itself was conducted in the Imperial Hotel. We were allocated one of the other top-rated hotels in the town. The big difference that year was that my darling husband would be attending in his new capacity as a prospective branch manager, and I would accompany him in the very proud role of a forthcoming branch manager's wife, something about which I was indeed extremely proud.

During that final month of his training, I had been at home planning our move. We were given a month or thereabouts to relocate to Newcastle, again all expenses paid. It appeared that we would have no problem selling our dearly beloved home, Pamanda Court. I did realise that it was going to be a very heartbreaking wrench, but the potential the move offered to Harold's future career convinced us both that it was going to be a very worthwhile move.

Leaving the children with my mother once again, we drove down to Torquay, leaving on the Sunday. My darling husband was truly optimistic that we could make the journey in one day. Very optimistic for the state of the roads in those days!

As had now become our custom, we took turns at the wheel. It was about three in the morning, we had just driven through Tewkesbury, and Harold was very tired. His plans to drive through the night had been too ambitious and he suggested we have a sleep in the car. Five hours later we both woke up and decided to stop at the next decent hotel to wash, freshen up and have some breakfast. The days of motorway service stations particularly in the West Country, were as yet a thing of the future, but we were able to stop at what looked like a delightful country house hotel just past Bristol.

We eventually arrived at our Torquay hotel somewhat the worse for wear, after hours of travelling, but managed a rest before facing the wonderful reception I certainly knew Harold would receive on the official announcement of his new appointment.

Not long after our arrival in the ballroom for the welcoming dinner we met up with Cyril and Renee Kenny, the outgoing manager and his wife. Harold had already met them at previous conferences, and I knew them also, but Harold was keen to renew their acquaintance to discuss his future takeover. They discussed with us the proposed visit after the conference for him to look over his new territory. He told them as always that all arrangements were to include me.

The conference was, as expected, very successful, with Harold again being the centre of attention, with much adulation, whilst I, as I was well known for my contribution to his success, received similar attention, with comments from other members of the company expressing the wish that their wives were as attentive and supportive as I was. I doubt that they observed Harold's avid attention to me. As at the previous conference, his jealous nature showed itself. He rarely left my side as he feared that I might receive too much attention from any of the other men present. Occasionally, I sensed that he felt threatened as he would grab my arm and steer me away even in the middle of a conversation with others.

We were able to return home, having had the highest of commendations and good wishes for Harold's future in Newcastle.

Chapter 33

The village of Chollerford lies in pretty, slightly undulating country-side, about 19 miles to the west of Newcastle-on-Tyne. At that time the village was sited on the main Newcastle to Carlisle road. The road ran alongside the remains of the historic Hadrian's Wall. The Kennys suggested that we might like to stay at the George Hotel near the village overnight, when we visited Newcastle to review the branch, and explore our future housing possibilities.

They told us that The George was quite exclusive and both the hotel and the restaurant were very popular. So we took their advice and arranged to meet them for dinner on the day of our arrival. It was our very first visit to that part of country, and our initial impressions were very satisfactory. We had a very pleasant evening, during which Cyril described some of the niceties of the branch, and some of the less appealing aspects.

The territory of the branch took in the whole of the northern part of England, from the Scottish border, west coast to east, and as far south as a line from the mouth of the River Wear on the east side of the country, and across to the Lake District and the Cumbrian coast. The territory included, in addition to Newcastle, the towns of Workington, Kendal and Keswick on the west side, and on the east, Stockton-on-Tees, Middlesborough and Hartlepool amongst others.

At that time there were about nineteen representatives. The majority were in Newcastle, a couple in Gateshead, two in the Lake District and Carlisle, and two in the Stockton area. It was a huge area to cover, and though monthly meetings were routine procedure for every branch, at which all representatives were expected to attend, the manager's duties included visiting the reps on their home territory. This meant that Harold was going to have to travel considerably around the area if he was to motivate everyone to the standard that he was aiming for.

In his remit, Harold had been advised that he was to increase the numbers of branch members to as many as thirty during the coming months in order to lift the branch from its position at the bottom of the branch table. This was in addition to motivating the current team to increase their production.

This was a most formidable challenge indeed, but one about which I had no doubts that my husband would easily handle. Making arrangements for us to meet up again in the morning at the Newcastle office, we wound up a very interesting and satisfying evening.

We were both now in a heightened state of excitement and anticipation at the prospect of meeting Harold's proposed staff and exploring the offices. These were situated in Collingwood Street, which was on the south side of the town. On the opposite side of the road was a brief hill which took one down to the Quayside and the site of the renowned Sunday Market, in those days a somewhat run-down area.

On arrival the following morning, and having been relaxed with the customary cup of office coffee, we were shown round the premises. They were of traditional design, with heavy dark wood partitions that separated the front office from the manager's office and the staff rooms, very gloomy and old-fashioned by today's standards.

We were then given the exhilarating pleasure of meeting the branch cashier. Ian Ferguson was a middle-aged gentleman. He seemed very amiable, but not much of a talker. He was highly commended for his part in looking after the branch's accounts by Cyril. I thought to myself that it was as well that the branch cashier was very capable at his job, knowing how hopeless Harold was with statistics. He did seem to be something of a dour Scotsman, but the two senior gentlemen, Mr Ferguson and my husband, appeared to hit it off immediately.

Cyril then asked for the lady who he referred to as his personal secretary to come to his office. The person who emerged from the rear offices was a very short, extremely skinny plain woman. She looked about 30 years old. With her short close-cropped fair hair, she reminded me of a stereotypical school marm, especially with the severe mien and miserable aspect with which she presented herself. Her features were small and sharp. I recall her eyes as being cold and totally without emotion, giving her face a sour expression. She appeared to be totally lacking any personality. Her dress was also very plain and nondescript. Introduced to us as Miss Wright, she said her 'Hellos' and retreated back whence she came without saying another word. She had given me the impression of being a very miserable, unpleasant person, not what one would expect of a personal secretary, at least that is what I remember thinking at the time.

The office staff included two other young ladies who worked at the counter in the front office, but who were not available at that time, so meeting them had to wait till later.

Once outside the office and back in the street, Harold wasted no time in expressing his displeasure at the person who had been introduced to him as the branch manager's secretary, and who presumably expected to continue in the role with the new manager. I could tell he had been on tenterhooks since meeting the lady, to tell me what he really thought of her. His remarks about her confirmed my opinion of her. He had also found Miss Wright a very nondescript and unpleasant person, and added that he was not going to have a person with such a miserable disposition working for him as his personal assistant. His first task would be to replace her with a younger, attractive and lively lady, someone who would be both pleasant and an asset to the office. He also announced that amongst the several changes he intended to make was to improve the relationship between the representatives and office staff by engaging a couple of pretty counter staff, so establishing a much happier working atmosphere.

After lunch, the afternoon was spent reconnoitring the recommended areas to house-hunt. Gosforth had already been suggested as the nicest area, but the Kennys advised us to take a look at Darras Hall. They explained that it was a fairly recent development at Ponteland, and was known as the locality's professional and executive commuter belt. Ponteland was a village 7 miles north of the city on the road that runs through Northumbria and eventually to Scotland. The Kennys had lived in Darras Hall throughout their time in Newcastle with the company, and strongly recommended the area to us.

Driving around Darras Hall, and seeing the quality properties that made up the estate, all detached homes, we became enamoured with the area. We were delighted with the rural atmosphere, and having looked over a few properties which the village estate agents put to us, we eventually were happy to find a suitable family bungalow, double-fronted and having three bedrooms. It stood in a third of an acre of land, which had been the minimum permitted by the local council, so enjoying a large garden. It was situated at the perimeter of the estate on its south side, so it overlooked green fields.

Our haven Pamanda Court was sold very easily and at a fair profit, though the sale was nevertheless gut-wrenching, but our home to be at Birney Edge, Darras Hall seemed to hold promises of being another haven, so we returned to Leeds full of hope and expectancy for Harold's new position and our family's future life at Newcastle.

Chapter 34

As part of our moving preparations, we decided to have a party. It was to be not just a farewell party for our family and friends in Leeds, but we wanted to make it a 'thank-you' party to all our colleagues with the Sun Life of Canada Assurance Company in Leeds for all their support. In particular, we wanted to show our appreciation to Jimmy and Maxie Johnson for all those happy fun nights we had had at Bond End, the Johnson's home. Maxie liked her drink when she was having fun, something she had in common with my darling husband. This seemed to bring us even closer together.

Their generous hospitality and Maxie's sense of fun, her frantic and agile antics and her humorous anecdotes that kept us entertained usually into the early hours, three or four o'clock in the morning, would remain in our memories as part and parcel of our history with the company.

When we totted up the numbers of guests, around sixty, Harold suggested we have the affair catered. He felt it would be too much for me. He preferred me to be able to mingle with the guests, and not to be constantly in and out of the kitchen, even when he was hanging on to my every move.

Addleman's, who had catered at our wedding, were called in. When we rang them to come and see us, Mr Addleman arranged to pop round during the week, but could not specify an exact time.

Harold was cooking his favourite snack, the only time he cooked anything for himself as I refused to cook it, but would not stand in his way. He was frying bacon, a forbidden food in our religion, when the front doorbell rang. A quick glance through the glass front door told us it was Ansell Addleman. Panic stations! The smell alone filled the kitchen.

I answered the door and showed Ansell into the lounge, the room the furthest away from my husband's 'gourmet' cooking. That was the last thing we wanted divulging to, of all people, a kosher caterer. I went to rescue Harold from his sudden nightmare, transgressing one of the gravest rules of kosher eating, to find he had used his creative skills most adroitly. He had put the hot pan and its contents in the fridge!

We made our arrangements for our party of the year, never able to determine whether our caterer detected anything suspicious from the curious smell that seeped from the kitchen. The party, held a couple of weeks later, was a great success and the food was superb, as we had come to expect from our caterers, although it was tinged with a hint of sadness at having to leave so many of our friends in Leeds. Family and friends we knew we would be seeing again very soon.

Chapter 35

We settled into our new home at Birney Edge, Ponteland very comfortably. A double-fronted dormer bungalow, it had two large bedrooms on the ground floor and a third very large bedroom, which had been built into the roof space at a later date. This was accessed by a staircase that separated the lounge-cum-dining room, and the kitchen on the left side of the property from the bedrooms and bathroom on the right side.

Harold and I had the large front downstairs bedroom, and Anne occupied the rear bedroom. The two younger girls shared the much larger upstairs room as it had plenty of play space.

Our routine to start with continued as we had lived in Leeds. Anne was enrolled into the local primary school in Ponteland. I continued to meet my husband for lunch with Pamela and Ruth as we had always done since he joined the company, that is, at least twice a week, on Tuesdays and Thursdays. The main difference was that Harold now had a nine-to-five office job, leaving him with much more free time in the evenings.

Within the first few days of Harold taking over as branch manager, he came home and told me that our first impressions of Cyril Kenny's private secretary had now been confirmed and there was no way he could work with Miss Wright. She was the same cold, miserable person we had met previously, and he had to replace her with a more pleasant and lively young lady as his personal secretary. He added that she could help Mr Ferguson, the branch cashier, and assist in the front office, but he also had his reservations about her dealing with the general public and their queries at the front desk.

He very quickly found himself two young ladies whom he called 'dolly birds' and whom he believed would bring some life and create a much pleasanter atmosphere in the office. This action proved very successful, particularly with the representatives.

As he had done in Leeds, he also made it known that he intended to recruit only married men, for the same reasons as previously, and which had shown the results he had aimed for. There were two single men in the branch when he took over and they continued to work for the company, but he enlightened his branch to his aims and methods immediately at his first monthly branch meeting.

From the beginning, as I had expected, Harold wanted me to come into the office and make my presence known as frequently as possible. I continued to write Harold's monthly bulletins for him, with all the branch material being provided by Ian Ferguson, and which were to contain any special stories or reports of the reps' successes. Harold acquainted me with the facts, which I then wrote out for him to insert into the bulletins. In fact, I more or less assisted him as I had been doing in Leeds.

My assistance was more visible at branch meetings, as I had anticipated. He asked me to act as hostess, and provide coffee and cakes. My home baking went down a treat, especially my sausage rolls.

Harold decided to hold a party at our home for the representatives and their wives, or girlfriends as the case may be, during our second month. As I always did, I went to town, and catered my usual lavish affair. Harold always wanted to create a lasting impression, and I am sure I did this. His main motivating motto which he came to use frequently, was, 'Look what I have done! If I could do it, so can you.'

The wives especially seemed to be very impressed. I had made some cheesecakes. Though a well-known and much-liked confection in Leeds, I learned that it was totally unheard of at that time in Newcastle, but my baking again proved to be a great success and my cheesecakes soon came to be in demand at our future functions. That party was to be the first of many and did much to establish a very happy rapport between Harold and his team.

Two new salesmen were recruited by the end of the year, and my husband's efforts had begun to show results. He held his first branch Christmas party in the office. As grand office parties go it was a splendid end to the year, and a great beginning for my beloved husband in his new capacity as branch manager.

We were both determined to maintain a good social life away from the office. Not knowing anyone in the area, we decided that our best option to make new friends was to join a synagogue. This was done very quickly. The members of the Newcastle Hebrew Congregation were very welcoming. When we explained our situation as newcomers to the city, it was suggested that we would make friends much more quickly if we joined the Bridge Section. We were introduced to Alex, a synagogue committee member, and explained to him that neither of us had ever played bridge before. Within the week, Alex arranged for us to have lessons at the synagogue, playing with Alex and his wife. They became close friends.

Over the next few weeks we had four hour-long lessons. I, myself, found the game rather tricky to learn, and I know Harold had problems remembering the various calls.

The Christmas season was approaching, so my darling husband was heavily involved at the office. He had also had to make his first trip to the Lake District to meet the salesmen there. One resided in Workington, and two in Kendal, so it meant he had to stay overnight, something that he disliked intensely. I was also unhappy about this, but I could not leave the girls, and it was impractical to take them with, especially as Anne was at school.

Having had an intensive start to our new vocations in the northeast, Harold suggested we take a long break over the festive season. He had been strongly recommended to the Peebles Hydro Hotel in Scotland, as being very family-friendly, so we decided to take the plunge and try it for the full period, including New Year's Eve.

The journey up to the border was very long and, being winter and snowing, it was very treacherous. The roads were narrow and winding over the hills, passing through Otterburn and then Jedburgh to the high peak at the Scottish border. We had been travelling over snow and very icy roads. These did become a little easier once over the border, but the roads were still narrow and winding. Nevertheless, the scenery was breathtaking. It took us a good six hours to reach our destination, and we decided even before our holiday had actually started that we were grateful we had decided to stay the full holiday period.

The hotel did live up to its exalted reputation. It was a beautiful, stylish building, The furnishings in our huge family room were the last word in traditional decor and very comfortable. Eating arrangements were made for the children to have their teas at five o'clock. I remember being surprised at the large number of children who sat down for tea, which helped to make us feel even more comfortable, knowing there were obviously quite a number of families who were also enjoying the facilities of this splendid hotel.

There was a very full programme of entertainments and seasonal festivities, especially for the younger clientele. However, one particular incident became an historic feature in our memories of experiences that Christmas of 1962.

The children were in bed, and we were both settling down, after dinner, sitting in the ballroom, awaiting the dancing, when a lady came round asking if anyone was interested in playing a game of bridge, as a fourth player was needed. She approached us, and Harold looked at me, jumped up and said he would play. I was startled at this, as having had only four lessons, I knew that Harold was insufficiently capable of playing with more proficient players. I called him to think again, telling him that he was too inexperienced to join these ladies. He just pooh-poohed me, and insisted that he was well able to play. I told him he would only make a fool of himself, but he was even more determined to prove that a few lessons made Harold Courtney a supreme expert. It was now becoming a habit with Harold that with anything new, he believed one lesson made him an expert!

He returned about half an hour later. His tail was firmly stuck between his legs, and the look of dejection and humiliation was even more firmly etched on his face. He then swore that he would never play bridge again. I never really found out what had happened in that bridge room, I could only guess, but I must have guessed correctly, as Harold never ever, to the best of my knowledge, played bridge again. Neither did I!

Another of the outstanding features of that holiday were the Hogmanay celebrations, which the children were permitted to watch. Bagpipes are not one of my favourite instruments, but they certainly gave a festive flavour to the New Year merry-making, with their midnight entrance. The whole atmosphere brought a lump to my throat. It was an amazing and splendid way to end our first holiday 'up North'.

The rest of the holiday was such a great success for the girls and ourselves, that we decided to return again the following year, and promptly booked for Christmas 1963. We were very surprised to learn on booking that the hotel was already heavily booked for a year ahead. I suppose I should not have been that much surprised as we did have a wonderful time that year at the Peebles Hydro Hotel.

Our return journey home proved to be much more wearisome than we could have anticipated, not knowing the customs of the country at that time. Not only was it New Year's Day, but it was a Sunday. In Scotland everything was closed. We had hoped to stop for a meal, but did not know the pubs and local hotels all closed for the day, so we were unprepared and eventually arrived home totally starved. Nonetheless, it had been a very happy time for all of us, and in spite of my husband's bridge 'glitch', one of our very successful enterprises.

Chapter 36

Two to three weeks after we returned from our holiday at Peebles, Harold renewed his efforts to persuade me how much better off we all would be if the girls were to go to boarding school. This man was unbelievable! I thought I had already convinced him that there was no way I was ever going to allow my children to be sent away from home, under no circumstances whatsoever. Yet he persisted in trying to make me believe that it was for everyone's good that the children be sent away so that I would have more time to devote to his needs as a branch manager. Clearly the only person's needs in his mind were his own. I was dreadfully angry again. I was never going to allow anyone else to bring up my children. Our home was their home, for always, and I tried to bring it to his mind that however much he insisted, this was one issue about which I would always stay strong.

I did realise that in his position he had increased responsibilities, and that he wanted me by his side as much as possible, although it was never a prerequisite of a branch manager in the company. And so with this in mind I came up with a compromise – in fact, two suggestions as a compromise.

The first was, I suppose, in the way of calling his bluff. I explained that if he was so concerned about the girls' education, though this argument never featured in his list of reasons for sending the girls away, that we should let them go to private schools in the area. He readily agreed, but said that I should deal with all the arrangements.

In deciding the best schools for our girls' education, I only had to consider Anne and Pamela at that stage. Ruth was well under school age and I was unaware of any nursery schools in the locality. I had no plans for her education as yet. After much researching and perusal of the schools' brochures, I decided that of the two top schools in Newcastle, or so I was informed, the Newcastle Church High School seemed the best option, in spite of its name. I was informed that while it was called a church school, the school did not restrict children of other religions. Both girls could start at the beginning of the autumn term in September, but that was conditional on them passing an

104

admission examination, for which we were just in time to submit their applications.

Though Pamela was only four at the time of the exam, I was able to enter her. I had taught her to read quite well for her age, as I had done with all three girls. She also knew the basics of numbers at the standard required for her to pass the exam, so I was quietly confident that she could pass the exam, just as I was equally confident that Anne's knowledge was up to the necessary standard. Ultimately, only Pamela passed with flying honours.

The second suggestion, my husband also agreed to without argument. To give me more time to spend with him, I proposed I should have a live-in help. This would assist me with baby-sitting arrangements, which had proved almost impossible living in a new city and not knowing anyone. In view of the previous disaster with the Spanish au pair, I renounced the idea of any foreign help. I hoped we would be able to find someone local. Harold jumped at the idea and said he thought he would be able to sort something out, which he did fairly quickly.

He searched several single mother and baby homes and was introduced to an Irish lady who had only just given birth and had given her baby away to be adopted. She had no family whatsoever and at the age of 23 was looking for a good home. We took to Marie immediately we met her.

She promised to be a willing worker and had a very pleasant personality. Tall and slim, and quite pretty, she had shoulder-length blond, almost white hair. Her references from the home were satisfactory. She was a reliable person, we were told. She seemed just the person we were looking for.

We had to adjust the loft area to the left of the staircase, putting floorboards down in order to make it into another bedroom. Marie said she was very happy with her living arrangements and was prepared to start immediately.

She told us she knew no one in Newcastle, and did not go out much in the evening. We had resolved our baby-sitting arrangements and Marie turned out initially to be a good help in the house, very cheerful and caring.

Even though we were so far away from the rest of our families, life was going so well now. Harold was happy that I was able to spend more time with him in the office, even though I still insisted in having Ruth and Pamela with me then, in the short term.

Harold came home one day around this period and told me that a gentleman had come into the office on official business. A Newcastle resident, the person was Jewish, originally French, so he had a slight French accent, and the two men had hit it off together immediately. Charles, an extremely jovial and friendly person, had invited us to his home to meet his family, his wife Phyllis and their two daughters. There began a very close friendship with all his family and friends. The family lived in Gosforth, which was several miles east of our home in Ponteland. They also had relatives in nearby Kenton. Nevertheless, we were welcomed into Charles's family circle and we all enjoyed a very happy and long-standing friendly relationship with them for the whole time we lived in Newcastle.

Marie had come into our family at just about the right time, when our personal social life began to escalate, and so we could get out and about more freely.

One of the most popular programmes on television at that time was *That Was The Week That Was*, a humorous satirical look at the week's news. It became the focus of our social life, such was its appeal. We each took it in turns to host a Saturday night dinner buffet and sat around the television set, determined not to miss a single episode. These tremendously enjoyable soirées continued for many weeks, and well after the series finished.

Chapter 37

Everything was going so well since Marie joined our family. Our social life, both personal, and in connection with Harold's business, was now making Harold very happy. I, too, was happy, now that I seemed to have made our compromises work well.

In my husband's delight with the way our life was going, he again displayed his generosity to the limit. Although he had not got his own way as far as the children were concerned, I believed that this happily no longer worried him. He was eager to show his gratitude for my perpetual support, almost reluctantly accepting that I had done the right thing.

Ever since I had started to learn to play the piano at the age of seven, I had wanted a grand piano. I had been learning on Mam's upright German piano, which was a beautiful piece of furniture as well as a lovely instrument. She gave it to me when we got married, but I still yearned for my grand piano. As soon as my talent showed itself, I pointed out that I felt my technique would benefit from a much superior piano. However, the answer I received from my parents was always the same, 'Your husband can buy you one when you get married', or words to that effect.

Harold knew from the beginning of my ambition one day to have such a piano, so that when he suggested we go out and try to find a suitable one, I was so elated. I could have jumped over the moon and back again, several times. Hopefully we would get a sensible exchange price for my upright. I was loath to part with my German piano. Having been my mother's it was of great sentimental value, but for me to achieve an almost lifelong ambition, I just had to have a grand piano, and now the opportunity had arrived.

It seemed Harold had already been looking up piano shops. He took me to the most prestigious of musical instrument shops in Newcastle, which happened to be in the centre of town. I was in my element. There were a number to look at. And there were a couple of Steinway baby grands! Of all piano manufacturers, the Steinway was the summit of my desires. I tried playing the ones of my choice and was easily able to pick the best. The tone, the technical details were as beautiful as one would expect from a Steinway. We were able to conclude a satisfactory deal with my German upright taken in part exchange. I had achieved my lifelong heart's desire, a baby grand piano.

It was not so long after buying my piano that Harold came up with another suggestion. As a teenager Dad had given me his Singer sewing treadle machine. This, too, had accompanied me to my marital home. I had always enjoyed the occasional dressmaking and had made some use of the machine as time allowed me.

Harold suggested I exchange it for a more up-to-date model. It would take up less room, for starters. It would be very nice to have one of the latest machines that had many useful embroidery and fancy stitching features. Once again, my lovely husband was able to negotiate a good deal on a new table machine.

During the next couple of months, during the summer of 1963, I embarked on a sewing spree that saw my girls fitted out with a very smart selection of 'Courtney' couturier designs for the summer. And not to feel left out, I presented my darling with two very fetching beach outfits for our forthcoming summer holiday, two sets of beach shorts and jackets in a very attractive Paisley fabric.

It seemed there was no limit to the extent that my darling would go to please me now, and I too, reciprocated in appreciation of his efforts.

Although we were all so tremendously happy, one thing did upset me. The results of the two girls' school entrance exams which they had taken earlier in the year, at least the fact that Anne had not passed hers.

I realised that her exam results were a cause for grave concern. During a subsequent meeting with the head of the junior school, I was reassured that Anne could have a second chance at the entrance exam the following year. I immediately embarked on an intensive course of coaching at every available opportunity throughout the whole period up to the time of the exam in 1964.

I concentrated on her arithmetic tables, particularly the eights and nines, and searching out and correcting her weaknesses. I really worked her hard, dreading the catastrophe that awaited us if she failed a second time. The one major break during all this was the summer holiday we had planned for the end of our first full year in Newcastle, in August 1963.

Chapter 38

Now that we had Marie to help me with the children, we decided to take her with us on our two-week holiday. Riccioni, just south of Rimini on Italy's Adriatic Coast, was to be our destination. I dreaded flying, and even though I had already been up above in a plane, as when we went to Jersey, my fear was mild compared to Marie's who had never flown before. When we asked her if she would like to accompany us on holiday, she was so keen that I doubt she gave the flying aspect of it any thought. It was only when we actually stood on the tarmac in front of the aircraft (covered corridors to the plane were not our experience at that time), that poor Marie went into apoplexy.

Harold insisted I have a brandy to calm my nerves, but it seemed nothing would help Marie. Of course, we eventually persuaded or perhaps pushed her onto the plane. The girls were highly amused. Flying seemed to come naturally to them. Well, they had flown from being babies. We were no sooner in the air than Marie became sick, and continued to be so for most of the journey. An unforgettable flight!

The hotel, a three-star, was a delight. We had booked two rooms. Marie agreed to share with the children. Being August, the temperature was very hot and we enjoyed being on the beach. The children played on the sands. The hotel was close by, though not immediately next to the beach. The days, too, were a delight. The evenings were another matter.

Harold and I had both looked forward to the holiday and having Marie with us, as we would be able to have some free time to ourselves in the evenings whilst she looked after the children. Much to our anger and our annoyance, this proved not to be the case. On the second day, after dinner, which we all had together in the hotel, when we were preparing to go out, there was no Marie. She had disappeared.

All along the beach were numerous bars and nightclubs which we hoped to investigate for an hour or so. This plan was soon thwarted by our help's unplanned absence. Harold chose to go out and look for her. It was dark outside and the bars were all very dimly lit. He did eventually find her – in one of the bars, chatting up some male! It would appear that Marie had found her niche, amongst the beach bars of Riccioni. However, we were having none of this. We had made it clear to her before coming away that we were taking her with us as a working holiday and that the rules of her employment would be the same as at home, with a few evenings off and some other daytime free by arrangement. This fact had escaped her mind, apparently, so Harold, having brought her back to our room, reminded her in his kindly manner. She was very apologetic, promising not to repeat the incident again.

This was not to be, and she repeated her untoward behaviour twice before she got the message and agreed to behave herself.

Once we decided we were able to rely on Marie to care for Pamela and Ruth responsibly, we arranged to take Anne with us on a coach trip to Venice for the day. It proved to be a very enjoyable experience, showing Anne the canals with their gondolas. We stood on the Rialto Bridge and the Bridge of Sighs so that Anne could watch the gondolas and the vaporettos, Venice's main means of transport and take photographs.

The Murano glassworks were a fascinating education, being able to watch the manufacture of the glass and the glass blowing, which was part of the manufacture of the ornaments. We took back some souvenirs, glass ornaments and figurines, but the one I treasured for many years was a large flower vase sixteen inches high, in crystal with green ribbon swirls circling the body. It took pride of place on my sideboard for a long time.

I had hoped to be able to see inside the Basilica: however, when I tried to enter I was stopped and informed that I was not correctly dressed. I was wearing a sundress and had nothing with which to cover my head and shoulders, so Harold took Anne inside to see the magnificent religious structure and icons whilst I waited outside.

After sitting and resting for a little while in St Mark's, known as San Marco Square, watching the world go by, we found a little café in a back street behind the square. It was obviously the haunt of the locals, so we knew it must be good. It was the first time we had tried Croques Monsieur and they were exquisite, toasted sandwiches with Italian cheese and various meat fillings. This all added to our very happy memories of that day.

The little principality of San Marino, which was only a very short distance from Riccioni, was the second main trip that we took with all the girls. It is a well-known tourist area, renowned for being on high ground, but we enjoyed the time we spent there, and again we were able to find souvenirs to take home, for the children as well as ourselves.

In spite of the problems of the first few days, Harold and I had a wonderful time with the girls and I am sure they also enjoyed their holiday, so much so that we resolved to return in the not so far distant future.

Chapter 39

Having Marie to help with the children had made it much easier for me to spend time with Harold at the office, much to his pleasure, or so he said, but since returning from our holiday in Italy, she had changed. She seemed to have reverted to what I believed to be her old self. She was no longer the subdued person who had originally joined our family. She wanted to go out much more in the evenings, and I suspected she was man-hunting or some such behaviour.

She never discussed her evening's activities, and since they did not impinge on our arrangements and prevent us from pursuing our own social life, I saw no point in pushing the matter. I had always told her that if she was in any way troubled and wished to talk to me, I would always listen, and since she seemed happy, that was all that mattered.

Harold's success at the office continued. He had engaged some more representatives and production figures were improving, albeit very slowly. One of the snags we learned in employing married men only, particularly in the northeast, was that the wives objected to their menfolk working in the evenings. Some of them confided in me that they found it difficult to trust them. I always did my best to reassure them, quoting my own experiences with my own beloved. The result of these 'honesty chats' was that I became much closer to them and our friendships proved beneficial to the general atmosphere in the branch. Some of the reps invited us to their homes. The increased amount of entertaining both at home and at the office also improved relations throughout the branch, hence the prospect of more sales and higher production.

Having Marie to help me made it possible for me to accede to Harold's wishes that I accompany him on his monthly day-trips to the Lake District and Kendal where two of his reps were based. Occasionally we were able to stay overnight.

This also contributed to the feeling of pleasantry and motivation which Harold hoped would result in more and more improved production.

As a reward for the improved sales figures produced during his first full year as branch manager, Harold decided to hold that year's

Christmas celebrations at the Royal Station Hotel. It took the form of a dinner for all the salesmen. That I would be the only lady at the event was not unusual, in fact I would have worried if Harold had not reminded me that I was again to be by his side, regardless.

The festivities and frivolities were no less than I had come to know of the northeastern folk. The highly intoxicated atmosphere was the best proof that the men were enjoying themselves. Once the dinner was devoured, a mad scramble to the bar heralded the true start to the evening, or so it seemed. I could not believe that so many pints of beer could be consumed in such a short space of time, especially after such an enjoyable meal.

Harold and I joined them, Harold with his usual whisky in his hand, and myself happy with my regular cup of coffee. Again, his boys were informed that I was able to enjoy myself and be full of life equally well on coffee.

It was nearing one o'clock in the morning when some of the men decided to call it 'a day'. A few, four others, suggested we adjourn to the station coffee room to round off the evening. A suggestion with which Harold was happy to go along. Another two hours later, we all decided enough was enough, and I with my beloved went home to collapse exhausted into bed at four o'clock in the morning. Another of Harold's successful office ventures.

On a personal note, and feeling the need for a well-deserved break, we rounded off the year spending the Christmas period as we had planned the previous Christmas by returning to Peebles Hydro in Scotland, only this time we only stayed the five days of Christmas.

Chapter 40

Marie was now going out in the evenings more frequently, and we came to the conclusion that she was either man-hunting or had now found herself a boyfriend. She was coming home later in the evenings, and on occasions she was much the worse for drink.

On one particular night, in spring 1964, we heard her coming in at about one o'clock in the morning. When we had converted that loft area into the fourth bedroom, some space beyond her bedroom was left untouched so that the joists above the lounge-cum-dining area were still in their original state, uncovered. We had advised Marie to be particularly careful not to venture beyond the end of her bedroom, as there was no flooring. With only the joists to balance on, if she fell on the joists, she could have a nasty accident.

We heard her go into her bedroom and within seconds we were jolted out of our efforts to fall asleep. A huge resounding crash shocked us out of our bed. We bounded down the steps to where the blast had come from.

There, in the centre of the lounge on the carpeted floor, sat Marie, completely dazed. She had fallen between the joists, through the ceiling into the room below. She looked a pitiful sight, sitting bolt upright amid the ceiling debris she had brought down with her. We checked her over as best we could. She insisted that she was perfectly all right, and apart from some slight scratches on the lower parts of her legs, she did appear unharmed. She was just very shocked.

Since she refused any medical help, I made us all a cup of tea. Harold had something a little stronger. He offered a tot of whisky to Marie, but as she was suffering the after-effects of both too much alcohol and the shock of the fall, I decided enough was enough and that a cup of tea was the best remedy.

It was now two o'clock and helping Marie back up to bed, we all ended that day knowing that we would have to sort out the damage in the morning.

About a month later, not hearing her come home by two o'clock, and thinking maybe we had missed her, we decided to check her room.

No Marie. No clothes. No possessions of any kind. She had left without saying a word. We never saw her or heard from her again.

Again I was left to cope on my own, not that I was worried.

Ruth had recently had her tonsils out in the Northern Hospital. In those days, mothers could not stay with their offspring overnight so I had to leave my little darling on her own for two nights. I did stay with her during the day, thankfully. I was able to bring her home safe and much better.

I had also been ferociously coaching Anne in a desperate effort to help her pass her school entrance exam second time round. Pamela settled into the school very comfortably, and I just could not bear the thought of how dejected Anne would feel if she did not pass the entrance exam the second time and could not get into that school. Thankfully, or so I felt at the time, all our hard work paid off. She did pass and she was able to start in the Junior Department at the Newcastle Church High School in September, the beginning of the autumn term and the new school year. We now looked forward to both girls enjoying their time at school and doing well.

Our friends and a neighbour helped out with baby-sitting, although we did have to curtail it a little. Conference time was coming up again and we were planning our summer holidays, a return trip to Italy. Mam was again taking the children for us so that I could again be with Harold at the July 1964 conference, so we deferred any decision to find a replacement for Marie for the time being.

Chapter 41

Our holiday in Italy's Adriatic Coast had given us so much enjoyment that we decided to return there for our summer holiday in August, only this time we would take the car and spend the whole month away so that we would be able to stop wherever we chose and explore the route.

We planned on spending about three days each way travelling there and back, so that we would be in Italy for about three weeks. A flat seemed more appropriate so that there would be more flexibility for us to move about as we wished. We made no prior accommodation bookings as we thought we would find no difficulty in that area. Cesanatica, a small town just north of Rimini, was to be our destination.

With three small girls in the back of the car and the boot packed solid, Harold and I took it in turns to drive us down to Dover for our first night's stopover. We hoped to have a very early start the next morning, 6 a.m., so happily we managed to find a comfortable guesthouse on the front overlooking the English Channel, very near to the ferry terminal.

The short crossing to Calais was uneventful and unmemorable. Faced with having to drive on the right side of the road for the first time in our lives, my darling husband insisted on taking up the challenge, informing me that there was 'nothing to it' in his typical nonchalant manner. Well, he did find there was 'something to it', more than he wanted to believe. Finding his way out of the terminal and manoeuvring the car the correct European way round the roundabouts, even following the French road signs, took more concentration than he realised, but we had a long way to go so I tried not to worry. After several circuits of the roundabouts around the port we eventually found ourselves on the right road north that would take us to the Belgium border and on to Brussels.

It was lunchtime when we arrived at the outskirts of Brussels, and we stopped at the side of a very broad highway with a wide grassy border to have our planned picnic lunch. So far there were no motorways. Our first experience of the autobahn was into Germany. I took the wheel and had the most enjoyable drive, flying down the perfectly straight road at 80 and over miles an hour. There was hardly any other traffic on the road and it was most exhilarating. We made a brief stop at Cologne on the bridge over the River Rhine to view the landscape, and made a mental note to have a longer stop on our return journey.

We planned to end the day's travelling in mid-afternoon to allow ourselves time to find accommodation and see some of the surrounding countryside. Thus it was at Heidelberg that we had our second night's break.

Again, we were soon able to find a small but delightful hotel near the town. The neon sign over the door announcing the hotel's name was most beckoning, and we found the large room assigned to us very comfortable for the five of us.

Heidelberg has one of the most prominent of German universities. The town is overlooked and dominated by its seventeenth-century castle, standing on a high hillside. There is an ambience of culture, presumably derived from its history and heritage, which I for one found fascinating, and which my husband told me he also felt.

I felt as though I was walking through a scene from the musical operetta *The Student Prince*. We had developed a love affair with the Italian Adriatic coast, and now it seemed that Heidelberg was also taking over our hearts.

We immediately went out to look for a place to eat. Strolling around, I found the quaint narrow roads very charming. There were cafés and restaurants at every turn, all announcing their menus on blackboards by the door. All the kinds of local food that I had often heard about were advertised, sauerkraut and German sausage, *sauerbrat*, *kartoffeln* (potatoes) in the German style. Just reading the menus made our mouths water. We picked a restaurant at random and did have a very tasty and enjoyable meal.

Regrettably, there just was not sufficient time to take in all the historic architecture and sites, but Heidelberg very happily imprinted itself on all our minds.

Leaving shortly after six o'clock the following morning, I took the wheel and sailed down the three-lane autobahn, which cut through the Black Forest. Two hours later, we reached the Swiss border at Basle. I had covered 200 miles in two hours! And thoroughly enjoyed every mile of it.

Harold took over the driving once through Swiss customs, which

117

enabled me to relax and enjoy the luxurious scenery, pointing it out to the girls. Our first encounter with the Swiss countryside was another unforgettable experience. The weather was perfect, hot and very sunny. The chalets with their window boxes dense and glowing with glorious colour from their beautiful plants, stood out amid the lush, green countryside.

Lunchtime found us at Lucerne, another beautiful town, so we parked near the lake and soon found a café. We chose Vienna Schnitzels for all of us, as they came highly recommended. These were served to us on a huge platter for the five of us. The owner must not have realised that three of us were children. The portions were colossal. They were served with another huge mountain of chips. The food was again beautifully cooked and tasted wonderful. The cost of the whole meal came to £2! It was unbelievable!

The price of the coffee did shock us. At the Swiss equivalent of 5 shillings per cup, I remember comparing it with the English price of a cup. It was then about 9 pence. Ah, happy days!

After lunch, we immediately set off, intending to make for the St Gotthard pass train station from where we would travel with the car under the tunnel under the Alps into the Italian side of Switzerland. I took the wheel and we started our ascent into the mountains. The road was very narrow, with single-lane driving along the numerous curves and hairpin bends. There were no safety barriers at the side of the road and I could see the dramatically steep drop into the abyss, which grew steeper and steeper the higher we climbed. It was quite frightening. One false move would be fatal. And yet the road was busy.

No one could be unaffected by the beauty of the landscape. Before long, I was driving through snow, and then I had taken us to the summit of the mountainous road where there was a very busy look-out post.

I had missed the train station. I suppose I was so keenly concentrating on my driving in such extremely dangerous conditions, and no one else remembered to look for the station, so taken up with the scenery were they that I had driven straight past it. But it was worth it. The children were disappointed to have missed the train ride, but the view was sensational, so devastatingly beautiful, seeing both the French side and the Italian side from the same position on top of the mountain, and with nothing to see but the mountains covered in snow, it was adequate compensation. We promised the children we would definitely go back through the train tunnel on our journey home.

The drive downhill towards Italy was not quite as treacherous, though still with many winding, hairpin bends. At four o'clock we were back in green countryside. We stopped to look for a café, and seeing some cottages at the roadside, Harold stopped and knocked on one of the doors and asked the lady who answered if there was a café around. Whether she clearly understood him remained a mystery, as she said she would make us a meal. She invited us to sit by her door where there was a table and some chairs. She soon produced a huge tureen of chicken soup, Italian style, of course. It contained masses of fine noodles and must have been one of the most scrumptious meals we had had on that holiday. We had certainly done ourselves proud in the food line so far.

Arriving at the Italian border, we continued towards Milan, took its ringroad and then drove east, across the north of Italy on the 'Motorway of the Sun'. It was time to find a bed for the night. We came to Bergamo and in the town we saw the most beautiful imposing building. It was a very fine baroque architecturally styled hotel. We expected it to be far too expensive for our budget, but it was getting late. We had travelled farther than intended that day and we were very tired, especially the children. Yes, we could have a family room.

The room we were taken to knocked us for six. In fact it was a suite, two huge bedrooms, each with monster double beds and an intercommunicating bathroom. The luxury was overwhelming. All the bathroom fittings were in very ornate gold with an elaborate lion's head as the bath's tap fittings. It was the height of luxury for us.

Once the children were bathed and in bed, Harold and I went to look for something to eat, or at least a snack and a drink. The children were safe, so the manager reassured us. We ventured out in to the dark streets and were amazed to find everything shut and not a soul around.

Back at the hotel, we learned that it was one o'clock in the morning. We had forgotten the two-hour change in the time. When we got our bill in the morning after a larger than expected Continental breakfast, we were blown away at the charge, £7 in total for us all. Another unbelievably cheap episode.

We arrived at our destination, Cesanatica, the following afternoon, having driven down the Italian Adriatic coast in blazing temperatures.

There was little problem finding accommodation, a two-bedroom

119

apartment. It was over a greengrocery shop, which was part of a parade of shops. We would be all right for shopping and buying Italian food, which we all really enjoyed.

For the second time, we had a glorious holiday lying in the hot sun on the beach and watching the children play in the glorious sands and paddle in the sea. Sightseeing was not such a priority this time. We made one excursion to the nearby town of Milano Marittima and made several trips to the local markets.

Our tenth wedding anniversary, 23rd August, occurred towards the end of our holiday. We had a small celebration there, going out for a meal, but planned to have a family get-together later when we got home.

Armed with boxes of peaches, watermelons and other delicious samples of Italian food, our return journey was just as enjoyable. We finally found the St Gotthard train station and travelled through the pass beneath the Alps. The children were thrilled to bits.

Four days in Switzerland, staying at a beautiful guesthouse just outside Lucerne, we were able to indulge in our shopping spree. The huge amounts of hot chocolate and gorgeous jams with our croissants were digested with gusto at breakfast. A large cuckoo clock was one shopping ambition achieved. We were yet to learn how annoying the constant call of a cuckoo in the home could be.

We even kept our promise to ourselves on the outward journey and spent a day in Cologne, allowing us time to look round the beautiful cathedral.

Once back home, we were able to look back on a very satisfying and happy holiday all round.

Chapter 42

Shortly after returning to the office, my husband told me that he had had enough of 'dolly bird' secretaries. They may look pretty and please the reps, but they lacked efficiency and common sense. He added they were very unreliable. Because of that, he had decided to reinstate 'misery guts' Miss Wright, as I referred to her, as his personal secretary. He declared that what she lacked in looks and attitude, she more than made up with efficiency and 'dedication to her work'.

Whenever I was in the office, during the two years since my husband took over as branch manager, I always found her the same, a 'non-person'. Without personality, she seemed to be without any emotion or character. However, I considered that Harold must know what he was doing by then, and the decision was his.

This made no difference to my role. He still expected me to be in the office whenever and as much as possible, being the generous hostess, and being a mentor to both the salesmen and their wives. I continued to write the branch bulletins, his speeches, and keep all our records. Life continued as it had done since he joined the company. Despite his constant jealousy and possessiveness, we were all happy and the branch prospered.

He informed me about the same time that he was pursuing his ambition to become a Mason. He thought that being a Mason would help to advance his career. He had been in contact with Rudolph again who had recommended a local Jewish lodge, and had named someone whom Harold could ask to sponsor him. This Harold had done, and he was now on the waiting list. The list was much shorter than the waiting list for membership to a Leeds lodge, he had been told, so things looked much more promising.

Our social life continued up to a point with our friendship with Charles's' family and other people who became friends through my husband's work. I did find it hard work, fitting everything in, and Harold agreed to find another help for me in the house. This proved more difficult than before, and it was to be some time before a nice pleasant and suitable lady was found.

Chapter 43

The telephone must have been the most widely used instrument to make life changes in those days. I never, in my wildest dreams, anticipated that the one phone call from my darling husband towards the end of 1964 would bring about such a tumultuous turnaround in our relationship which would be so devastating to me.

When he told me that he was unable to meet me, thus breaking a perpetual lunch arrangement that we had had for over eight years, almost since he joined the Sun Life Company of Canada, I was not unduly concerned, but to put to me that I still come down to the office and have lunch with another man ... I could not believe what I was hearing.

Up till now, if Harold thought that a man was as much as looking my way, he was extremely annoyed and often angry. If I had suggested meeting another man for whatever reason, I know there would have been a scene. I would never have even had such a thought, let alone made the suggestion, loving my husband so much and knowing how jealous and possessive he was.

But the worst aspect of the whole conversation was that he had insisted that I dine with the man who I considered to be the most obnoxious member of his sales team.

Harold had appointed Edward Brown as a representative soon after he became branch manager. At the time he seemed a pleasant enough man. Almost as tall as my husband, and about the same age, he was very slim. He was, as I soon learnt, a very good salesman, very charming when he wanted to be. Unfortunately, in my opinion, he was a very heavy drinker. He was also quite good-looking and in time he let it be known that he considered himself extremely good-looking. In fact, he regularly boasted that he was irresistible to women.

His wife, Mae, was a very pretty lady, shy and retiring, and in the few times I had met her at branch functions, seemed oblivious to her husband's behaviour and attitude. Either that, or she turned a blind eye to it.

By the end of his first full year Edward had produced the highest amount of business of any salesman in the branch. That he was a good salesman was in no doubt, though in no way could he be compared with my husband. I believed that because of Edward's success, my husband was drawn to him. They seemed to develop a close friendship. This relationship must have given Edward more confidence in his behaviour to the ladies in the office. He became increasingly arrogant and egocentric. Whether this behaviour, which I found extremely offensive, extended to any other ladies he came into contact with, I could not know at first. I was to find out.

Edward was unable to keep his hands to himself, and as the era of sexual harassment as an offence was still many years away – in fact, I do not remember the term 'sexual harassment' ever being used at that time – Edward took great delight in pinching or stroking the ladies' bottoms. If he got the opportunity to rub up to one of the office ladies, or make what I considered to be offensive gestures, touching them in the most inappropriate places, he would certainly do so. At least that is what I saw whenever we both happened to be in the office at the same time.

To my knowledge no one ever complained. It seemed to be accepted behaviour.

Over the weeks, whenever I was in the office, Edward's bravado came out and he started making offensive remarks to me. I had heard compliments about my support for my husband for a long time now, and I knew them to be complimentary.

These types of remarks, now in a somewhat twisted form, started being uttered by this man. From how he wished his wife was like me, and variations on that theme, he advanced to making sexual innuendoes. Eventually, these developed to him making even more offensive suggestions, such as that he would like to take me to bed. Offers to spend the night or the weekend with him, and other similar remarks, were made on many occasions.

My problem was twofold. I was worried as to how my excessively jealous and possessive husband would react if I told him about his super-salesman's obnoxious behaviour. I did not want to sabotage my husband's branch's improving production record. I could not put Harold in the position of having to dismiss the man. I could not stop going into the office, as I sometimes wished were possible. To avoid any unpleasantness, my only recourse was to ignore the man, whom I had come to dislike and resent immensely, especially as he showed such lack of respect to myself and, as I thought at the time, towards my beloved husband. I maintained my decorum and tried not to let it influence my behaviour in the office. After all, as I have already remarked, sexual harassment was something that we ladies just had to put up with.

Such were my feelings about Edward Brown when Harold suggested that I have lunch with the man, because he, Harold, much to his dismay as he put it, had to miss out on a regular and longstanding feature of our lives.

I had told Harold I would explain my reasons when he got home in the evening. Though I had considered telling him on several earlier occasions, this was now crunch time and I was worried and full of consternation all afternoon. He had been so insistent and seemed angry when I refused the offer. I could almost just imagine Edward's remarks when Harold told him of my refusal to have lunch with him during our phone conversation.

The whole situation was of such great concern to me. I could not understand my husband's sudden desire to pass me off to another man, let alone someone like Edward. I just found the whole scenario weird and unbelievable.

The afternoon passed very slowly, thinking how best to explain everything. I was just overwhelmed by my feelings of trepidation, wondering even if I would be believed, so strange was the whole situation.

As soon as Harold arrived home that evening, he demanded to know my explanation. This in itself was significant. I tried to persuade him to have his dinner. The children had eaten. I suppose I was trying to delay the dreaded moment, but my husband wasn't having it. He had to have my explanation immediately.

Harold listened impatiently. Then he amazed me with his reaction. He was completely calm. There was not the jealous outburst or expressions of dismay that I had anticipated. He seemed annoyed, but there was no anger. His response was to tell me that he would speak to the gentleman and tell him to keep away from me. His reply was very reassuring.

The following evening, he told me that he had spoken to Edward and that he would not be annoying me any more.

A couple of days later, I was waiting for Harold to come home from work when a knock at the door disturbed my meal preparations. I was absolutely dumbfounded to see the offending gentleman on my doorstep. He said he had to see Harold. Happily, Harold turned up almost immediately.

He called Edward into the house. I felt shattered. Nothing further was said to me at that point in time, but I resented having such an ignominious person in my home, especially as Harold had told me that Edward had promised to keep away from me. Feeling very disturbed, I waited for Edward to leave, eager to ask why Edward had turned up having been told to keep away from me.

We had a small row when I told Harold I did not want the man in my home. I never wanted the man in my home. Harold protested that as the man had come on business, I was being unreasonable. He eventually agreed never to ask Edward to our house, and to tell him he must never come here either.

I was thoroughly shaken again when a few more days later Edward turned up at my home and said that Harold had invited him to the house to speak to him. I did not know who to believe. I could not even believe that Harold would do such a thing after he had promised to keep the man away from me. And yet, Edward was here on my doorstep telling me that yet again Harold had asked him to come to our home.

This time a more acrid row developed between my husband and I after Edward left. He told me that Edward was an important member of his sales team, and as such he sometimes needed to speak to him urgently. Business was business, I was told. I responded by telling him he should conduct his business in the office and not in my home. Harold replied that if he wanted to speak to Edward in our home, he would do so.

Harold had been telling me that he would make sure that Mr Brown stayed well away from me, and yet here he was making excuses to have the gentleman at my home. My husband was pushing my wishes and feelings to one side. This was something that had never occurred before.

The reps would never come to our home uninvited. It seemed that now my beloved husband was telling me one thing and doing another. Had he actually told Edward to keep away from me? I was beginning to wonder what was really the truth.

Two doors away from the office on Collingwood Street there was a café which was frequented by the reps sometimes for a coffee and a snack. Harold and I had the occasional tea or coffee there and we met in the café from time to time before going into the office. I decided that rather than go into the office first, I would meet Harold in that café. I always had Ruth with me, so it seemed easier for us all.

It was not long before I noticed that Edward would follow me into the café. I always got there before Harold. Sometimes other reps were also there, which eased my feelings of discomfort, but his sudden perpetual presence seemed too much of a coincidence. He still offered his unwanted remarks, although they were much toned-down now.

Nevertheless, Edward continued to turn up at my home on a regular basis over the next few weeks, then months. Not only were my feelings being ignored, but I felt as though I was being stalked. Harold would tell me he wanted Edward to keep away from me, and yet Edward seemed to be around us more than ever. My husband no longer behaved as though he wanted to please me. The times when he would do anything I wanted were no longer happening. He said one thing and was now doing something totally different. It looked to me that Harold was deliberately bringing Edward to our home so that that man would be more and more in my presence, giving him the opportunity to say the horrible things that Harold had told me he had admonished him for.

The arguments between my husband and I became equally more frequent and accusatory. Our relationship became more and more tense. It had changed, and seemed to be deteriorating. I just could not understand what had brought about this change in Harold's attitude towards me. Nor did it occur to me to ask anyone else for advice. I still trusted my husband to keep his word, and that the nightmare would blow over as suddenly and quickly as it had started. In spite of this, our personal and social life continued as though nothing wrong had happened. He still showed himself to be the most loving of all husbands when with our friends.

Chapter 44

Our regular weekend tête-à-têtes with our friends continued, with Harold behaving as though nothing was wrong, so providing me with a very welcome and helpful diversion. I was beginning to feel the stress of never being sure of my darling husband's extraordinary change in character, with regards to his company colleague. Our friends certainly could not be aware of the way I was now feeling, nor of the strain that was creeping into the relationship between Harold and myself. I do not think they ever knew what was happening to us.

I was still very happy being the supportive wife, doing whatever Harold required of me in the office, hostessing the branch meetings, writing his bulletins and speeches, as well as keeping his records personal and financial, and whatever came along.

We still continued to have our lunchtime rendezvous, but they became more and more irregular and at varying times. Some of our most enjoyable times during that period were spent on occasional lunches at the Red House restaurant on the Quayside.

When time permitted, usually during school holidays, I took the children out into the countryside, visiting the various historic and beauty sites in Northumberland, of which there were many, including Otterburn Castle and Alnwick Castle. I usually found somewhere where we could have tea.

At the weekend, if the weather was favourable, and mainly in the summer, we would all take a day trip to the Northumberland coast, visiting Whitely Bay, Tynemouth, or further north, Alnmouth, Amble and the very popular Seahouses, and some of the many other little quaint villages along that coast. The beaches around that part of the country were some of the most beautiful I had seen, with their clean white sands. Our friends, Charles and his family, had a cottage near Seahouses and often spent the weekend in the summer there, so we visited them on some of those occasions.

The weather was not as one would have wished for much of the year for us to have full enjoyment of the area, but the girls and I certainly tried to make the most of whatever time there was to spend there.

They were able to learn so much about the countryside in that part of England.

Early that summer, Harold told me that he fancied a short break in the western side of Scotland, in Galway. He had already done his homework when he told me of this, and said he knew just the hotel. He had found it in a tourist brochure. It was a small private guest-house at Kirkcudbright on the southern coast of Galway. The brochure gave it a glowing report, including the food, so I looked forward to it, hoping for an opportunity to have a happy time with my husband and the children.

What I had not been told was that Harold had arranged a couple of meetings on the way, with prospective salesmen, thus dragging the journey out and tiring the girls. Finding the hotel then proved to be very difficult. Once at Kirkcudbright we searched the town, looking for the address. On making enquiries, we were told that the hotel stood at the end of a lane, and to follow the seacoast round to the bay. The hotel stood in the bay.

The lane was in fact a very narrow, muddy track, well over a mile long. There was no room for other cars to pass, although there were two passing places at wide intervals, and one side of the track fell away straight into the sea. That drive to the hotel was terrifying.

I cannot tell you of the immense disappointment we all felt when finally arriving at our destination. The weather was utterly awful. The promised accommodation was an old Victorian stone-built house, which in the misty atmosphere looked as though it had come out of some horror film. Our room, though quite spacious as a family room, was very ordinary, and I felt not too clean. The bathroom and toilet were communal in the hall.

Our biggest disappointment was the food. As we were all food lovers, it was absolutely horrific. Every meal was the same. We had booked full board, and each meal was exactly the same as the previous, a slice of meat and squishy, overcooked cabbage with the same watery hard-boiled potatoes. The pudding was some weird concoction which was described as sponge, floating in even worse watery custard. The less said the better!

On viewing the outside, to our consternation, the hotel was the sole occupant in the small bay. The tide came in but a short way, but the beach, which was completely mud flats up to the edge of the sea, was just useless as a place for the children to play. Complaining to the proprietor got us nowhere. His attitude was 'Take it or leave it'. He could not have cared less. His business would have never got off the ground in today's world.

We had to find something to make the most of our time there, so a couple of times we struggled with the track and made our way in the car into Kirkcudbright to see the town's sights. On another occasion walking seemed a better option, but that too was an ordeal. We put up with the situation for three days and then decided we could take no more, and left.

Deciding to continue with our break, we drove west and north through very narrow, very picturesque winding lanes following the west coast of Scotland, making for Ayr. There the guesthouse we settled for was the complete opposite to the disaster we had left behind. Bright and welcoming, even the town was beyond comparison, and we were able to enjoy the next couple of days.

Since our arrival in Newcastle, we were able to enjoy the occasional visits of various members of my family and our friends from Leeds. Mam and Dad spent a few days with us from time to time, as did Cyril and his wife Chana. These events were always eagerly looked forward to, especially by the girls. To me they were a welcome break from the confrontations by my husband and which were on the increase, both in frequency and intensity, but which never occurred in the presence of our house guests. At least not up until then.

Our lives were quite hectic now. I realised that, perhaps I should have help in the house again. Harold was only too eager to agree with me and to pursue the matter.

Chapter 45

Elizabeth was a student at Newcastle University and had had a brilliant academic record at school. She was living in university accommodation when she decided she preferred to live with a family. I do not know how Harold found her, but she told me at her interview that she felt she would be happier and more able to get on with her studies.

She seemed the ideal person to us. At nineteen years old, and quite pretty, she told us that she was a willing worker. She had plenty of spare time away from her studies to help me.

We liked her immediately. Her personality was pleasant, and the children took to her immediately. She soon found that she was able to relax and enjoy her life in our home.

Having Elizabeth's assistance, we were able to return to a fuller social life. She rarely wanted to go out, particularly in the evenings, and encouraged us to make use of that time. Having more freedom to go out brought me, however, more problems. Harold now decided to make one of his regular monthly visits to his Lake District agents, only this time he wanted me with him so we could stay overnight. We were to visit the Cowells who lived in Kendal, so a hotel in the town was booked.

Telling me about this, he then asked me how I felt about leaving 'loverboy' behind. I knew what he meant. He had recently been accusing me of encouraging his nasty colleague to visit us so often. He insisted that he told Edward to keep away from me, so why was he still coming to the house? I sensed that Harold was twisting things around, but there was no way I could be sure, as I had now learned that confronting him with such allegations only inflamed him more and brought strong denials.

During an argument I very mistakenly, but in my naivety, announced that Edward was a good-looking man, that he believed he was irresistible to all women, and that this gave him a licence to treat all women as he did, obscenely. He apparently thought that the women enjoyed his mistreatment, which was totally untrue. My darling husband had digested everything I said and then used it against me, accusing me of leading the man on. This was a new move, but one that he was to use frequently. I had always trusted him, and still could not understand why he was doing this. This taunting me was just the first of many similar instances, and worse, that I was going to endure.

That visit to the Cowells was constantly interspersed by my husband's horrible and malicious referrals to my so-called 'absent lover' – 'was I missing him?' and similar uncalled-for declarations. Sometimes I was able to counter-respond by insisting he ensured that the gentleman (if he could be called that) not be invited to our home, but these protestations fell on deaf ears. He was also reprimanding me for not supporting him sufficiently. The man whom I adored and worshipped, and for whom I would do anything, indeed I thought I was doing everything he wanted, was lecturing me repeatedly about wifely loyalty and that 'a woman's place is by her husband's side, not encouraging lovers'.

My nerves were now being stretched and suffering from his verbal battering.

The questions were piling up, but I was getting no answers.

Chapter 46

During the whole period of our marriage, my darling husband had objected to me going out anywhere socially without him. The difficulty with this was that his interests in the main were dissimilar from mine. He also, as already been chronicled, refused to allow me to go out socially on my own or with my own friends. All of which resulted in me not being able to pursue my concert-going hobbies.

There had been one notable exception already recounted. Before moving to Newcastle, Rose Hardy had invited me to go with her to a performance of the ballet *Swan Lake* at Leeds Grand Theatre. Perhaps Harold did not class her as one of my own personal friends. Maybe, because she was one of the office staff, he had been caught in the predicament of not being able to refuse. Of course, it meant that someone would have to look after the children during my very brief absence. Whatever was in his mind then, I was quite taken by surprise when he agreed that I could go. And thoroughly enjoy it I did.

Now, a few years later, I was asked if I would like to join Charles's wife and sister-in-law at a symphony concert at the Newcastle City Hall. Certainly not Harold's cup of tea. To my complete amazement, he actually agreed, though why, I was unable to discern. I made the most of my opportunity and thoroughly enjoyed the outing. It made a lovely diversion from the hassle that seemed to be exacerbating in my life.

Towards the end of the year, when the weather had become distinctly wintry, Harold and his friends had taken to playing cards, poker I think. That December evening, the game was held in our home. We ladies decided to go elsewhere and leave the men to their diversion. I had prepared a substantial repast to satisfy their hunger needs, as I was accustomed to do.

We ladies enjoyed a delightful evening at one of the ladies' homes in Gosforth, making the most of our evening's freedom. Gosforth was a northern suburb of Newcastle. My home at Ponteland was some eight miles to the north west of Gosforth. When it was time to go home, we found that snow had been falling heavily. It was bitterly cold and the roads were now icy. It was just after eleven o'clock.

I took one of the ladies home, just up the road from where we had spent the evening. Then I had to traverse some narrow country lanes. One of the ladies wanted to join her husband at our home. Another friend, Sylvia, and her husband lived not far from my home down the road at Kenton, so the two ladies were in the car with me.

I had just started driving onto the very twisting and winding narrow country lane in the driving snow, when I sighted a car behind me. It seemed to be following me and sitting on my rear bumper. It kept up with me. Though it was dark and snowing, I could make out a small saloon car. I decided to increase my speed, as I wanted to get away from it. I knew there were no turn-offs for about three miles. However, the car increased its speed as I increased mine. Then its lights started flashing. We were all getting terrified. The road was treacherous, yet I felt I had to keep up the speed to get away from our pursuer. Dinnington village was at the halfway stage. There was a police station there so I made for that. All the while, the lights of the car were flashing constantly and keeping up behind me.

It was with great relief that we arrived at the police station in one piece. But the car also stopped directly in front of me. Now we were really petrified.

Then the driver scrambled out of his car and ran straight up to us, and banging on the window, he shouted to us, 'What do you think you were doing? Speeding like that on such treacherous roads!' Or words to that effect.

I refused to lower the window as he asked. I shouted back to him that he had terrified us following us like that. The gentleman told us then that he was a policeman. He opened his overcoat to show us his policeman's uniform. But I retorted that he was not in a police car and he had a heavy overcoat over his uniform. I did not know who he was in the dark, or what he was doing. All I knew was that he was a strange man in an ordinary car chasing us in the late evening.

His reply was that I would be reported for dangerous driving and speeding.

When we got home the boys could see that we were upset. After describing our experience, one of our friends, Sylvia's husband Gordon, who was a solicitor, immediately rang the police station up, spoke to the officer in charge and made a very strong complaint that a plain-clothes policeman in an ordinary car had terrified us ladies by trying to stop us in the middle of the night, on such a dreadful night as that was. The policeman told Gordon that he flashed his lights to get us to stop as we were speeding, whereupon Gordon replied that it was wholly incorrect to expect a lady driver to stop at that time of night, especially in the middle of nowhere, for someone in everyday clothes driving a small saloon. Was it any wonder the ladies were terrified?

The policeman had had no way of making his status recognisable until I had stopped my car out of sheer terror.

Gordon threatened to sue the policeman concerned, if the allegations against us were not dropped. They were.

That was the last time I was allowed out socially without my husband for a very long time.

Chapter 47

It was around this time, 1965, that gambling casinos in nightclubs were legalised. I had never thought of my husband as gambler. Yes, he liked the occasional card game, mainly poker, but it never occurred to me to think of him as a gambler. He was quite a heavy drinker. But gambling, this was something that I could never have associated with him until these nightclubs with casinos opened.

These nightclubs, at that time, housed a dance floor where cabarets took place, as well having a restaurant and casino. Harold now had a new and for him an interesting hobby. I was never a gambler. To me it was a waste of hard-earned money, and I found no enjoyment in watching the gamblers playing. As had always been the case, I had to go wherever my husband chose. My desires went unheeded. Now that we had Elizabeth to look after the children on an evening, what at first seemed to me a harmless hobby when Harold and I alone visited the Dolce Vita, on Tuesday and or Thursday evenings soon developed into a dreaded ordeal. Casinos were the place where my husband now chose to spend much of his spare time and he soon developed a taste for gambling on the roulette wheel. We agreed a limit of £5, to which he stuck for the time being. He passed me the odd chip, possibly to appease me, as he knew I did not enjoy betting.

Two particular ones in the Newcastle area now became the curse of my life. La Dolce Vita, and sometimes The Cavendish nightclub. They played a significant role in Harold's and Edward's unpleasant behaviour towards me.

One evening, when we were preparing to go out, Edward turned up at our home. To my intense dismay, Harold asked the gentleman if he would like to join us for the evening at the casino. He enthusiastically accepted. I felt my stomach somersault. This seemed to me to have been a planned move.

It was not enough the man repeatedly coming to my home unwanted, in spite of all my protests. My darling husband, who I worshipped and adored, now sought out this person's company socially and in public. There seemed nothing I could do to make

Harold see sense. He must have known by now that he was upsetting me. Or was he deliberately trying to upset me? Worse was to come.

Once at the nightclub, Harold made straight for the casino and a roulette table. I followed. As Harold sat down, he turned to me and told me to go and have a dance with Edward while he played the tables. It took me all my strength not to cry, but I was not going to dance with that man. Feeling very angry and mentally dazed, I ambled around the gambling tables trying to avoid my tormentor, but Edward, with a glass of beer in his hand, followed me. He seemed to be around me all the time. The evening was a nightmare.

Over the next few weeks, the pattern was repeated several times. It became a regular event. During these evenings, Edward repeated his earlier behaviour and made offensive remarks and suggestions to me, asking me to spend the night with him and similar variations whenever he thought Harold could not hear, or so I believed.

It occurred to me at the back of my mind, that there was some kind of plan, but I tried to dismiss this thought.

I have tried to relate these events exactly as they happened, without the bias that was to evolve over time. As the two men's joint behaviour towards me continued, I was able at a much later date, and again now, to say with hindsight that I felt that a conspiracy had been planned, but at the time, if that suggestion had been put to me, no way would I have believed it. What purpose would a conspiracy serve? The idea was preposterous to me. My darling husband would not do such a thing to me. At other times, especially with our personal friends, and in spite of the escalating rows, he was still very much the loving husband. And so I was helpless to stop it.

As time went by, from time to time Edward brought his wife along. This made no difference to the situation. Harold esconced himself in his seat at the gambling table for the evening, whilst I walked about trying to avoid the other gentleman, who still tried to gain my attention, always with a pint of beer in his hand. Mae, his wife, appeared to enjoy watching the gamblers and showed no awareness of my predicament.

There seemed no end to my dilemma. I could find no way out, no way of bringing back some peace into my life.

That Christmas, Harold decided to hold the branch's annual party at a nightclub in Northumberland Street, in the centre of the town. It was to take the form of a dinner dance to which all the wives and girlfriends were invited, also all the office staff. Every representative was expected to attend, including those from the outlying areas of the branch's territory.

The party went with a swing, the meal was fine and everyone was enjoying the dancing. During the evening, whilst everyone was enjoying themselves, Harold came over to me and told me that he had to take a couple of the boys with their wives to the station to get the train to Carlisle for the Lake District. He wouldn't be long and Edward would look after me while he was away. I protested at this, but he called Edward over and told him he had to keep an eye on me, adding that he would be back soon. This angered me intensely. This was the last thing I wanted. I did not need a bodyguard, and certainly not this person. I walked away in disgust wanting to avoid my appointed escort.

He was constantly around me. I told Edward that I did not need an escort, but he just ignored me. After several minutes of this annoyance, I thought that if I were to go to the Ladies' Room I could get away from him for a while. The Ladies' Room was upstairs, so without a word, I walked out of the ballroom and made for the stairs. Edward ran after me. As I climbed the stairs, he followed me and called to me to wait. At the top, he caught up with me on the landing. He very swiftly and suddenly grabbed my arm and pulled me towards him. He was trying to kiss me. I was stunned and outraged. I pulled myself away from him. I was horrified. I ran into the Ladies' Room having disintegrated into tears, and tried to pull myself together being so distressed. My thoughts frightened me.

The incident seemed planned. I emerged from my sanctuary when I heard voices. Harold was coming up the stairs. Mae was coming up with him. She had gone with him to the station. Relieved, I ran to my husband at the top of the stairs whilst Edward looked on.

Harold was trying to throw Edward and myself together at every opportunity. It just seemed so far-fetched, that my husband could do this to me. And yet it all fitted into the scheme of things. I refused to believe the possibility. The journey home that night was one long argument. That happening, with its implications, tormented me incessantly, as much as I tried to dismiss it from my mind.

What I found even more bizarre about the whole situation was that Harold had now found that he had another outstanding salesman who appeared to be competing for the top position in the branch, but my husband took little notice of him beyond the necessary office courtesies.

My husband had recruited the two gentlemen to the branch shortly after he had gone to Newcastle. I had scrutinised both men for Harold and formed the opinion that they were both very suitable at the time. It seemed that I had made a grave mistake in the case of Edward.

Gordon was a real gentleman, a devoted family man. Usually quiet in the office, he did produce results. This was what induced Harold to make his appointment. Harold also did not fuss over Gordon, or befriend him as he had done with Edward.

Edward was still producing results, and had introduced another salesman to the branch. But it is the results that count in business, and whatever feelings I held about Edward, it was clear that Harold was using him and had no intention of changing the situation.

Harold must have had a purpose in his behaviour, but I still could get no answers from him, only arguments.

Chapter 48

The winter of 1965–66 was for me, in Shakespeare's words, a 'winter of discontent'. Apart from anything else, I suffered from heavy bouts of 'flu and bronchitis, which laid me low. During this period, my beloved husband was the most caring and attentive person I could have wished for. He called in the branch doctor who prescribed a strong dose of vitamin C. It was the first time I had heard of this as a cold cure. He recommended one tablet of the soluble variety, 1,000 mg daily. In those days, we were unaware of any other form of the vitamin. It certainly helped, and I have taken the vitamin ever since. Even when not ill, I have always had a small amount for protection, as I seemed to develop a propensity to bronchitis in the winter months.

Having recovered from this setback, a little while later we were shopping in the town with the girls when I felt unwell. Harold took me into Boots, where the pharmacist prescribed me aspirin. Within minutes I was collapsing and passed out. I came to almost immediately, but felt very unwell. Harold took us all home. The doctor told me I was allergic to aspirin and must never take any again. I have never been able to have anything containing aspirin since.

Perhaps the ultimate setback, particularly for my other half, occurred when he took me out for dinner. It was meant to be a special occasion for my birthday.

Although I hated strong drink, over the years, because of the many business events, my husband had been trying to wean me onto wine. Starting with the sweet variety, La Flora Blanche, which I believe was somewhat fashionable then, I did succumb to a small glass on these special occasions, branch dinners and company conferences, if only for the sake of peace. I certainly found wine more enjoyable than spirits or other intoxicating drinks. My one fear was still getting drunk. I could never be able to stand the awful feeling of being out of control of oneself. I was gradually introduced to the less sweet varieties, but insisted on the one glass only.

As this was a special occasion, Harold asked me to try a red wine with our dinner. He told me that Chevrey Chambertin was a particularly good vintage wine and most suitable for the occasion. I had barely had a sip, when again I started to feel ill. Another sip and I felt really ill. Harold took me to the foyer for some fresh air. I was almost passing out. We sat there for a while, but in the end we had to go home. I had no doubts that the wine upset me. I have never touched red wine since.

I had now become aware that I had put on a considerable amount of weight. I always had something of a weight problem, and had tried to keep it down, but after giving birth to Ruthie, my girth had increased a little. All efforts to control it were in vain. With the aggravation of the last few months, my weight increased considerably. Loving food so much, I resorted to comfort eating, especially after those very uncomfortable and unhappy evenings at the casino. A late-night cheese sandwich went some way as compensation.

Whether or not it was the additional avoirdupois, I was now 2 stone heavier. Perhaps I must have had a low allergenic threshold or, with hindsight, the aggravation was taking its toll, for my health was not as good as it should have been. Thankfully, with having all these apparently petty illnesses, I had Elizabeth to help look after the children.

Harold now came up with one of his blockbuster suggestions. As our personal lives had gone into turmoil, he explained, he thought we could reverse it by moving. A new home would make everything right. At least, he was accepting that we did have problems, but he was blaming the house for our problems!

My immediate reaction was to object strongly. We had settled down nicely and for the most part enjoyed living where we were. Apart from all the friends we had made, we had wonderful neighbours. On all sides of our cul-de-sac, friendships had blossomed for the children as well as ourselves. Wally M. and his wife in particular, and who lived directly facing us in Birney Edge, had befriended us and made our reallocation so much easier. Anne was also extremely welcome in their home and enjoyed all their attention. She was often there. It was as if they had adopted her.

Some of our now much wider group of friends had persuaded us sometime earlier to join the B'nai Brith, a Jewish organisation in Newcastle, where we both, Harold and myself, soon found ourselves elected onto the committee, such was the warmth of their friendship. Harold's initial idea was to move away outside of Newcastle but still within commuting distance of the office. I felt this would affect our newly found friendships. No sooner had we established ourselves, and my darling husband felt the desire to move on. This was in spite of the fact that he was building up his branch so successfully.

In recent months, certain aspects of the policies of my daughters' school had caused me some consternation and I had considered removing them. Now that Harold had brought up the subject of our moving house, this would give us the opportunity to change their school. This thought and my husband's plausible powers of persuasion convinced me to agree with his decision.

Within days of my agreeing to the move, Harold came home and said he had found just the place. I should look it over right away. It was a four-bedroomed detached house in Sunderland. Harold told me that it was such a beautiful house and that it had been featured in *Ideal Home* magazine when it was built quite recently. He made it sound all cut and dried. Of course the final decision was up to me, but it sounded as though Harold had already made his mind up, which I thought somewhat unusual. It was if he was telling me that I should agree before I had even seen it. Now he was trying to make decisions without asking me. Another change to his usual behaviour which gave me more cause for bewilderment.

This was meant to be a new beginning for us, so I went with him to see the house. It was situated on one of the main roads through Sunderland, Queen Alexandra Road, and straddled an elongated curve along the road. The drive stretched the length of the house's frontage. The outside of the house itself was of all-white cement. With gardens to the sides and rear, it looked most imposing.

The interior was truly modern, with an open-plan ground floor. An open-tread polished wood staircase reached the first floor. The huge lounge section had a parquet floor with a central well for a carpet. The dining section was elevated by a curved step and the floor was all parquet wood. Four large bedrooms added to its attraction. All the fixtures and fittings, including the large fitted kitchen, were of the best quality. I had to agree with my darling that the house was great. Moving to Sunderland was far less appealing. It was even further to travel to the office. Harold said it was not a problem for him. We were also near the beach. He had made his mind up. I could think of several reasons not to move but there were more in favour. The sale was made.

We now had to sell Birney Edge, which proved to be no problem. Elizabeth had been a godsend and I hoped she would come with us to Sunderland, but she felt it was too far for her to travel to the univer-

141

sity. I do not know who was more disappointed, the girls or myself, but she helped us to pack and prepare for the move.

As the move became more real, somehow I had the feeling that we were doing the right thing and everything was going to be all right. How wrong I was.

Chapter 49

Euphoria overcame me the morning my husband rang me from his office to tell me that our purchase of 129, Queen Alexandra Road had been completed and I could pick up the keys. The jubilation in his voice infected me. I just knew that a new turning point in our lives had arrived and everything was going to be all right. He asked me to phone him as soon as I had let myself into the house.

I immediately went to collect the keys and dashed over to Sunderland to the house. As soon as I let myself in, the open spaciousness of the empty house greeted me. The absence of any furniture gave the place a forlorn atmosphere. The telephone was looking very dejected in the middle of the floor of the empty lounge, beckoning to me. It was still connected as we had requested.

Harold was eagerly awaiting my call. He sounded so ecstatic when I told him I was 'in', phoning from the house. It was an extremely happy day for both of us.

The sale of the house in Birney Edge had gone through smoothly, so we could now transfer ourselves to Sunderland. The two elder girls were still at the same school till the end of term, so I had Ruth with me on the day we moved house.

That was the day certain realisations came to me. We were on a main road. My kitchen was at the front of the house so that I could see the activity happening around the area within view if I chose to watch. It was not until lunchtime that I became aware of the frequent comings and goings of the well-dressed people to the building directly across the road, and it came to me that it was Yom Tov, one of our religious festivals. The building was a synagogue. We had bought a house immediately facing the main *shul* in the town and it was Shavuot. Not the most important of our festivals to Harold and me, but one of importance to the orthodox. Sunderland's Jewish community, we were to learn, were on the whole a singularly orthodox one. I felt most uncomfortable that our move was very noticeable to those passers-by on the other side of the road. Harold said he could not care less. We were here now.

Another realisation that was yet to hit me was the fact that Queen

Alexandra Road was on the direct route to Edward's home. We had moved more than 10 miles nearer to my antagonist. When travelling to and from Newcastle, Edward could pass through Sunderland and past my home more comfortably and much sooner than when his journey ended on the far northern side of Newcastle where we had hitherto lived. I dismissed the thoughts from my mind, and settled down to turning our 'Ideal Home' into our castle.

I enrolled Anne into the local comprehensive school for the coming September. The local Menorah School was highly recommended for junior and primary children. Ruth was now of school age. The school was happy to have both Pamela and Ruth in the coming autumn term. The headmistress, Mrs Shochet, was a delightful lady, and I felt that the girls would now all settle happily into their new educational environments.

As the first few weeks passed and we continued to establish a new routine, my confidence in our resurrected happiness became more assured.

Chapter 50

That summer we chose to have a holiday in Tenerife. It would have to be in August before the children started at their new schools.

The hotel we booked was on the outskirts of the northern town of Puerto de la Cruz. We did not realise at the time of booking its exact situation. We knew it was a little way out of the town, within walking distance, and quite high up. How high became known to us on our arrival. It was a huge hotel complex at the top of a mountain. The approach was very steep and really only suitable for the very fit. There was thankfully a courtesy coach, which ran both ways every hour.

I was not all that impressed with the beach. It was very pebbly, so we tended to stay at the hotel by the pool. The girls enjoyed that, as I could not let them near the sea for bathing. Our visits into town were mostly to enjoy the beautiful shops and boutiques. We also took advantage of the local market, as one does on these holidays.

One day, Harold told me he would like to take me into town without the children. They could stay by the pool. My darling husband was insistent, not unexpectedly, that we have some time alone.

After wandering around the interesting streets looking at the shops, my escort suggested we should have a drink. Not my favourite occupation, so Harold said he knew just the drink for me. I should try it as it was very sweet, and he was sure I would enjoy it. He found us a small tavern in one of the side streets which announced on its billboard 'Homemade Sangria'. Harold jumped at that and said it was 'just the job'. I, in my ignorance, went along with him.

We sat at the bar, whilst the barman, presumably the proprietor, poured various drinks into a large jug. Many of the drinks were unknown to me, but I recollect seeing a large quantity of brandy and a bottle of wine poured into the jug. I learnt then that the whole jugful was solely for the two of us. Just watching the concoction being made up made me feel drunk. The whole creation was then topped up with masses of sliced oranges, banana, pineapple and other fruits. This was finally topped with a sprig of mint. The fruit alone would have made a meal in itself. The display had already intoxicated me.

I was beyond drinking it by the time the whole jug was finished ready for consumption, but my devoted husband kept challenging me to try it. Amidst feelings of guilt at the prospect of the drink being wasted (I should not have worried; my husband would not allow that), I decided to give it a go. I took a sip from my glass and immediately felt it going to my legs. Yes, it was a pleasant drink, but it was awfully potent. My other half insisted I should at least try some more. I did, and rued the moment. My already wobbly legs seemed to vanish from beneath me.

How Harold managed to get me back to our hotel was beyond the capabilities of my memory, especially as he had continued to enjoy a substantial amount of the explosive liquor before we left the bar.

When we got back to our room, the children were already there, and witnessed their mother as they had never seen her before. I was absolutely out of it, stoned drunk, falling all over the place, and on practically nothing! The girls thought it hilarious. Their mother absolutely drunk. They had never seen me in that state before. Needless to say, I soon fell asleep on the bed and missed the rest of the afternoon. The girls had a tale to tell, and I am sure they remembered the incident for some time afterwards. As for myself, that was the very first time and the very last time I was ever drunk.

'Never again,' I swore to myself, later that day.

Nonetheless, it did not spoil our holiday, which in fact was most enjoyable. It was another confirmation to me that not only my legs, but also our marriage was back on terra firma.

Chapter 51

Although we now lived a few more miles from the office, our business relationship continued as before. Harold still wanted me in the office for the monthly branch meetings, preparing his speeches and branch bulletins as well as whatever came along that would help him with his position, the frequent socialising and parties at home.

Whenever I had to go into the office, I got a feeling of trepidation at the thought that I had to meet Harold's 'co-associate in trouble', as I now thought of him. The idea of the man starting with me again still haunted me. Since moving to Sunderland, for those few weeks, though he was usually in the office, I was not approached, as I feared, and I kept a very clear distance. It was not really the way the branch manager's wife should behave towards any of her husband's team of representatives, but I felt I had no alternative to avoid any confrontation in the office.

A new circle of friends had begun to gather around us. These were initially family and friends of friends in Newcastle. I did notice, however, over the next few months that our Newcastle friendships seemed to be diminishing. Invitations became fewer and fewer. I do believe Harold remained friends with Charles and his family personally in Newcastle, but they no longer visited us in our new home. They said they found the distance, about 12 miles from their own home, too far.

We made several friendships which helped the girls. Anne became particularly close to the son of neighbours. John attended the same school as Anne and he became a regular daily visitor to our home, as did Anne to John's home. They seemed inseparable. Harold and I were delighted, as it proved to us that we had done the right thing in changing my daughters' schools.

As the children settled into their new school life, I felt more able to relax. A couple of weeks after the girls started school in September, during a Sunday morning, an unexpected and for me certainly unwanted visitor arrived on our doorstep. Edward was accompanied by another gentleman. I was given the impression from the introductions that this was a pre-arranged plan between the two visitors and my husband. I had not been informed, but the ensuing conversations left me in no doubt.

The unknown gentleman, who I was told was called Keith, was a prospective salesman. Edward had brought Keith to meet Harold. Had it been anybody else, I would have been only too pleased to have them in my home at that time. Did I not interview all Harold's prospective representatives for his unit at our home in Leeds? But this arrangement, which had been kept secret from me till now, was very disconcerting.

Keith was interviewed to Harold's satisfaction and would work with Edward. The manner in which I had been taken unawares was another matter. I did not know how to tackle Harold about it. Was it to become a regular event, Edward bringing prospective salesmen to our house? The implications worried me, and my nerves became edgy again.

Two more weeks later, and my worries seemed to be justified. Harold told me he thought we ought to have a dog. He said he had always wanted a dog, and he thought the children would love to have one, too. I had never really been a dog enthusiast, and at first refused. Over the next few days, Harold persisted in asking me to reconsider. Labradors were wonderful dogs, mild in temperament and very lovable, definitely a dog for beginners, I was informed. Harold put on his best salesmanship tactics to sell me the idea.

He then came up with his ace card. He told me that Eddie (Harold always used the familiar version of the man's name), had a dog, a Golden Labrador. So that was what was behind his persistence! Why did I not have a look at it? By now the girls had been brought into the situation and were eager to have a puppy. Harold had played his ace card to perfection. The plan had worked out as Harold wanted.

As much as I detested the thought of having to put up with Edward's presence once more (it made me feel sick), my husband now had the girls on his side, and I could not say no.

I could not help wondering what my husband's real motives were. No one had ever suggested us having a dog before, and as Harold was the first person to raise the suggestion, the idea that this was another of his ruses to bring Edward back into our home filled my mind. I found it hard to believe that my husband was genuine in his desire for us to have a dog.

At Harold's invitation, Edward brought his animal over the next Sunday. As much as I hated to admit it, it was a beautiful animal. The girls loved him instantly and pleaded with me to let them have a dog. I found myself agreeing that perhaps we should try having a puppy. But I insisted that it had to be the same breed, and male.

A week later, we made the journey down to the Midlands, to the kennels that Edward recommended. The kennels bred only Labradors. They were all so adorable. They had to be at least six weeks old before they were allowed to leave the kennels. Our choice was ultimately unanimous. The little ball of fluff's pedigree name was Sandylands Rockabee Teak as registered with the Kennel Club of Great Britain. To us he became Troy.

Troy brought the family much joy. The girls loved him, but he was a little terror throughout his puppyhood. Very destructive, we tried to restrict his activities to just tearing paper, for the most part in vain. That and puppy training was indeed hard work.

Then a dreadful incident occurred through which we were able to show just how much that little fellow had come to mean to us in such a short time.

Living on a main road had its setbacks. When Troy was just three months old, the main gate must have been left open. He escaped out of the house into the drive, ran into the road and was hit by a car. When I reached him lying in the road, he was severely unconscious. He was carried into the house and the vet called.

The diagnosis was dire. The vet did not think he would pull through. He advised us that our only chance to save him, and that was extremely remote, was to put ice-cold compresses on his forehead non-stop round the clock for the next twenty-four hours or so. The compresses would have to be renewed every twenty minutes or thereabouts. It meant staying up all night, but we were determined to save him.

During the long evening a friend, Joe, came round. We had not known each other for very long, but he only lived across the road, and wanted to help. We arranged to take it in turns to look after Troy, changing every four hours to allow us to get some sleep. Harold insisted he start the rota first and Joe stayed with him.

When I came down during the night to take my turn, there had been no change in the dog's condition, but he was still alive. Joe insisted in staying with us and we all persevered through to mid-morning.

Then the miracle happened. A little whimper, and we knew the battle was being won. Within minutes Troy came round. He made a full recovery and was with us until he was 14 years old.

One of the bonuses of living in Sunderland was its beach. Whenever

I had the odd spare hour, I was able to go there with Troy, and with the girls from time to time, to wander on the sands whilst Troy enjoyed rolling in the sand and playing in the sea. He soon became very wet, covered in sand and very filthy. I had to bathe him and clean him up after every visit to the beach, but the pleasure I derived getting away even for a short time helped me to cope with my problems that started to accumulate again.

We could never thank Joe enough for his devoted help. That is what I call a true friend. He remained so during our stay in Sunderland.

Chapter 52

I could never find out whether the 'doggy situation' was my husband's way of deliberately bringing his associate back into our personal lives or not, but either way, that is just what happened. As I had foretold, once Troy joined us, it was not long before that man resumed calling in to our home on a regular basis. It was then that it was brought home to me just how convenient the location of our house was for Edward to stop by, on his way to or from the office, or so was his excuse now.

I had to plead even harder with Harold to stop his so-called friend from tormenting me with his resumed regular unwanted attentions, as that is what his behaviour was doing. As before, my husband's promises belied his actions, and the situation continued.

My bewilderment and confusion intensified. Not that long ago, Harold would never have allowed any man to speak to me the way I was now being spoken to. The nightclub visits continued, with our 'escort'. My husband's predilection for the roulette wheel became an excuse for his regular trips to the casinos, insisting I accompany him and his cohort. There seemed to be no escaping Harold's repeated bullying.

About a year prior to us moving to Sunderland, my husband's desire to become a Freemason was granted. My cousin, who had promised to help Harold, arranged for the necessary sponsors to refer him to a local lodge in Newcastle and his wait was over. He was voted in, in accordance with Masonic procedure.

He acquired the requisite regalia and proudly attended the Masonic meetings in the Newcastle Masonic Hall up to the time of our removal to Sunderland. He then continued to attend meetings in Sunderland for a short time.

Towards the end of the year, Harold delighted all his branch team by telling them that they were all invited to the Ladies' Night together with their wives and partners. It was to be held in the Sunderland Masonic Hall, which was in the centre of the town. It took the form of a grand ball and required full evening dress.

On the actual day, about a dozen representatives and their wives were able to join us at our table, Edward and his wife included. It was a very grand but fascinating evening. It seemed that none of our guests had previously experienced such an event, and though they initially seemed a little out of their depth, the vast amounts of wine and liquor that were consumed mellowed the evening and all were soon much more relaxed. None as much as my own spouse.

The evening seemed to be a rollicking success from my husband's viewpoint. Before the close of the evening, he went round to all our guests and invited them back to our home for coffee. We lived about three-quarters of a mile from the hall.

I left in my car with Gordon and his wife to get home and put the kettle on. I saw Harold organising the others, I presumed to ensure everyone knew where to go.

Seeing that we were all back at my house, I put the kettle on. Then we realised one of us was missing, that one being my own dear husband. We checked around the house and the front drive, but definitely, Harold had not come home. I said I would have to go and look for him. Gordon insisted in coming with me. It was one o'clock in the morning and we had become very concerned.

Leaving everyone in the house – the children were fast asleep in bed – I took my car and drove slowly back to the Masonic Hall. All the while Gordon was looking around to see if he could spot the missing husband.

On driving into the small square that fronted the Masonic Hall, we spotted a body lying face up in the middle of the road. Fearing the worst, we both ran up to it to see that Harold had collapsed, paralytic, absolutely stoned drunk, and had fallen asleep right in front of the Masonic Hall.

With great difficulty the two of us dragged Harold's huge and uncooperative bulk into my car. We were just relieved to find him virtually unharmed. He was so lucky that he had not been found by the police; or even worse, he could have been run over. He was fortunate that at that time in the early hours of the morning there was hardly any traffic. It was a happy escape for him.

When we got home, a couple of the men took Harold upstairs and put him to bed. Everyone then bade their farewells. I never got to make anyone any coffee.

After that evening, I cannot ever recall my husband going to any more Masonic meetings. To my knowledge, that was the end of Harold's affair with Freemasonry.

It did unfortunately give my husband more time play his cruel games with me. In spite of my constant nagging to keep Edward out of our personal lives and the ensuing arguments that returned ever more frequently, my pleadings were ignored. I became the butt of more and more sarcastic remarks. My 'lover boy', as my husband called him were words which were repeatedly hurled at me and I was constantly accused of encouraging the man. Nothing I said stopped the flood of insults. From time to time, I had visits to the house on Sunday mornings. Mr Brown brought Keith with him, supposedly for a business meeting. At least, he was less obscene on these occasions.

Our arguments were still sometimes followed by my husband's demands for wifely loyalty and support. To me, these were more accusations. I could not think of what else I could do to convince him. I do not think any husband in his position could have had more help and support than I had given him over the years. Yet as before, there were times when my husband was the most caring, adoring of husbands when it suited him. Particularly in front of other people, he became the charming, charismatic person with whom I had fallen so madly and deeply in love.

I suppose I must have become more and more confused because there was no way I could account for Harold's erratic behaviour.

The new life that I had been promised by moving to Sunderland became a faded dream.

Chapter 53

Shortly after moving to Sunderland, I had to attend the Queen Alexandra Eye Hospital. This hospital was a mere 50 yards from home on the other side of the road.

The appointment was mid-morning on a Friday afternoon. I usually prepared our Sabbath evening meal during the morning, so I managed to do some cooking before I left. After the appointment, I walked out of the hospital and began walking up the road towards our house, when I saw smoke belching out of the chimney on our rooftop. It was dense, thick smoke. I was absolutely horrified.

A number of labourers were in the road in front of the house, doing road repairs. When they saw me running towards the house they shouted out to me, 'Your house is on fire', as though I could not see it!

I yelled back to them, 'Has anyone called the Fire Brigade?' Someone yelled back at me that they had.

At that point, the fire engine arrived. I had stayed out in the road, frightened to try and enter the house. I was more upset because Troy was in the house and I was worried about him.

Fortunately Troy was safe. He had inhaled a little of the smoke, but thankfully the vet said he would be fine in a day or two.

When the firemen went into the house very thick, very toxic fumes greeted them, or so they told me. The whole house was filled with absolutely dense black smoke. There were no flames. The smoke had come from my pressure cooker on the top of the cooker. I had prepared chicken soup and forgotten to turn the gas off. All the plastic parts of the cooker had melted and this produced the toxicity. The firemen opened all the windows to get rid of the smoke, which took several hours to clear. A friend living round the corner kindly invited us in in the meantime.

The fire chief told us we were very lucky there was only smoke damage. A few more seconds and the pressure cooker with its charred contents would have exploded and burst into flames. As it was, the whole house up the staircase and into the two bedrooms nearest the staircase were badly smoke damaged. This demonstrated one of the disadvantages of having an open-plan staircase.

154

Thankfully, we were well insured and were able to get the whole house redecorated. No one was hurt. Troy, poor dog, made a full recovery, again. And I had a very valid lesson on ensuring that the cooker was completely turned off whenever I was going out.

Chapter 54

By the middle of 1967, I think I was beginning to feel the effects of the stress I had been enduring during the past two and a half years or so, my husband's Jekyll and Hyde behaviour, then the smoke disaster, and the usual stresses of dealing with a difficult teenager, not to mention Troy's two close shaves with eternity.

In spite of all this, little was I prepared for the shock I was about to receive.

This year, the biennial company conference was to be held in Bournemouth in June. Harold told me that it was a manager-only conference, and that I would not be going with him. This was really a bolt out of the blue. I was so astonished. I never in my wildest dreams thought I would ever hear my darling, beloved husband, whom I believed adored me equally, tell me he was going anywhere without me, and in particular, a company conference. He was full of apologies and pronouncements as to how very much he was disappointed and was going to miss me.

Apart from the very first conference, which was due to pregnancy problems, I had never missed accompanying my darling to any of the conferences since. At every conference, he had always taken the opportunity to boast to the company executives, usually in my presence, about the large contribution I made to his success, as a salesman, then a unit supervisor, and now as a branch manager. He had brought his branch up to the top quarter of all the branches in the country. I just could not believe that he would want to go without me. My possessive and intensely jealous husband had made so many demands on having me by his side at all times, that I would never believe it possible that he would go without me. It was not that long ago that he would have moved heaven and earth to ensure that I accompanied him, even if I could not attend the sessions. I knew that managers took their wives, even though they could not attend the sessions. There was plenty of other things for wives to do. This change in his attitude perplexed and confused me.

Even if it was a managers's conference, I could think of no reason why I could not go with him. It was beyond my comprehension.

Harold left home to go to the five-day conference on the Monday morning. That night I never slept a single minute. It was not just that I was alone in my big bed. I had been left alone for a little time when Harold was training at Reading and had no sleepless nights then. I was deeply troubled. Somewhere deep in my mind my instincts told me that something was going on, though what, I was unable to determine. I kept dismissing the thought, but it kept resurfacing.

The following night, though dreadfully tired again, I failed to get any sleep at all. The four nights passed without my having had one minute's sleep. By the time Harold came home I had had no sleep the whole week, and I was excruciatingly exhausted. I decided not to say anything to my darling husband, as I was so sure that now he was home, sleep would come easily.

My travelling husband was so very excited when he got back that he told me he wanted to take me back to Bournemouth immediately. He described having had a wonderful time, staying in the five-star hotel, The Carlton, overlooking the sea on the Eastcliffe side of Bournemouth, and he wanted to show our girls and me where he had been. He told me that he wanted us to stay in the same hotel to make up for him not being able to take me to the conference.

I was overwhelmed by his eagerness, especially being so tired. I told him 'immediately' was not possible, but we could be ready the next day, Saturday. I had to pack for the girls and myself. This was Harold at his most impatient, and in spite of my exhaustion, I was pandering to him, glad to have him home. We arranged to have an overnight stay in London at our regular hotel, the Regent Palace.

I so truly expected to fall asleep, but I had yet another sleepless night, and I was dragging myself around in a stupor. I just could not bring myself to tell Harold what was wrong. Nor could I understand why I was unable to tell him.

Travelling down in the morning, I found it impossible to take the wheel, and Harold had to drive the whole way. He said nothing, but I wondered if the unusual, that I had not offered to drive, had occurred to him.

Even a night in the comfort of a top-class hotel failed to restore my sleep habits, so that by the time we arrived at Bournemouth I was in a dreadful state.

My husband pulled up at the side of the road in front of the Carlton Hotel, and said he would go and see if they had a room for us. We were to wait in the car. I had understood that he had booked the accommodation, and found this curious, even more so when he returned to inform us there were no vacancies. He then suggested we go next door to the Langham Hotel. They could accommodate us. Though I was past myself with exhaustion, this apparent mix-up over our hotel accommodation continued to worry me, but at least I had somewhere to rest my head.

The next two nights still remained sleepless. I went out in a fog, dragging myself around, head throbbing and on the point of tears fighting myself to keep my eyes open – something that I tried desperately to hide, especially from the children, as I did not wish to spoil our holiday. I still could not bring myself to tell Harold. I do not know why. It might have been because I was too exhausted even to talk. I could not say anything, even when Harold did make a few remarks about me being slow and dragging behind them.

On the Tuesday morning, after another unbelievable sleepless night, we went into town to look at the shops. We went into the large department store then known as Binn's. I followed at a snail's pace, struggling to keep up. We went down to the furniture department in the lower ground floor. I could sense that Harold was getting impatient and irritable at my slow steps. We looked at some of the carpets, when he started to make offensive remarks about my straggling behind. I managed to catch up as he stood viewing the carpets, and then he shouted at me that I was lazy. I wanted to cry, but words failed me.

It was then I felt a sudden sting across my left cheek. He had hit me on my face. Whether it was the force of the blow, or my weakness, or maybe a combination of both, I could not say, but I fell backwards and lay on the floor, sprawled between rolls of carpet in full view of the children.

The shock caused me to burst into tears, and with what little strength I could summon up, I managed to yell at him, 'Can't you see I'm ill? I need a doctor. I haven't slept for days', or similar words. I do not know how I managed to find the strength to shout at him.

I think the force of my outburst brought my husband to his senses. A few words of apology were followed by him offering to take me back to the hotel, and calling a doctor. The doctor prescribed me sleeping tablets and I hoped that that would solve my problem. That was wishful thinking. I did fall asleep but only for about two hours. This pattern repeated itself over the remaining nights of our stay and did very little to cure my acute exhaustion.

I could still feel that sting from when the man I loved so much struck me across my face. I knew I was never going to forget it.

We had booked to see the show *The Fiddler on the Roof* in London on the Saturday night, staying over at the same hotel, but we returned to London on the Friday in the hope that I could get some rest beforehand whilst Harold took the children out to see the sights of London. He was trying to make up for his lapse and could not have been more attentive and caring. I kept hoping that normal sleep would return, but it did not.

How I ever made it to the theatre with such extreme fatigue, I do not know. Harold had booked our five seats on the front row of the dress circle. We occupied the last seats but two nearest to the left aisle. Harold had sat down first, followed by the children. I seated myself last.

We had seated ourselves a good ten minutes before the performance started. Once seated, I peered over the balustrade to look down at the stalls below. They seemed to be inordinately far away. Then in a sudden flash everything turned pitch black. All I could see was a huge swirling, dense abyss. I was falling into a whirlpool, being sucked down and down. I heard someone letting out the most excruciating, piercing scream as I sank into what felt like eternity.

I felt someone touch my hand, and I came to, realising that it was I who had screamed out with such terrifying intensity. I stood up from my seat and ran into the aisle and out into the foyer. I must have looked like a crazy woman as I realised later that I had no idea what I was doing. Harold must have followed me. I was about to go down the steps when I was grabbed from behind and prevented from going any further. Harold swept me into his arms to comfort me as I was sobbing heavily. Somehow he managed to calm me down and persuaded me, though with great difficulty I know, that I had to go back into the auditorium for the children's sake and see the show through.

Holding my arm tightly, he took me back to my seat and sat down next to me. He held me tightly throughout the show. He must have realised the state I was in. I managed to absorb some of the performance, but it was probably the greatest ordeal I had ever had to suffer. I was never able to sit in balcony seats after that for many years.

I have never been able to remember going back to the hotel or being driven home to Sunderland with my family. The next thing I remember was being attended by a doctor in my home who had me immediately admitted to Sunderland General Infirmary, suffering with extreme exhaustion and a nervous breakdown. It was noted and recorded in the medical notes that I had shed several pounds and was suffering from 'irritable bowel syndrome' and colitis. I had not been aware of this until I read the notes much later. My husband's and his colleague's constant offensive behaviour had affected me far worse than I had realised.

Harold rang my mother, so I was told at some point, and she came and took the children back to Leeds whilst I was in hospital. I was sedated and kept asleep for four days. I was then put on strong sleeping tablets, which at least helped me to sleep through the night. By the end of the week, when my doctors were satisfied that I had resumed a normal sleeping routine, albeit with the help of medication, Harold was able to take me home.

Chapter 55

Four weeks after leaving the hospital, I had a check-up. I was told I was fine and told that I no longer needed sleeping tablets. I was discharged. During that month my home life returned to what I lovingly called normal. My beloved husband was once again the caring and attentative person I had known during the first half of our marriage.

I was fine and sleeping well for the first two weeks or so without the sleeping tablets, but then Harold decided to resume tormenting me with his accomplice, and once again I was having that unwanted visitor in my home with his unwanted attentions. Not as frequently as before, but the couple of times my husband's accomplice did come to my house during the next few weeks were very unsettling. Harold resumed his name-calling and made his usual demands for wifely loyalty. These were very hurtful times, as I still felt vulnerable from my recent illness. It seemed very unfair that the man who I loved so much should turn on me once more. I still could find no reason for this, but it appeared to be a deliberate attempt to undermine me. Now that I had recovered from my setback, with hindsight it looked as though my husband did not want my recovery.

This mental and emotional abuse which was being directed at me, again took its toll. I continued to be helpless and unable to get any answers as to why, in view of the illness I had so recently suffered, my so caring husband had turned on me again. As I was already sensitive to such behaviour, it affected me more easily this time and again I stopped sleeping properly. By mid-September, the nervous exhaustion had once more enveloped me and I collapsed.

My doctor was again called and he referred me directly to Cherry Knowle Psychiatric Hospital, at Ryhope just outside Sunderland. Once again, my mother came to take the children back to Leeds at Harold's request. The consultant was the same person under whose care I had been three months earlier. I was once more sedated, only at night this time. I remained in the hospital for three weeks.

I think the doctors were trying to find the reason for this recurrence, but I doubt they were able to find the answers any more than I could.

I know they spoke to my husband on several occasions, but I was never told the contents of these meetings.

I again found myself relying on sleeping tablets, and when I was eventually discharged from the hospital, I continued to take them. In fact, I was to continue having to use sleeping tablets for a very long time to come.

My husband did modify his behaviour for a while, and our lives seemed to be a little more harmonious. All the same, two nervous collapses in a short space of time, together with the conflicting behaviour of my other half, took its toll on my general health.

Chapter 56

My husband had sprung some momentous surprises on me during our lifetime together, but the one he sprung on me at the beginning of 1968, 'took the biscuit' – except for the very first, that is, his marriage proposal!

That evening remains clear in my memory for two reasons. One, the suddenness of it, and two, it was put to me as a *fait accompli*. There was no 'What do you think?' about it as he used to ask when making decisions. Such decisions had always been a joint effort. Here was a statement of fact.

He had decided to set up his own business and go back to Leeds. He then explained that the next step on the promotional ladder with the company would involve a move to head office in London as a company executive. This would mean he would be sat behind a desk twenty-four hours a day, so he said, and that was something he could not do. He would no longer be able to sell. He intended to form his own business as an independent insurance broker.

It all sounded very reasonable to me, but I was not so sure at having to move again, in spite of the fact that we would be going back home to Leeds. I knew instantly that I would miss my walks along the beach with Troy. He loved playing in the water and getting himself covered in sand and mud. There was one thing about which I was very certain. I would no longer have to put up with any more torment from his accomplice's Don Juan tactics, or so I thought at that time. It was going to be worth it to get away from all those stresses and start a new life, again, just the two of us and the children.

We discussed it further for several days, as the more we spoke about it the more there was to talk about. It would not be as straightforward a move as on previous occasions as we had to find suitable office premises in Leeds as well as moving house. He said he wanted to be in the town centre in the business area. On this, my husband displayed his arrogant naivety. His 'think big' policy came rambling out of his head, before he had had any time to think things through, especially the financial arrangements. At least, that is how it came over to me.

Ten days or so later, he came to me with what sounded at first like a logical suggestion. He said that he was going to need a secretary. What better than to employ someone he already knew and was familiar with the insurance business? I could not begin to think whom he meant until he told me he was referring to his personal secretary, Miss Wright. I can honestly say that I was appalled at the idea.

This was the woman who on our first introduction nearly six years ago, had shown herself to be a sour-faced, miserable being, bereft of any personality. I had found no change in her after all this time. I could not imagine Harold working with this person in a brand new environment and building up a successful business. I had never found her manner and attitude with all of us in the office anything but curt and impersonal. In an independent business such as he was planning, I failed to see what she could bring to the business. I pointed out to him that I could see no reason in taking such a person out of her job with the company where she had worked for many years, to go to a business starting from scratch. It was taking her from security to an unknown commodity, not to mention her having to move to a different town where she knew no one. I was informed that she had never been to Leeds. I was sure that a more personable and professional person could be found locally in Leeds. Our discussions over that period were proved to me to be a waste of time. Harold was determined to take her. No longer did he want my advice, let alone to listen to me.

Not long after, I was further shocked and deeply hurt when he told me that he had decided to make her his partner. Now suspicions were gathering in my mind, but I could still not convince myself. I could not accept that my husband could have any relationship with any other woman, never mind this insipid, lacklustre character.

I asked him what kind of money she was putting into the business to warrant a partnership. His reply was that she did not need to put money in. Her efficiency and experience made up for her lack of funds. This did not please me, as the more we discussed the matter the more it was obvious that whatever I said was not going to dissuade him. He intended taking Miss Wright to Leeds at all costs.

I asked him what part I was to play in the business, as surely, I was his partner. He agreed, telling me that I would look after the general side of the business as I had always done. Again, all was cut and dried. My input appeared to be no longer wanted.

And still I refused to accept that there was anything going on between them, even with the persistent murmurings in my head. My husband showed that he was still very devoted to me, in spite of what

I considered slight lapses in his behaviour with Mr Brown towards me, and I knew he would never do anything to hurt me. Well, not intentionally, so I still believed.

My beloved told me that under his contract conditions as manager he had to give three months' notice to allow time for a replacement to be found. Six months was mooted as giving us sufficient time to sell up, buy a house in Leeds and set up the business in the type of swish offices that Harold was planning. It was finally decided that the end of July, the end of the school term, was the time for the planned change.

The next totally unexpected and hurtful move was when Harold told me that his partner-to-be would be taking over all the work that I had been doing for him whilst we still lived in Sunderland. It would be good practice for her. So from then on she would write his bulletins and do all his paperwork until he finished with the company. This made me feel quite redundant, as though he was cutting me off from his life with the company, even before he had left. When I queried this, he insisted on trying to reassure me that I was imagining the worst. He still needed my help in the office. But as time passed and developments were occurring, as much as I tried to ignore them, my suspicions were taking stronger root.

To set up the company, a visit to our accountant was necessary. Harold did agree on that, so arrangements were made for us both to go down to Croydon to see Bill Smith. We did need guidance on various aspects, which my husband realised only I would understand at that time, in particular the tax and VAT situation.

On arrival at our hotel, the same one in the High Street as we had stayed at on our first visit to meet our accountant, we had dinner with Bill.

The following morning, the meeting with our accountant took place as arranged. We were shown how to set up the necessary books and given some much-needed advice.

Now, we had to start arranging our move, which involved travelling backwards and forwards to Leeds on several occasions. We looked at a house in Shadwell in the countryside just north of Leeds. West & Company was building these houses when we were planning our first move in 1959. We could not afford any of them at that time. This stone-built detached house suited us, although it only had three bedrooms. And now it was in our price range. I fell in love with it and we bought it. The move and all that it involved did not turn out to be as happy and straightforward as I would have wished for.

165

Chapter 57

If my darling beloved husband wanted to spring more hurtful surprises on me, he certainly knew how to pick his time. He had been gathering information about available office space in his chosen area, and we arranged to visit the premises to check them out, or so I was informed. He insisted that his so-called future partner join us on our trip to Leeds.

He took us to premises in South Parade, in the heart of the business area in the city centre. It was a very prestigious address and typical of my husband's 'think big' attitude. He was determined to impress, regardless of cost. I asked him if the rent and outlay for a brand new concern were justified. He did not want to know, or even discuss it. It seemed that he had made his mind up, together with his secretary, that these premises were ideal, even before seeing the place. I concluded that he must have talked Miss Wright into the proposition, as she knew nothing about Leeds and the importance of addresses and their location there.

The suite of offices was on the first floor, with wash and toilet facilities in the basement. There was no lift, so that going up and down between the two floors involved two flights of stairs. A major insurance company occupied the ground floor. Harold took me into the first-floor room and immediately ordered me to sit down and say absolutely nothing, just watch. I was taken aback by his abrasive manner towards me and then I realised that everything was cut and dried between the two of them. He had not only settled on taking the offices without discussing it with me, but in reality he had brought his partner-to-be to choose the furniture and fittings, and I had virtually been told in front of her to mind my own business and sit quietly. She had been given a free hand to make her choices. She had even brought a tape measure to measure up for the curtains. The windows were very tall and narrow, and my husband was giving her an affectionate helping hand.

This to me was certainly his statement that there was some kind of relationship – more than just business – between the pair of them, and she came first. My husband repeated a couple more times that I must not interfere. He must have noticed how angry and hurt I was, but he did not care, or so it seemed.

Once the pair finished what they were doing in those rooms, I was then ordered to follow as we made our way down to an office furniture and equipment store on Wellington Street, about a 100 yards from the premises in South Parade. My husband was engrossed in conversation with his lady friend, presumably discussing the plans. I could not have been more hurt and humiliated. I felt as though I was deliberately being made to feel an outsider.

Again, in the furniture store I was ordered to sit down at the side and keep out of the way. Miss Wright was given free rein to look and choose whatever she wanted for the office. I could not believe that I could be treated so badly. It would have been better had I not been there at all, and yet Harold had insisted I be with them on this outing. Long afterwards, I often wondered if my husband was deliberately flaunting his relationship with this woman. Or were they so deeply besotted with each other, as it looked to me, that he did not realise how badly they were behaving towards me, his wife?

It was certainly the case that I still could not accept that my beloved and doting husband could so much as look at another woman. If I had been told to my face that they were having an affair, I know that at that time there was no way I would have believed it, in spite of what I was witnessing.

Their conduct towards me was repeated once more at another office equipment shop further along Wellington Street. That day proved to be one of the most humiliating in my life. I understood that my husband liked to schmooze his business associates, but he had never before humiliated me at the same time, and in front of that woman.

Later that evening, when we were on our own, I confronted him about his treatment towards me. He denied treating me badly. When I asked him what was going on between the two of them, again he denied there was anything going on and said I was imagining things. I could not confront him outright, as I refused in my own mind to believe that their association was anything more than business. In any case, I had nothing more tangible to go on. Yet their close behaviour left me with a gut instinct, a sickening feeling in the pit of my stomach.

I also took the opportunity to ask Harold where the lady intended living when we got to Leeds. I had not been informed of any plans in that direction.

'Isn't it time she looked for some place to live?'

The reply was not what I wanted to hear, nor what I expected. She was not going to look at anything until she was more familiar with Leeds. She would be living with us.

I was not going to stand for that. I could understand the logic of what I had been told, as Leeds was an unknown quantity to the person concerned, but in view of what I had seen and what my instincts told me, I was not having that woman under my roof under any circumstances. I had always been a hospitable person and made any guest welcome to stay in my home, but in this instance my instincts warned me against this person (I refuse to call her a lady) staying in my home.

I came up with all the reasons I could muster from announcing the lack of space – we were buying a three-bedroomed house, with three children – to the impropriety of such a situation. All my efforts fell on deaf ears. Here was something else that my husband was demanding. The rows escalated. The move was supposed to be a new start and this was to be the beginning. We were rowing the whole time even before we had moved into the house. My husband was a control freak, determined to have his own way regardless.

Time was moving on. His partner was making no effort to find her own home. My nerves were being shattered and my resistance was weakening. I could not find the strength to keep on fighting him. He was continually taking sides with his intended partner against me. I just did not know which way to turn. The character of the relationship between my beloved husband and myself had completely changed from those wonderful earlier years of our marriage, and I did not know how to recover it.

Chapter 58

Everything was going well with the sale of our house at 129, Queen Alexandra Road. The purchase of the house in Leeds was all sealed with a completion date agreed for the end of July, when Harold's notice terminated. Then several weeks prior to our agreed removal date, my husband rang me at home to tell me that the purchasers of the Sunderland house wished to complete and move in towards the end of June, one month ahead of our planned move. He added that the estate agent told him that the sale would fall through if we did not agree, and then we would have to put the house back on the market, giving ourselves an even bigger problem trying to resell it. Harold remarked that he saw no problem with that, and would discuss it with me when he got home that evening. I was very uncomfortable with the idea, as I could foresee difficulties ahead even if arrangements could be sorted out.

Harold told me what he had in mind later that evening. I could take the children to Scarborough for the month and rent a flat. He would join me at the weekends. His own accommodation for that period he had also prepared in his mind. He could stay at a bed and breakfast. In fact he had already looked into it, he told me. Our furniture could be put into store.

It all seemed so simple. He had got it all planned in his mind and had already given the estate agent the go-ahead for the new completion date. We would have to be out of the Sunderland house by the beginning of the last week in June, and Harold had taken my agreement for granted. After all, the profit on the sale, according to Harold, made all the upheaval worthwhile.

We had to journey the short distance to Scarborough to find somewhere to live for those four weeks. It would be summer, so that was a consolation. We also had to find a place where Troy would be welcome. Luckily, so I believed, we found a suitable place on West End Road near the Valley Bridge and not far from the beach. It was a first-floor front flat with two bedrooms, a lounge, kitchen and the usual toilet facilities, and had been converted from an old Victorian three-storey dwelling, now used as holiday homes. It was pleasantly furnished and decorated and reasonably cheap for a holiday flat. Although there was no phone in the flat, I decided it was adequate for the month.

Thankfully, my stalker, Mr Brown, had stopped his outrageous activities towards me, but he decided to arrange a farewell party for us at his home to which he invited all the salesmen with their wives and partners. It was held one evening some two weeks prior to my leaving Sunderland.

I was not happy about attending in view of the way the proposed host had behaved towards me during the three and a half previous years, and I made my feelings known to my dear husband. I really did not have much option in refusing the invitation, being the manager's wife, but it was with great apprehension that I did go.

The Browns lived in an ordinary three-bedroomed semi-detached, with a small lounge and dining room. Harold and I arrived at the Browns' home and were shown into the lounge to find that there were six reps and their wives present. There appeared to be plenty to drink, which was mostly beer. This came as no surprise.

We had been at the party only about five minutes, when I saw Edward Brown going to each of the women present, all young wives. He was groping them and stroking their breasts with his right hand, all very deliberate actions, whilst holding a glass of beer in his left. I looked on in horror for a few moments, not able to believe what I was seeing. He was sexually harassing and behaving in a grossly obscene manner towards his female guests.

I called Harold into the hall and told him what I had seen. He was genuinely shocked and he took me back into the lounge to see for himself. Edward was still behaving indecently to the ladies. I was relieved to see that Harold was equally disgusted. We thought about it for some seconds to decide the best way of handling the problem, for a problem it truly was. Harold and I called his wife and we all went into the other room where Harold told Mae how Edward was behaving, and that it was totally unacceptable. She agreed, but did not seem surprised. She asked that we should all speak to him. This gave us the belief that she knew the character of the man, but could do nothing about him, at least not by herself.

She went and brought Edward from the lounge to the dining room where she told him in front of us that his behaviour was improper and she wanted it to stop. He responded very angrily that this was his house and he would do what he liked in his own home. Harold told

Edward that he could not behave as he was doing to the women. It was very embarrassing for them, and he was not showing a good example of company morals. Edward replied characteristically that no one could stop him doing as he wanted in his own home. I had become even more outraged and irritated and I then told Edward that if he continued to behave as he had been doing, which was grossly improper, I would walk out.

We rejoined the other guests in the lounge and horror of horrors, Edward put on an even more aggressive display of his harassing conduct, upsetting the wives. He was determined to show us that he could do whatever he wanted in his own home. No one made an outright complaint that I knew of, but the expressions on the ladies' faces told me all and I felt for them. I told Harold to collect our coats, as I was sticking to my word and leaving. No doubt my husband was just as disappointed in his salesman colleague's horrible reaction to his reprimand, and we both left the party in disgust.

For some weeks, Harold's secretary had now been doing some of the written work that I had been doing for years. Whilst I still would not accept that theirs was anything more than a business relationship, in spite of my subconscious telling me otherwise, I did believe that Harold's attitude in transferring my previous responsibilities to Miss Wright was an act of affection towards her. I think he felt that by giving a person such responsibilities, he was in some perverse way displaying his feelings towards that person. I now felt that he had demonstrated his love for me previously by letting me take charge of so many business duties. Now that he had transferred these duties to his secretary, I felt humiliated and let down, that I was no longer needed.

The morning after the Browns' party, we woke up at about eight o'clock. Still in bed, Harold's first words were that he wanted me to ring Wright straight away. I asked him, 'Whatever for?' He replied that he wanted me to tell Wright about the party and Eddie's behaviour. I was amazed.

'Whatever for?' I repeated. 'You can tell her when you get to the office. What's the hurry at this time of the morning?'

Harold demanded that I relate the story, but I steadfastly refused. He would tell her if I would not. I saw no point in speaking to her then, so Harold took the phone and dialled her number. Listening to their phone conversation as we lay in bed, it occurred to me then, like a thunderbolt, that all my husband wanted was to speak to her, just to hear her voice, even at that early time of the day. The sacrilegious events of the previous evening, and my walking out of the party, had given him an ideal excuse to do just that. He would talk to her even before we had got out of bed.

Chapter 59

Scarborough has always been one of my favourite holiday resorts for short breaks and weekends in England, always staying at the St Nicholas Hotel, so having to spend a month there in the summer was no problem for me. I did have my reservations at having to take the girls away from school before the end of term, but I sought to deal with this by arranging for the girls to go to school in Scarborough.

A month off school was far too much, especially as that month would link up with the regular summer holidays through August. I managed to get Anne into a secondary modern school at the far side of town, from where she could get a bus back to where we were staying. Pamela and Ruth were accepted into the local junior school for the period.

I took the girls and whatever possessions we thought we would need down to Scarborough that weekend. Harold followed in his car, ever the dutiful husband, and then went back to Newcastle early on the Monday morning. We arranged that he would return on the Friday evening for the weekend, a weekly arrangement that was maintained for the duration of my so-called vacation.

There were, however, two areas about which I was very unhappy. Harold told me prior to moving out of my home in Sunderland that he had found a bed and breakfast accommodation on the Westgate Road not far from the office, but he repeatedly wriggled out of giving me the address.

I was told that there was no phone at the residence, and since there was no phone in the flat, the only way I could keep in touch with him was for me to phone him from a public phone box during office hours. I did phone him as frequently as possible, as he could not always come to the phone if he was working. These niggles that had stuck at the back of my mind tried to resurface, but I was determined to try and make the most of this break, which being mostly in July, was generally very pleasant. The weather was to my favour and I made the most of the beautiful, warm sunshine.

In the mornings, when I was not busy in the flat I would take Troy for a walk along the promenade, or on the beach so that he could enjoy a paddle, and get thoroughly filthy. I made a point of meeting Anne off the bus from school. I had already collected Pam and Ruth from school and we all enjoyed going to the park, where we spent an hour or so before going back to the flat for tea. I am sure the children enjoyed those after school outings, playing round the lake and watching the ducks.

At the weekends, when we were all together, we spent time looking round the town and shopping, doing our usual treat of having tea out. If it were not for the circumstances that necessitated us being at Scarborough at that time, it would have been a very happy time. Harold having to return to the office put a damper on the situation.

Monty and Leila visited me a couple of times. They drove over from Leeds in the late afternoon and had dinner with the girls and myself, spending the evening with us. This broke the midweek loneliness, as I knew no one around and I did not have time really to get to know anyone. I was at least able to have some peace, even though I missed my darling husband and could not wait for the weekends to arrive.

Eventually I had to think about going home to Leeds. I was in two minds about this. In one way, I earnestly desired to move into my new home, sort out all the furnishings and decorations, and get settled. I was also dreading having to put up with my husband's obsession with having that woman live in my home. I had no idea how long she intended to be with us, and I could find no way round it. Being isolated for the immediate weeks prior to moving, as I felt at the time, there was less than nothing that I could do about it. I would just have to wait until I got back to Leeds and our new home to deal with the situation.

Chapter 60

Bright canary-yellow! The brightest, vividest yellow that any car could be, a bright canary-yellow Ford Anglia with the scooped-out back! That was the first thing I saw as I drew up to my new home at 7, Gateland Drive, Leeds, that late July day in 1968. It was squatting on my drive, and a surge of nausea swamped me as reality dawned. That woman had already arrived at my home, and the sight of her car standing on my drive, as the first view of the home I was moving into, suffocated me.

Harold came over to Scarborough for that last Friday to help me move out of the flat at the weekend and return to Leeds. We each drove in our own cars back to our new life, as I had been hoping it would be.

I now felt certain that Harold and his secretary were having much more than a business relationship. I had nothing concrete to go on. I did not dare to question my darling any further without more to go on. The thought that I might rock the boat if I did query his behaviour held me back, but the sight of that car as I pulled up behind it in my drive reinforced my instincts that the relationship between my husband and his secretary was more than business.

The furniture arrived soon after us and Harold and I set about the task of organising the removal people. The three bedrooms were arranged so that the main bedroom, a through room was at the right side of the house. A store cupboard was placed between that bedroom and the two other bedrooms with the smaller of the two at the extreme left. I reasonably planned that Pamela and Ruth would share the bigger of the two and Anne would have the end room to herself. With having an unwelcome visitor, it meant the three children had to share the larger bedroom. It was very annoying. I was being thwarted at every turn.

As I was sorting the bedroom furniture out, my husband came upstairs and stated in very firm terms that he wanted the visitor to have the end room. He expanded by remarking that he wanted her to be as far away from our bedroom as possible so that we could not be overheard in our bedroom. I found this a most curious, if not a significant statement. I again requested to know for how long was I going to have to put up with her presence in our home. And again he refused to give me any sensible reply. It was a very infuriating and frustrating situation I found myself in. He was trying to make himself appear to be the loving husband, but with equally infuriating and hurtful innuendos.

We settled down to a semblance of family routine, but the arguments increased with the passing of time as I saw no move to let me have my home to myself.

As soon as the August school holidays were over, I enrolled Anne into Allerton Grange School, and the two younger girls were accepted into the local primary school, Shadwell Primary, which was only a few yards up the main road.

Anne's teenage tantrums had started to exhibit themselves. This gave my husband another excuse to have a go at me. He blamed me for her outbursts, demanding that I make a bigger effort at controlling her.

'Shut her up! Shut her up, can't you?' he would bellow at me as he washed and dressed. It became a regular morning calling card.

'I can't stand it! I've got a day's work to do.' His voice would bellow through the house as he rushed out to start his day, and leaving us all more stressed than was warranted.

Any suggestion that he reprimand her himself met with more accusations that I was a bad mother and that she was my responsibility.

I tried to avoid confrontations with my husband whenever the children were around, but he never gave them any consideration. He could not care less about them, and any reaction they might suffer from whatever they saw. He continued to play cat and mouse with me, being loving and caring and then suddenly turning aggressive towards me whether the girls were around or not.

Now that we were all back in Leeds with my parents and greater family near by, I was hopeful that Anne would be happier, as we all were. Anne adored her grandma as all my children did, and now that we were able to visit all the time, my mother would be a steadying force. Anne did become a regular morning visitor at my parents' home, which she passed on her way to school.

Once the children were back at school, Harold asked me to go in the office to work on a part-time basis. We had tried to organise some form of working arrangement whilst still in Sunderland. The company would be registered as Courtney & Co Insurance Brokers, though specialising in life assurance. I would be working in the office some of the time, though I was unsure how this arrangement would actually work out when it seemed that the other woman seemed to control the office, and my husband.

I had agreed to having £1,200 pounds put into a separate account in my name only, which was to pay for immediate domestic needs, food, cleaning materials and suchlike, for a year. This was so that all or any money earned during the first year could be ploughed back into the business and help to get it established, as well as ensuring there was money to fall back on if the business did not get off its feet. It was to me a wise arrangement.

The main bills, utilities, would be paid from the office. I was informed that Miss Wright would handle that side of our affairs. I took immediate objection to this and told my husband so. I had always dealt with such matters and I objected to that person knowing my business. Whilst it could take a weight off my mind, I found the significance of that woman taking more responsibility very disturbing, suspecting that their relationship was of a more romantic nature than my husband would admit. The thought occurred to me that as the new partner was not putting any money into the business, and had no money, as Harold insisted, she would be taking money out of the business for her salary. I felt that this was something that had to be discussed, under the circumstances. When I raised this point with my husband, he became very angry and I was told that it was not my business. I had now learned that any questions I had involving the new partner were taken as an attack on her. I walked on eggshells.

It was with mixed feelings that I started working for my husband in his new business. At the start, Harold produced a partnership form, which he asked me to sign. I was delighted. He had conceded to my requests that I should be a partner. If Wright was to be a partner, then so should I. There would never have been a new business but for me, I honestly believed, and I had to put my foot down to preserve my own self-respect. I was to deal with the general business as I had always done and there were new agency forms for me to sign. I would deal with these accounts.

On my first day in the office, Harold told me that he had been approached by a friend who we knew was working for another insurance company. He had asked Harold if he could join us as another partner. The gentleman had only been working for his company for a

177

year but had been very successful and wished to start his own business. My opinion was sought as Harold felt that the gentleman was too inexperienced. I suggested that Harold should go along with his gut feeling, but I also felt that his current other partner would not be happy having a new person in the business, a thought that stayed inside my head. The gentleman did not join us, but he did create his own company, which went on to become a prominent insurance brokerage.

I tried to be as cooperative as I was allowed to be, but the longer Wright resided in my home, the worse the arguments became, as I repeatedly demanded to know when she would be moving out.

My husband's parents could now put their oar in as well. Harold usually visited them on a Sunday morning, sometimes taking the girls and myself. These trips were something of an ordeal as his parents were still fighting, and about the same thing, money. His mother always complained to us that the old man still did not give her enough housekeeping, and she had to go on working to make ends meet. She was still working part-time, as a gown sales lady, at Wallis's.

I felt that her complaints were an excuse to avoid making anything to eat, other than a tasteless cup of tea, and the occasional small tin of salmon between us. It was also served as before, in that tiny kitchenette where there was only room for two to sit, and the rest of us stood in a crush.

The rest of the house was crowded out with even more antiques and ornaments of every size and description, so there was hardly any space to walk in, let alone sit down. The old man told us frequently that they were the children's inheritance. Their value must have been very substantial. However, the children never liked their grandpa, or Zaide, as he preferred to be called. Most times he still looked a sight, very unkempt. I do not ever remember seeing him with his false teeth in, and his uncouth and ragged appearance frightened the children. He had not changed his avaricious ways, trying to bribe the girls for a kiss by showing them one sweet or toffee. It never worked, but only made the girls recoil even more. I doubt if they ever enjoyed their visits to their father's parents' home. I never did.

One day, after having had to put up with my unwelcome visitor for several weeks, and whose miserable face and hostile attitude provoked me even more, for she made no attempt to be friendly or at least civil to me, my mother-in-law called in to see us. During conversation she let me know that she had made dinner one evening earlier in the week

178

for Harold and his 'partner'. This was the first I had been told about this, and it sounded as though Harold had meant it to be a secret. Harold and that woman had apparently become regular visitors at his parents' home. I do not know whether I was more angry or more hurt. I became even angrier then, and told my mother-in-law that she was out of order. Did she not realise what was going on? How dare she make a meal for them, knowing her son's wife was waiting at home with our children? It was bad enough making a meal for her son and his girlfriend but the matter had been kept under wraps. She had never made dinner for Harold and myself, with or without the children, the whole time we had been married, and I wondered just what kind of a meal she had cooked up, or in what part of the house they had dined.

This was even more confirmation to me of my husband's extra-marital affair. I told Harold's mother about my thoughts on that, and that she was encouraging them. She then told me that I was being ridiculous. I was always rude to Wright, she informed me, and I had refused to make a meal for the visitor. She was just trying to make it up to her by being friendly towards her. It was obvious now that my husband was lying to his own mother. I could not get over that incident for some time. There was even more going on than I had wished to believe.

Whether this incident had prompted Wright to act more quickly, I never knew, as I tried to avoid her as much as possible, but I blessed the day that Harold told me she had found a flat and was moving out. She had been under my roof for three hellish months.

Chapter 61

Wright had only just moved out when I bumped into an old friend whilst out shopping. I had not seen Cynthia for so many years. Certainly, well before moving to Newcastle. She was one of my many friends whom Harold had prevented me from keeping in contact with. We had so much to talk about. She told me that she and her family lived in a large old Victorian stone house at Oakwood. Her husband, Peter was keen on cinematography as a hobby and he had converted the attic into a cinema where they entertained friends with film shows.

She told me that she worked for a charity, fundraising (again, which one I have forgotten), but she was having a coffee evening with a film show the following week, and invited me. I had no hesitation and accepted immediately. It would be a break from the agony I was living with.

When I told Harold about the invitation he was very angry and told me I could not go. This was so unreasonable. He was back to his possessive behaviour. His reason, so he said, was that it was not his cup of tea, and I was not to go out with out him, either.

Harold had soon resumed his forays to the casino. He went to the Moortown Casino once or twice a week initially, insisting I go with him, although as far as betting was concerned he did listen to me and still kept his bets on the roulette wheel to a maximum of £5 a visit, win or lose. He usually gave me a couple of pounds to use, although I was not really interested in playing.

When he stipulated that I could not go to Cynthia's, with or without him, he was making one rule for himself and another for me, so I was determined to go. For once, I felt that I had to stand up to him, so I went to Cynthia's coffee evening. It was due to start at eight o'clock. I had not been there more than about fifteen minutes when there was a phone call. It was for me, and a very irate husband was calling me, ordering me to come home immediately. I told Cynthia that he sounded in such a terrible temper that I should go home.

He was waiting for me, and must have been dwelling on my 'disobedience' as he called it. I could not recall him being in such a state before. He was shouting and insulting me. I could not get a word in edgeways. He followed me up the stairs as I went to see if the children were in bed. They were. He was bellowing and screaming at me. I tried to reason with him, and then I felt the heat of his hand as for the second time, he slapped me across my face. I was stunned that he could do this to me again. I think he must have shocked himself. He had gone out of control, but slapping me with such ferocity must have brought him to his senses. He stopped cold. I ran into the bedroom.

The next morning, I gathered together some of his belongings. I put them in a small suitcase and planted it on the back doorstep. I told my precious, darling husband that I wanted him out. I never wanted anything more to do with him. No man was going to treat me like that. I was so very, very angry. Without a word he picked up the case off the doorstep and walked away.

After I had calmed down, I had to get the children off to school. I rang Cynthia to tell her what had happened. When I told her that he had hit me, she practically burst into tears herself, she was so stunned by my news. She said she would be round in minutes, and true to her word she soon arrived. She lived a mile or so away, but her husband, Peter drove her. She tried to comfort me. Just having her there in the house with me, was a tonic. I knew I had a true friend in Cynthia.

The next couple of days were an ordeal. I started to miss Harold, as I truly loved him in spite of all that he had put me through. I was so shaken at the knowledge that my husband could hit me again. It never occurred to me that this could possibly be the end of my marriage. I tried to carry on as normal, although I did not know where he was, and I did not even try to think about where he was.

I could not tell my mother; I was too embarrassed. But by the fourth day, I realised that I had to say something to her. The girls were missing their father and no doubt would tell her he was away. I tried to make out he had gone on business.

I rang her and told her what had happened. When I explained that he had hit me, she exploded into a fury,

'How dare he!' Her anger was then explained as being due to the fact that not only had he hit me, but he had actually gone to her and was staying there at my mother's. He had had the gall to go to my mother with some cock and bull story about me. Sympathetically, she had given him a bed. I had never known my mother so angry, that he had hit her daughter and then made up a fairy tale to her. She cried out that she did not want him in her house any more, and would not let him in again. He had to get out immediately.

I told her to tell him he could come home, but it was never to happen again. When he did walk through our door, he was so full of remorse. Promises that it would never happen again could never have been more effusive. He would make it up to me. Apology followed apology. My beloved could not be more loving. I knew that all that time his secretary was still on the scene. Even though she had moved out of my home, she was still in our lives, but for the moment that did not matter.

As soon as she moved out, it was soon to be half term so we arranged to take the girls to Blackpool, staying at the Norbreck Hydro Hotel. We all had a lovely week there. Harold could not have been more loving and caring. It was as if all our, or should I say all my, problems had never existed. Everything was once again all right.

We returned home on the Saturday evening. As we drove along Gateland Drive towards our house, we saw that all the downstairs front windows were open. We had been burgled.

Harold opened the front door and entered the house with great trepidation. I slowly followed. Once in the house, we found the back windows to the lounge were also open. Stacks of our silver, the candelabra, tureens and plates, cutlery as well as Wedgwood and other valuables were piled onto chairs by the windows. The thief must have been disturbed before he was able to remove anything out of the house. No doors were forced, only the back lounge window. Ironically, we had locked the hall door to the lounge. It had a Chubb lock and could not be opened from the lounge side, but there was a hatch from the kitchen through to the lounge, and it appeared that the burglar had climbed through the hatch into the kitchen, as much of the silver that was kept in the kitchen cupboards now sat on chairs in the lounge ready to be removed.

We rang the police and then made a search with them, looking in all our cupboards including the sideboard, and were happy to believe that nothing had been taken. The bedrooms were still locked and had not been entered.

It was bad enough to think that our house had been broken into, regardless of whether anything had been taken or not. We collected Troy from the kennels and then tried to sort things out.

During the following week, the girls had returned to school and on the Wednesday evening, Pam and Ruth's school held a concert. We were sat watching the children perform and thoroughly enjoying the occasion. Harold rarely came to school functions. He usually excused himself, either with business commitments or his lack of patience to sit and watch children. However, on this occasion, he went with me. He sat, playing with a penny coin, rolling it between his fingers, from side to side.

He suddenly stopped and exclaimed, 'My coin collection!'

Rolling the coin over his fingers had reminded him of his collection of valuable coins of various denominations. They were kept in a cigar box in the sideboard, which had been sealed up with Cellotape. He remarked that when he had looked in the sideboard he had seen the box, but had not thought to look inside it. Something, he felt, was wrong and he could not wait to get home.

He was right. Having rushed home as soon as the concert was over, he found the box empty. His valuable coin collection had been stolen. The police were informed, but unfortunately the collection was not covered by insurance. It was never recovered.

Eighteen months later, we received a letter from the police saying that they had arrested a man for another job, and he had asked for the burglary at our home to be taken into consideration. He received a jail sentence.

Chapter 62

Harold was now paying all our household bills from the office, but had given responsibility for their payment to his partner-cum-secretary, so that when I received a letter from the Local Government rate office demanding immediate payment of an overdue rates bill together with the threat of being summonsed, I was shocked and very angry. (Rates were the predecessor of our present Council Tax.) I have never, ever been in arrears, and have certainly never been threatened with a summons for an overdue payment of any kind.

I was at home at the time and rang Wright at the office to explain the letter and to ask why the rates bill was in arrears. She immediately went on the defensive and sharply retorted that she had paid the bill. Her tone of voice was very aggressive from the start, but I tried to be as tactful as possible and told her that the bill could not have been paid if I had received such a letter. I then went on to explain that the bill was in two parts, the first to be paid on receipt of the bill, and the second half to be paid in September. I went on to suggest that it could be that she had only paid the first half, and it was the second part that was overdue.

Her reply was that she had never had to deal with those kinds of bills so she could not be expected to deal with them correctly. This told me so much about her work. She had apparently not read the bill carefully, as payment arrangements were clearly explained, at least to my way of thinking. And this person was responsible for running my husband's business! Despite my thoughts, I said no more, as she said she would deal with it.

A few hours later in the day, I answered the phone to an exceedingly angry husband.

'How dare you talk to Barbara like that?'

I was taken aback.

'Don't you ever speak to her like that again, and if you have anything to say, say it to me, but never, never find fault with her again.'

This was unbelievable. My husband's secretary was complaining about me, and he was taking her side against me without even asking

184

me my side of the conversation. How much more hurt and humiliation was I supposed to take?

Harold was in a filthy mood when he arrived home during the evening, and immediately burst in to a tirade about my behaviour towards his partner. He accused me of trying to make out that there was more between Wright and himself. I was imagining the worst, and deliberately finding fault with her. All of these so-called accusations against her he denied strongly. Nevertheless, he was defending her against me, when once there was a time when no one, but no one, dare say a wrong word about me.

I put the children to bed with this husband of mine agitating and complaining at me. As I have already pointed out, the one thing I have always tried to avoid, and tried to tell Harold, was to not argue in front of the children, but he was not listening. By the time I walked out of the children's bedroom, he had worked himself up into a ferocious lather.

I looked at him as I stood at the top of the stairs, about to step down. He charged up to the top of the stairs, forcing me to step back. His eyes glared at me. His pupils had sharpened into jet-black points of ice. I could feel his glare piercing through my body as though I was being stabbed. At the same time I felt the blow as he punched me in the chest with his closed fists. He had worked himself out of control and was throwing punch after punch at my chest. I tried to push him off me, but he was too strong and I fell backwards against the wall. He knocked me to the floor and then started kicking me. I was unable to help myself. The girls had come out onto the landing and must have watched the whole episode in terror but did not say a word.

The beatings stopped. He ran down the stairs, and struggling to get up, I screamed at him to get out. He went there and then. The last thing I could ever have wanted was to have my girls seeing me, their mother, being attacked by their father, and so ferociously. The only thing that mattered now was comforting and reassuring my children that I was alright. Apart from a few bruises, I was not hurt physically, but the pain of knowing my children had witnessed the attack with all its viciousness, and the strain of having to put up with so much aggravation, was affecting my nerves.

Left alone with my three beautiful daughters, I had a sleepless night in spite of still having to take sleeping tablets. First thing in the morning the phone rang. It was Cynthia.

'He's been hitting you again, I can feel it.'

185

This was to be the first of a number of what Cynthia and I called her 'psychic revelations'. She always sensed what was happening to me, and she was right every time. She came to the house in moments to comfort me once more.

I had no idea where Harold had gone to, and at first I did not care. I was happy to have some peace and spent time with the girls after school taking them for walks round the local countryside. Pamela liked to ride on her bicycle with us sometimes.

But as the time passed, first one week, then into the second, I started to worry, as I did not hear from him. Mam and Dad were concerned for me being left on my own with the children. Even Monty took a great interest and came to see me frequently, expressing his disgust at his brother-in-law.

One morning, at the beginning of the third week, Dad rang me up and told me he had been making enquiries and had found out that Harold had gone with his sister Doreen to Majorca. They would be away for two weeks. My husband had not had the decency to let me know.

The girls were very distressed at their father's absence and were missing him, in spite of what he had done, though we did not talk about it. I doubt that they understood the severity of what their father had done to me. All the same it must have been very traumatic for them. I was missing him. After all, I still loved him. The girls, and especially Pamela, kept asking me when he was coming home.

Towards the end of the fourth week, when we knew my husband was back, Monty went to see him to give him a piece of his mind and to sort things out. Harold told Monty that he was very sorry and wanted to come home. Monty reported back to me that Harold was missing us, and that he was very remorseful and apologetic. Pamela got very excited and asked if she could phone her father to ask him to come home. I agreed, but only with certain conditions. It was decided that I would see Harold on neutral territory, and Cyril and his business partner and friend, George, were asked to be mediators.

When Pamela spoke to her father, she asked him to come home, which he said he would, but I would not speak to him until I met him and sorted things out. I could not let this situation happen again. Monty arranged with Cyril and George that they would all meet us at the Griffin Hotel, a prominent hotel on Boar Lane, in the town centre.

Cyril and George had booked a room, so we had privacy to discuss our problems. and that was where Harold and I with Monty met up with our mediators. We spoke for a while, and everyone told Harold

186

what they thought of him in a friendly manner. Harold could not have been more full of remorse. He apologised profusely, declaring how much he loved me. He insisted that there would never be a repeat. Words that I had already heard before. When everyone was satisfied that Harold really meant what he said, I agreed to spend the night with my husband at the hotel.

I was so grateful to my brother and our friends for settling everything so well. They had managed the situation to everyone's satisfaction as though it was a foregone conclusion that I would take my husband back. Arrangements had even been made for the girls to be looked after for the night. We were both happy to be back together, and returned home to the girls' welcoming arms in the morning.

My nerves were nevertheless playing up, and I felt drained. That week we had a visitor, Harold's cousin Lionel. He was the son of Harold's father's sister and her husband. He was over from Los Angeles, where they had lived for some time. Lionel was the same age as Harold and they had always been close friends. That first Saturday back together, we took Lionel down to the Red Lion, the local pub in Shadwell. Lionel and Harold were close drinking companions. Harold explained to Lionel that we had had some minor problems, as he called it, and that he had been away. Lionel suggested that as recompense Harold should take me away. He should return to Majorca with me, as he thought it was the best way to make it up to me. Harold, unhesitatingly, said he would. I was not too happy, as I was nervous of flying, and my fear seemed to have been exacerbated as a result of feeling so nervy. I dismissed the idea.

A couple of days later, Harold came home with the news that he had booked for us to go to the same hotel where he had just stayed in Majorca. He had even arranged with Mam to have the girls. She said she would do anything to help our marriage. We were to go immediately.

It was now late November. The hotel was right on the coast at Magaluf, which at that time was an exclusive resort, so everything was first class. That could not be said of the weather. Harold told me that he wanted me to have a memento of his eternal and undying love and devotion to me. We went into Palma to find a jeweller's shop. He wanted to buy me an eternity ring. We chose a white gold ring, set with three oblong Majorcan rubies, side by side. We had a pleasant week, and I was able to put my memories of the past few weeks behind me, at least for the time being.

Chapter 63

When we returned home from Majorca, I did not intend going into the office to work alongside his secretary, even though she had continued working in my husband's absence, and Harold did not discuss this with me, but within a day or so I was called in.

At breakfast, he usually asked me how I was spending the day, and then went to the office without making any comment. But within the time it took him to get there, he would be on the phone frantically asking me to get down as soon as possible. The phone was ringing non-stop, and he could not cope, or so he proclaimed.

During those days back in the office, I noticed that the business registration certificates were not displayed on the walls, and asked him about this. He replied somewhat sulkily that they had not yet been sent to him.

One of my duties was to answer the phone. I did so, on that particular day, answering with the usual Courtney and Company introduction. The voice answered in a friendly tone and stated that she was ringing to thank Harold and 'yourself' for the lovely meal that they had all had the previous evening. I was stunned. I felt as though I had been kicked in the stomach yet again.

I realised that the caller believed that she was talking to Wright, and in view of what I had already been told, I made a quick decision not to inform the caller who I really was so that she might continue to enlighten me more about my husband's nefarious activities. The caller was a lady doctor policyholder from Harold's days with Sun Life whose name I recognised, but had never met, and now my beloved darling husband had been wining and dining her with someone whom the doctor now believed was his wife, or at least that they were a couple, according to the contents of our conversation. This, on an evening when he had told me that he was out canvassing on his own. He had lied again.

Harold had only entertained what he called his important clients or policyholders to dinner on rare occasions. This follow-up phone call gave me some of the answers I had been seeking. If this was not confirmation of his relationship with Wright, I do not know what was. I decided not to say anything for the time being. It was just one phone call, but over the next few weeks, I was to hear several similar phone calls from other policyholders or prospective ones, when I was in the office. I just did not know how to handle the situation, as I was not sure how I wanted the situation resolved. I did want Wright out of our lives, but in view of my husband's earlier response to my complaining entreaties, I feared further reprisals from him.

It now came to light that during my absence, a new firm of accountants had been called in. Wright had apparently had problems doing the books, or so I gleaned from glimpses of conversations. I was responsible for the accounts of the general business, dealing with the bills, and paying the companies concerned. Wright had difficulties with these during my absence, and a large local firm of accountants had taken on our bookkeeping as well as the auditing.

To me, this was adding on unnecessary expense, but I was in no position to point this out to my husband. It would be castigating his revered partner, and I had already suffered too much after having complained about her work. Nevertheless, I could keep my thoughts to myself, even though I felt it was affecting the business in a negative way.

At the same time, Wright started making the occasional derogatory and snide remark that I was too clever for my own good, or that I was 'snooty', or words of a similar nature. I ignored them to her face, but I wondered if she had heard these remarks at my in-laws' house. I know they thought that I looked down on them. I did not, but I could never really like them. The fact that Wright could be rude to me, all the same, was very hurtful. Complaining to my darling, devoted husband would have been a waste of time. I was sure of that now.

During the next couple of weeks, a daily routine developed whereby I was told I was not needed that day, and then I would be called into the office urgently by phone, as soon as Harold got to the office. There were occasions when I had to cancel hairdressing appointments and other arrangements at a moment's notice. I wanted proper arrangements so that I knew where I was. The girls were at school, but I still had to have a routine at home as well.

Unfortunately, Harold failed to see my reasoning. I could see his point, knowing the kind of person he was, impetuous and headstrong, that he never knew what each day would bring. But this only added to my discomfort, knowing he always expected me to be at his beck and call without any consideration for my feelings.

From the outcome of my plea to him, I assumed he must have talked this over with the other partner, as it was decided that she could cope without me, and after all, her wishes came first, regardless of whether it was good for business or not. In any case, I felt most uncomfortable working in the office. I felt like a stranger in what I believed to be partially my business.

I was told not to come into the office to work, ever again. It seemed like a happy escape for me.

And all this, after my husband's recent undying pledge of love and devotion.

Chapter 64

I suppose it was a crazy idea, and I cannot remember who suggested it, but since I could not work in the office with that other woman, and I felt I needed to work, even if only part time, the idea of running a restaurant sounded like a suitable solution.

Harold made out that he was keen on the idea. It would be an extension of his business. (Was he planning on a business empire?!)

Within days, he came to me telling me he had found just the right property. We had agreed that something just out of town would serve our purposes and he had apparently started our quest for suitable premises with great zeal.

It turned out that the property was an established grocery shop in the village of Burley-in-Wharfedale, a very few miles out of Leeds on the way to Otley and Ilkley, popular tourist spots. It was on the shopping parade on Main Street. This we surmised would give us considerable passing trade on which to build. The property was owned by two elderly sisters who according to Harold agreed to us developing the property. The shop occupied the ground floor, with a small area at the back as a stock room. The upstairs could be used as a café in the meantime. To turn it into a restaurant involved considerable rebuilding, not to mention the refurbishing to make it into a high-class establishment.

I did point out the cost, starting with the architect. My optimistic husband told me not to worry about those things. He could deal with it. We could run the grocery shop as it was until all the plans had been passed and building work could begin.

Throughout all our discussions and subsequent negotiations, which I was led to believe were being arranged and conducted by my husband, I never saw a contract or legal binding agreement. I could never find out the cost of the lease or the amount of the rent. Harold insisted that he would run the administration of the restaurant from his office. He would look after the bookkeeping and all other paper work, including the paying of my bills. It sounded to me as though he again was sharing control of my affairs with the Wright woman, as those were her current responsibilities as partner with Courtney & Co. All I

191

had to do was to run the grocery shop for the time being at least. I was also told that anything I wanted or needed to run the business, I could have. Just ask the office, my judgement was good enough, I was told.

Thus it was early in 1969 that I took over the business. The food that was sold was very simple. I thought I would try to introduce some variety. The customers were clearly only used to the plainest of fare, so I knew I would have to introduce new lines gradually. I also arranged for a daily supply of fresh cream pastries. These were supplied by a well-known Leeds bakery, which produced the most gorgeous of delights, so I did not anticipate any problems there. It was just a problem of controlling the stock.

Everything started well, but I found that being on my own was proving tricky. I needed an assistant. Some of the suppliers wanted payment on the spot. I was supposed to give Harold the bills, and he complained that paying the bills on the spot complicated things. I put a small advert for an assistant in the shop window, but it drew no response. Harold then told me he would advertise in the local paper. When I still failed to get any response, I started getting worried. I asked Harold several times if he had placed the advert, as I desperately needed the help. I kept getting very peculiar replies from him. He had forgotten, or Wright was dealing with it. My gut instincts were playing up again. I sensed that trouble was brewing. Was the advert ever placed?

I tried to open the café at the weekends. Anne and the girls liked to come over and give a hand. They thought it was great fun. Without them, I would not have been able to manage satisfactorily.

Sometimes Harold himself offered to help, but I became aware that he was making a mess of things, taking the wrong orders, causing me considerable problems. Was this deliberate? I did not want to think so, but doubts were plaguing me again.

During the month of February, we had a spell of very bad weather. The snow blocked some of our roads. My husband became ill with 'flu and had to stay in bed for some time. He seemed unable to shake it off. He insisted I go to the shop. I had no one to take over. This meant I would do my own books. I always cashed up at the end of the day and recorded my takings. Now, something was wrong. Figures did not tally. There was money missing. I realised I had to keep my finger on the pulse. The bank statements went to Harold's office. When I asked to see them, I received very unsatisfactory answers. They were a put-off, so I could never audit my own accounts accurately, even though many of my bills were paid in cash on the spot.

192

I asked Harold many more times what had happened to my advert. The takings were not adding up. I sensed that things were not going to plan. In fact I started to think that my efforts were being sabotaged. I suspected that no advert had ever been placed in any paper. It was once more affecting my nerves and I was becoming exhausted.

Money was going astray. Harold made out that I was mistaken. He declared that the business was not being run properly. No architect had been hired, so the agreed plans for the restaurant were not proceeding. He was not helping me. I felt as though I had been here before. Harold was promising one thing and doing the opposite, agreeing to my wishes, but ignoring them or contradicting them behind my back. I was losing my grip.

In the middle of March, I was informed by my beloved that one of the sisters who owned the property had died and the remaining sister had decided she did not want the property converting. Our dreams were being eroded. I still could not help wondering whether I was being told the truth. I had been caused to doubt my husband's word for so long now, that I found it hard to believe everything he told me. If the conversion had been agreed legally, where was the contract? I could get no answers. Either way, true or not, my sensibilities took a terrific beating. It was as if there was yet another conspiracy against me. I was not going to be allowed to make a success of anything, if my husband had his way. I struggled to keep going, but I was too tired. I felt as though I was fighting my husband and I could not go on. I was feeling so browbeaten.

A little later in the month, Harold came to the shop as I was closing. At the sight of him, my knees buckled. I felt as though all my breath had been driven out of me. I crumpled up and fell to the floor.

Harold asked me what the problem was. I could hardly speak and he had to help me to my feet and hold me to prevent me falling. I was too ill. He helped me into his car and told me he would take me straight to hospital.

At Casualty, at the Leeds General Infirmary, I was found to be suffering from extreme nervous exhaustion and colitis, and was admitted to Ward 6 under the care of Professor Hamilton. Mam was once again called to the rescue to care for my girls.

Whether my husband seemed to be angry with me, or at the situation, or both, I was too ill to decipher. On reading the hospital notes at a later date, it was recorded that 'the husband was very uncooperative and unpleasant'.

193

Harold made himself out to be a very loving and caring husband. He visited me every day, staying for hours, holding me as though everything was all right. He brought me flowers, fruit and various other little gifts that one takes to patients in hospital. To the hospital, he must have looked like the wonderfully perfect husband. The doctors nevertheless, must have seen through him, judging by the hospital records.

One week's stay in hospital provided me with the rest I desperately needed, and I was allowed home as an outpatient. Apparently, an appointment was made for me to come back a little later, unknown to me, as it was also noted in my records that the appointment was never kept.

During my stay in hospital, my spouse informed me that he was getting rid of the shop. There were now so many unanswered questions mounting up. Why was my husband behaving like Dr Jekyll and Mr Hyde towards me? But I no longer had the strength to worry about them for the time being.

After a couple of weeks at home, it was suggested that I could go back to the office for a few hours. It looked as though my husband was trying to throw me to the wolves again, but I felt as though I needed to get out of the house a little. I was then given no option. My husband's desperate phone calls from the office first thing on a morning, demanding my help, could not go unheeded.

On returning to work, I was met with a big surprise. Harold had moved into other offices. These were in East Parade, on the first floor. I had not been informed of the move until now. The décor and furnishings of these premises were not up to the high standard of the previous suite in South Parade. The rental and overheads must have been considerably lower, and I could not help but wonder why the move had been made, though I did not ask and I was never told.

Chapter 65

Not long after leaving hospital, my dearly beloved husband came home from the office one evening and started lashing out at me in front of the children. I had no idea what this beating was about. I tried to push him off me, but I could not get through to him. He was totally out of control. I managed to get to the phone and dialled 999 for help. This calmed Harold.

Within a short while a policeman came to our door. When the door was opened, Harold pushed me aside and tried to explain the fracas to the policeman, not allowing me to get a word in. The response was that this was a 'domestic disturbance', and of no concern to the police, or words of this nature, and the policeman left.

Harold immediately rang our GP, Dr Feldman. What I could make of the conversation implied that I was out of my mind. The doctor agreed to come round. I was terribly distressed. I could not make out what was happening. I was certainly not out of my mind. But in those days, a wife did not have a leg to stand on, as I learnt to my horror.

When Dr Feldman came to see me that evening, he suggested I return to hospital. Harold was obviously not satisfied with the treatment I had received at the Leeds Infirmary. So it was suggested I go to a private hospital, The Retreat, a psychiatric hospital at York.

I was admitted the next day under the care of consultant Dr White. After two days of examinations, Dr White told me he could find nothing wrong with me mentally. I was suffering from nervous exhaustion as a result of stress and anxiety.

He then told me something that I had long been waiting for. He believed that the cause of my condition was my husband. He considered Harold to be very unstable. The fact that he put up a show of devotion and caring in public, whilst treating me badly at home, pointed to Harold having mental problems. At last I had a sympathetic doctor. He was the first doctor to recognise and accept what I had been putting up with from my husband, though I never knew if Dr White told Harold that he thought Harold was to blame for my bad nerves.

I was put on a course of medication that included Valium. I was still on sleeping tablets, but they did not always help.

After three days, I wanted to go home, and the doctor consented. Harold had been to see me with the girls every day. He again made himself out to be the adoring, caring and loving husband to the hospital staff. At least I knew that Dr White could see through him. He promised the doctor that he would look after me. However, Dr White recommended that I be referred to St James's Hospital as an outpatient. I consented.

A referral was made quickly and I found myself attending Dr Rose, one of the chief psychiatric consultants at the hospital. Dr Rose was the most sympathetic and understanding doctor I ever attended. He wanted a full history of my problems, and he listened to my story. I recalled all the events that had happened since that eventful phone call over four years ago. How we had been so happy until that event.

The psychiatrist explained to me, when I told him about my experiences with my husband's supervisor, for the three and a half years before returning to Leeds, that often husbands try to make out their wives are having affairs for any or all of several reasons.

They may just want to discredit their wives, or if they were having an affair themselves, it would be a way of salving their own conscience. Alternatively, the most usual reason was for a man to divert attention away from his own affair by directing it at the wife. As I had not had any real proof of my husband carrying on with his partner-cum-secretary, Dr Rose said he could not make a proper analysis. Any attempt to extract a confession always met with a complete denial. It seemed to me as though Harold just wanted to hurt me, for whatever reason. Dr Rose added that he believed my husband to be a compulsive liar. I found myself looking to Dr Rose as my salvation, though I had no idea how he could help me at that point in time. I continued to see Dr Rose regularly for some time.

During the early summer, Harold learned that he had to have a haemorrhoid operation. Arrangements were made for him to be admitted to the Clarendon Nursing Home, a private hospital off Clarendon Road, near the city.

The hospital had been converted from a huge mansion. My husband had a room on the first floor immediately facing a wide staircase that led up from a large Victorian-styled foyer.

He was scheduled to be in the hospital for two weeks. The operation was deemed to have been successful. I visited him every day for the first ten days, from the afternoons till the close of visiting at 9 p.m. That tenth day, I stayed as usual till nine o'clock. I was walking down the stairs when Harold's parents arrived in a hurry. They were running up the stairs. They commented to me as they passed me on the steps that they had not been able to get to the hospital any sooner.

The driveway to the hospital was accessed from an unmade road leading from the main road. It was a run-round drive leading from the lower gate to the exit at the top of the road. The road had a muddy surface with a slight incline down to the end about 30 yards or so further along. There, a fence blocked further passage. A similar muddy border, with trees spaced along it, edged the road.

My car was parked in the driveway directly in front of the main entrance. I got into my car and my gut instincts started playing up. I drove slowly out of the drive, and as I pulled onto the unmade road, I stopped to look down the road. To anyone watching me, I would appear to be obeying the Highway Code and looking both ways. To me, something was guiding me. As I looked to my right down the road, parked at the very end by the fence on the border under a tree, which being summer was in full leaf, I could see a bright canary-yellow Ford Anglia. *That* bright canary-yellow Ford Anglia! It was so clearly an attempt to hide the car. To the best of my knowledge, there was only one such car in the area and that belonged to Wright.

'Why does she feel the need to hide herself under a tree?' I wondered to myself.

I drove off left into the unmade road, and then almost immediately turned right into Clarendon Road, drove down the hill for several yards, stopped my car and waited a few minutes. I then turned my car round and drove back to the hospital. Sure enough, the canary-yellow Ford Anglia was now parked in the hospital driveway in front of the main entrance. I pulled my car up behind the parked yellow car. Something told me that I now had my chance to find the truth.

I re-entered the building and climbed cautiously up the staircase. There at the top of the stairs sat my husband's parents outside the door of their son's room. I looked at them. They looked at me, lost for words. They were obviously shocked to see me having come back. I stood in front of my husband's hospital room door for a brief moment, quaking. I was convinced that I would see the evidence that I had been seeking, but could I face it? Slowly, I grasped the door handle, pressed the handle down, and very gradually and with much trepidation, I pushed the door open. My heart was in my mouth. The door to Harold's room opened wide and I could see right into the room. I filled up with horror and my stomach turned over.

There, lying in bed under the bedclothes, were my beloved husband and his mistress, Wright. They had their arms around each other. I looked on stunned, choking. I could not move. I could not open my mouth. I was frozen for what seemed like forever. They looked up at me, obviously in surprise. Now I had the confirmation that I had been wanting, for such a long time. Not a word passed between us.

I turned round, totally mortified, and ran to the stairs. My mind was a blank. I could not think. I heard my in-laws shouting at me that it served me right. If I had brought them they would not have had to ask Wright. They were actually blaming me. They clearly knew what was happening inside that hospital room, otherwise why were they sat outside?

I ran down the stairs, out of the building and into my car. How I ever managed to drive myself home I have no idea. From then on I remembered nothing for some time other than the sight of my husband in bed with his inamorata. His fancy lady lying with him in his hospital bed! I had been right about them. My suspicions were now confirmed. At least I had an answer. The jigsaw was coming together. But there were still some answers I needed to complete the whole jigsaw.

Chapter 66

The idea of leaving my husband was never an option. In fact, the thought never entered my head. I still loved my husband very much, and although I had seen him in bed with that woman, I had the proof that he had been lying to me about her all along.

I could never leave him. I needed a roof over our heads, especially for the children. I had nowhere to take them even had I given the matter any consideration. I only wanted the pain to stop. I wanted her to go away. So, when Harold came home from hospital, life went on as normal, if normal could describe the way we had been living for the last few years. Once he was home, my husband tried to convince me that there was nothing going on. He tried to make out that it was not what it looked like. Did he really think I was that gullible?

By now, I was in a worse state of anxiety, and Dr Rose did his best to help me.

One day, only a short time after my husband's return from hospital, I prepared myself to go out. I had put my coat on and with my handbag, made as if to go out of the kitchen door. As I put my foot on the threshold, I froze. I could not move. It felt as though a wrought iron gate had come down from the ceiling to the floor in the doorway in front of me and was blocking my exit. I stood there for a few moments, but I could not move myself. Inside, I was panicking. I could not think. I felt totally paralysed and had to stay home. I knew I wanted to go out, but something was preventing me.

I tried several more times over the next couple of days, but always the same thing happened. Harold could not understand it. I could not even go shopping. Dr Rose was consulted after discussions between Harold and my doctor. I wanted to cry, but even that did not happen.

I was informed that I had developed agoraphobia, fear of open spaces. Nobody could understand me, or what had happened to me. I was advised that hypnotherapy could help me, but that was still in its infancy and not well received as yet. Then it emerged that Dr Rose was the only psychiatrist in Leeds known to practise hypnotherapy. He told Harold and I that he thought he could help, but he would have to come to the house and he only treated patients privately. It would cost £5 a session, but how many would be needed was an unknown quantity. Harold gladly agreed to pay for the treatment. He told Dr Rose that he would do anything to make me right.

I felt that perhaps my beloved was gloating because now he believed that I had been proved to him to have some kind of mental problem. Dr Rose informed me that I did not have a mental problem. The agoraphobia had been induced by all the extreme stress I was under.

One session a week lasting about three-quarters of an hour was recommended. The number of sessions could only be determined by the progress made.

The treatment consisted of me being taken into deep relaxation by Dr Rose's instruction, and then under hypnosis, he instructed me step be step. At the first session he asked me to pass through the doorway where my condition had originated, walk over the doorstep and take one step onto the drive. He had described that he would take me one small step at a time. I had to practise this as much as possible, at least every day till the next session. The more I did it, the more comfortable and easy it would become.

I did find the effort excruciatingly difficult. I felt as though I was pulling a huge steam engine. It was very tiring.

The next week, Dr Rose instructed me to walk to the end of my drive. Immediately after the session, he took me through the walk, as he did in all the sessions, but I found each and every step so very hard to do. It made me breathless and exhausted.

By coincidence, I learned that Dr Rose was a neighbour. He lived in the corner house at the end of the street, just four houses away from ours. He told me at one of our early sessions that because of my husband's violence towards me, he had taken to walking his dog regularly, each morning and evening, along our street, past my home deliberately so that he could come to my rescue should he hear me screaming.

My parents found the situation totally beyond them. Mam kept going on at me to pull myself together. She made me feel as though she thought I was a big kid, playing up. So far both my Mam and Dad had been supportive, but this development was too much for them to understand. This just added to my distress.

I was now walking a few steps up my road and feeling a little easier, when Harold decided to have one of his violent sessions, though why he went for me on that occasion, I never knew. He had started getting ideas into his head that I was disobeying him. Sometimes he asked me

200

to do things, and ten minutes later or so he would ask me what I was doing and why, and lashed out at me. He had forgotten what he had told me, or so it seemed.

He disappeared for several days. This was an incident that came to be repeated more and more frequently with time. During his absence, the agoraphobia disappeared, and I went back to normal. When he turned up again, so did the agoraphobia. I know there was a message within this behaviour, but I was always helpless to do anything about it. I always missed him and had to take him back.

I was making some progress after several sessions when Dr Rose told me that he had had a meeting with my husband, our GP Dr Feldman, and a close solicitor friend. He had called the meeting in an attempt to help me. My husband only consented to the meeting if everything that was said at the meeting was in total confidence. Nothing was to be repeated to me, ever. Dr Rose then continued by telling me that the purpose of the meeting was to glean anything that would help me recover, so that everyone present agreed to complete secrecy. My psychiatrist then revealed that he had had no intention of keeping his word if the meeting produced anything he could use to help me, which he told me it had.

Harold had eventually admitted his affair with Wright, but I must never be told that! He was then told that his behaviour was not only endangering my health, but that he was putting my life at risk. Harold was going to have to make a choice between the two women in his life. Apparently, Harold was angry about this, but he could not argue with the other men at the meeting. He stated that he still loved me very much and did not wish to give me up. He told them he could not leave me and would do anything to get me well again. He was then persuaded into leaving his 'lover'.

The two doctors and the solicitor made him agree to not seeing Wright ever again from that moment on. At the office, she would be subject to 28 days' notice in lieu, and during that time could not go into the office under any circumstance. At the end of the 28 days Wright would be out of our lives.

Dr Rose then explained my part in this plan. I had never to let Harold know that I knew about that meeting. I would have to go into the office to work every day throughout the 28 days, no matter how bad I felt. I was warned that the two conspirators were likely to try every scheme on earth to try and worm Wright back into Harold's life. If that happened then I would be out! I would lose my husband. I was promised Dr Rose's full cooperation and help to get me through that endurance test.

My husband later told me that Miss Wright would not be coming into the office any more, but he never gave me any reasons. In view of Dr Rose's warning not to discuss the matter with Harold, I was unable to ask him any questions about her leaving.

I had to go into the office the very next day. Dr Rose's warning was well advised. As soon as I arrived I was asked to make coffee. This involved me filling up the kettle, so I had to leave our office and go down into the basement to the ladies' room for the water. When I got back to the office, Harold was on the phone. He told me it was Wright, asking if she could come back into the office. I thought to myself that that call was well timed, wasn't it!

Throughout the day, I was given every errand that Harold could think up to get me out of the office. I had to go across the road to the newsagent for some cigarettes. Would I get him a sandwich from the café across the road? A bacon butty? Harold loved bacon butties. Make some more coffee. We both must have been drowning in coffee by the end of the day. The excuses were endless to get me out of the office, and each time I returned, Harold was speaking on the phone. His story was that Wright was ringing him. I thought how convenient that she managed to time her calls when I was sent out of the office. How right Dr Rose was when he warned me that I had a battle on my hands.

The siege continued in the same way every day. Goodness knows how much coffee we went through during those four weeks. And the kettle was always empty, however much water I put in it each time. I noticed that I was being sent on messages at certain times. Always around 10 a.m. and 4 p.m., and from time to time in between, and always when I returned to the office, the phone was working full out, following which I was regaled with the same question,

'Can Wright have her job back?'

Dr Rose warned me I would have a hard time, and that I would have to stand my ground to keep my husband, but this dreadful constant onslaught could never have been forecast, I'm sure. How I managed to keep going day after day, the whole four weeks, I could never understand. On reflection, I wondered how I did not succumb to the ordeal. I suspect that it was the strength of my love for this man that kept me going, my determination to keep my man and be rid of that woman.

Those nightmarish four weeks, however, did pass. No work was done but my ordeal was over. Wright was out for good. Harold never once queried me on my knowledge of that meeting with the doctors and our solicitor friend. Neither did he ever admit to me that he had had an affair. At least, she was gone for good, so I believed at the time. And at no time in the future was I given any reason to doubt that.

Chapter 67

I now went into the office every day but finished about four, to get home to the girls. My agoraphobia was gone, although the fear that it might return has never left me. Temporary secretarial staff were supplied part-time by a local agency until a permanent secretary could be found. I had no worries that a suitable, and probably a better replacement was to be had.

The subject of the business registration had to be dealt with. The original partnership certificate had never appeared, at least to me, despite my occasional queries. I reminded Harold from time to time that the certificates should have been framed and displayed on the office walls, but I was ignored. I wondered about this, but walking on eggs with him prevented me from pursuing the matter more strongly.

He now produced another form, which showed Harold and myself as the only partners. I signed this and saw Harold write his name in the appropriate place. I now looked forward to receiving the full business registration in due course so that it could be framed and placed with pride in its correct place on the wall.

On the Friday of the third week, Harold asked me to work the full day. As soon as the day's work was over he went to the safe and took out the company's chequebook and paying-in book. He told me he wanted me to take them home for the weekend and asked me to put them in my handbag and look after them. He then stated that he wanted to show to me that I could trust him. I found this a curious statement. It made no sense, and I found myself turning it over in my mind repeatedly. I took the two bankbooks and put them straight into my handbag.

The weekend passed pleasantly enough. On the Sunday evening, after dinner, at about seven o'clock, Harold asked me if I had the bankbooks. Of course I had them, I told him. I hadn't even looked at them in my handbag since I put them there on leaving the office on Friday. Of course they must be there.

'Are you sure?' he demanded.

I repeated that of course I was sure. I could see he was growing agitated. I could not understand this. He then insisted that I look in my handbag and made sure they were there. I found this unbelievable, but I had to obey him even if only for the sake of peace.

I opened my handbag, and looked inside for the two items. They were not there. I felt bewildered. I was so sure I had never taken them out. But my bag was bereft of those books. Harold immediately pounced on me.

'Where are they?' he demanded to know.

I had no idea. Now in a rage, he accused me of hiding them. I could not answer him. I could not tell him where they were when they should have been in my bag. I had not looked for them the whole weekend.

The accusations came fast and furious. I had taken them and hidden them.

'Why would I want to do that?' I queried

'You've hidden them in the sideboard!' he growled at me.

He ran to the sideboard and pulled at the door handle. He tried both doors. Neither door would open. He pulled hard on the handles, but the doors refused to give. He screamed back at me in full fury that not only had I hidden the bankbooks, but I had put them in the sideboard, locked the doors and hidden the key! He demanded I give him the key.

I could not do this, as I had no key. Even the key was missing. I tried to convince him that I knew nothing about the lost books. I had not hidden them in the sideboard and locked it. Nor had I taken the key and hidden it. There was nothing I could do about the books or the sideboard key as I had not done any of the things he was accusing me of. His temper was going out of control again.

The next thing I was aware of was that he was phoning the police. He then rang a friend of his family. A policeman and the friend arrived at almost the same time. I was terrified. I was in torment at the chaos of the situation and what might happen.

Harold managed to calm himself down sufficiently to tell the two gentlemen that I had stolen his two bankbooks and refused to return them to him. I had then hidden them in the sideboard, had locked it and would not hand the key over.

I tried to tell them that I knew nothing about either the books or the key, I had not taken them. But no one would listen to me. The policeman was the typical stereotype of his day. The wife is always in the wrong. She had no chance against that attitude.

Harold asked the policeman if he had his permission to break into the sideboard and retrieve his books. The policeman replied that he could do what he liked in his own home. The policeman even offered to help him. Harold then went out and soon returned with an axe, a smaller chopper, which he gave to his accomplice. He gave the hammer to the policeman. I did not know we had such tools. The three men set about chopping up my beautiful sideboard. The doors were smashed in, but not content with that, they continued to hack at the furniture until the sideboard was totally destroyed and they were satisfied that no books could be found. I could only look on, petrified, worried to death as to what would follow.

I now feared for my life. Anything could happen when Harold was in that mood, and the others were going along with him.

Whatever had happened to the police's attitude of not acting in cases of 'domestic violence?' It seemed that the police acted to suit themselves.

Hadn't I gone through enough? And now to see my furniture hacked to pieces. There were no bankbooks.

Not finding the books, the men ended their destructive spree. The two accomplices seemed satisfied with their efforts and concluded that the books must be elsewhere. They then left, leaving me to my husband's machinations.

The atmosphere in my home was unbearable, stultifying. The last thing I needed was such tension. What was to happen now? How was I going to cope with my husband's repeated ravings? Not a word was said. I went to bed with my mind agonising over the havoc that the man I loved so much had wreaked on our home. At least, I did not have to suffer one of his violent outrages on myself on that occasion.

The next morning, he left for the office still without anything being said. I could not go to work myself. I decided the office was no longer an option for me. I did what I always believed was the correct thing to do in the circumstances. I rang the bank as soon as possible to notify them of the missing books. I was told that new books would be sent immediately. I then rang the office to tell Harold that I had informed the bank of the missing books. He again flew into a rage on the phone and told me I had no business in telling the bank. He then made a remark that was most bizarre. I was interfering with the bookkeeping and I should keep out of his business.

Then it dawned on me. The whole scene was a set-up. It had all been engineered for my benefit. I was being punished for having got rid of his sweetheart, or so it seemed to me. It was like a scene out of Patrick Hamilton's play *Gaslight*. The villain manipulates his actions to make it look as though his wife has done whatever is planned, and then accuses her of it! In the play, he is trying to turn his wife insane. My husband was seeking revenge. The books had never been lost. Harold had taken them from my handbag when I was not looking, and then accused me of taking them!

Harold had manipulated situations before, as when he tried to set me up with Edward Brown in Newcastle, for just one example, and now he had done it again.

I have never been able to prove my thoughts on this. I decided against challenging my husband on this one, but I was as sure as when I also believed my husband was having an affair, and then proved right. I have always been sure that I was set up.

Chapter 68

It was time I started doing the things I enjoyed for myself, I thought. I had been a devoted, loyal and deeply loving wife all these years. I had brought about the success in business that my husband had craved. Brought about, not just helped. I gave up most of my own hobbies, mostly my music, to work with Harold. During the whole of the period of my marriage up to that time I had only been to three productions. I went to see the ballet *Swan Lake* in Leeds with Rose Hardy. When in Newcastle, I went to a concert with my friends at the City hall, and more recently to the film of *Madame Butterfly*. Anne wanted to see it. As in all these instances, Harold could not refuse under the circumstances. And for all my loyalty and much, much more, I had been so badly ill-treated in recent years with cheating, beatings and perhaps the worst of all, his lying.

With hindsight, I realised how confused and disoriented I had become as a result of all his twisted behaviour. Avowing his great love and devotion, whilst simultaneously trying to humiliate and hurt me. But nevertheless, I had to do something for myself. I decided to give piano lessons again. I had not taught professionally since the beginning of my marriage when I was pregnant with Anne.

There was no way I would go back and work in the office, but I still needed to have an interest other than the home. I had given my girls piano lessons from time to time throughout my difficulties. Now Anne and Ruth asked me if they could stop, as they were not really interested. It was a different kettle of fish with Pamela. She had taken to the piano and I now thought it was time she had a more advanced teacher. When I suggested this to her, she replied that she preferred to learn to play the violin. This was fine with me, but there was no violin available.

I put this to Harold and he told us that he knew someone who had a very good violin, and had been waiting to sell it, but only to a genuine artist who would appreciate the instrument. The lady concerned had been a representative with his former company Sun Life. Her hobby had been playing with an orchestra and she had since retired. Harold was positive she would sell it to us, so he went to see her at her home in the Lake District.

He returned with the instrument. It truly was a beauty, though still not a Stradivarius. When Harold regaled our benefactor with promises of Pamela's ability and that she would make good use of it, she gave it to us for nothing, but only with the promise that Pamela would make something of herself with it. I could not have been more delighted for Pamela.

A leading violin teacher, who coincidently lived nearby, took Pamela on and she did well with her new teacher. Pamela was never keen to be a soloist, but went on to play with groups at concerts arranged by her teacher. She was eventually accepted as a violinist with the Leeds City Schools Orchestra, with which she played until she left school for university.

But back to my own endeavours. I planned to give piano lessons initially on two days a week after school, Tuesdays and Thursdays, teaching young children. I hoped to add Wednesdays as the news spread about my lessons.

I discussed the whole project with my beloved husband. He said he wholeheartedly approved and sounded eager to support me. I soon found two pupils amongst the ranks of my family and friends, and another quickly followed.

At the same time, I thought I would polish up my own technique and made arrangements with Bessie Waterman, a renowned teacher in Leeds, to have piano lessons once a week. I knew I needed to practise to get back up to standard. My playing had become somewhat rusty.

I had given the first couple of lessons, when Harold came home whilst I was teaching and demanded I make him a cup of tea. I asked him to wait till I had finished the lesson. He insisted he was in a hurry and I had to make the tea now! This was ridiculous. He was insisting I disrupt the lesson. He would not make his own tea. He never came home from the office at that time. During the next three weeks, he came home at that time during every lesson. He was deliberately breaking up my efforts. He also objected to me practising during the evenings.

I soon recognised that this was another of my husband's efforts to sabotage my plans. He had made it plain that he had no objections to my teaching, but as he had already done on several occasions, as with the shop in Burley-in-Wharfedale, his behaviour was the opposite of his spoken word. It was as if he resented me doing anything for myself in case it became a success. Needless to say, it was hopeless me trying to continue the piano lessons. I could not even go on with my own piano lessons as he interfered with those. He had won again. I was once more becoming despondent. I still saw Dr Rose as an outpatient at St James's Hospital, and he now prescribed antidepressants for me.

I had always done my best to stop our troubles being aired in front of the children, but as I have already recounted, it was a waste of time talking to Harold as once he was out of control, he did not care who heard or saw us, in spite of my pleadings.

Harold now appeared to have had some change of heart, yet another personality change. He became a much more amenable person, more like his old self. He suggested a break, a holiday. The last vestiges of autumn were upon us, the year was soon coming to an end. 1969 had been another truly traumatic one not just for myself, but also for the whole family, and a holiday seemed a way of escaping from our troubles.

Within a day or two, he came home from the office with a brochure and details of the Treganna Castle Hotel at St Ives in Cornwall. This was a five-star luxury hotel, with full amenities and entertainment, so if the weather were bad, it would not affect our enjoyment. It seemed ideal. I really felt the need for just such a break, and the arrangements were made. We drove down, taking it in turns to drive, as we usually did.

The hotel was indeed very beautiful. It was as its name implied a castle and we had a very enjoyable time. The food was good, the weather held for the most part. We made several trips around the county, in particular to Land's End. The scenery was breathtaking, even for that time of year. The girls seemed to enjoy it and the holiday was a success.

I felt confident once we were home, that the New Year would turn over a new leaf for the whole family. Everything was going to be all right, at last.

Chapter 69

The New Year did not work out as I had hoped. Over the Christmas holidays, the promises made by my converted husband were soon abandoned. He decided to have one of his tantrums, though I could not understand why, and I was attacked again, though not as viciously as in previous assaults. He then took himself off and disappeared for a time. I was left again with the children.

I was not to be on my own for long. Mam took ill and was rushed into the Leeds General Infirmary in an emergency. She had an acute appendicitis and was operated on straight away. I had to look after Dad. He refused to move into my home and insisted I move with the children into their bungalow.

This was to be a major upheaval for us all. My parents' bungalow had two spare bedrooms but insufficient beds and bedding for the girls and myself, so a removal was necessary.

My close friend and support came to my rescue, as reliable as ever. Cynthia and I were frequent visitors to each other's homes. Not only did she comfort me and help me on the frequent occasions when I had been beaten up. She was always ready to lend a helping hand with other things. This last occasion was no exception. Now she offered to help me move my things with the help of her husband Peter and his car. They took two beds to my parents together with everything else I needed. They were wonderful the whole time.

Mam was to be in hospital for two weeks. Dad had sold his business to retire, but now worked for a friend part-time. He said he could never really stop working. It was his life. He got up at seven o'clock to be at work for eight. I had to make him his sandwiches for lunch, which he had before coming home. He insisted that his routine be undisturbed, even though Mam was in hospital.

I had to take Pam and Ruth to school. They now attended Middlethorne Middle School on Shadwell Lane, near to my home but some distance away from Mam's home.

My days were hectic. I tried to visit my mother nearly every day. During the second week, I was sitting at my mother's bedside when Harold turned up. He said he needed to see my mother. He was still very fond of her, but I asked him to leave. I did not want him there. Towards the end of the second week, he came to the hospital again. This time, he demanded that I speak to him. He wanted to come home. I told him that it was not the time or place to discuss it, and he would have to wait until Mam was feeling better and at home. He was most reluctant to leave. At least he avoided a scene, which I half expected.

Mam did come home after two weeks, and my workload escalated. I was run off my feet for the first week. She was very demanding, as she always was, but not feeling so well seemed to make her even worse. She took over after a few days, and by the end of her second week home I was feeling redundant. We were under each other's feet. I wanted to suggest that it was time I went home, but did not know how to put it for fear of upsetting her. Mam must have felt the same way and I was more than relieved when she told me she could cope and would I like to go home.

Cynthia and Peter removed me back whence I had come. For that, I would be eternally grateful. No one could have had better friends than I had with Cynthia and Peter in those awful days. They were there for me constantly.

Once home, I more or less collapsed. I was totally exhausted.

Within a few days, Harold was phoning me full of apologies and requesting to come home. Yet again, he was full of remorse, promising me it would never happen again. He was never going to lay a finger on me ever again. I realised he was repeating himself, but I loved him so much. I was missing him in spite of his behaviour. The girls were missing him. I suppose that I wanted to believe him, trusting him to mean what he promised. So, for the umpthteen time we were reunited.

At last, his promises seemed to be holding. I had resumed some of my friendships whilst he was away, and he made no objection. Our social life improved. I had persuaded him to let us join a charitable group, The Friends of Donisthorpe, a home for the aged. The group raised funds to buy much-needed extras for the residents in the home. We worked with the group for quite a while.

One evening I had a party, which was attended by some friends, two couples of long standing. The evening progressed very well and we were enjoying ourselves when the subject of hypnosis came up. It may have arisen as a result of some discussion about my earlier hypnotherapy.

Phil, one of my longest standing friends, announced that she was into hypnosis and asked if anyone would like to be hypnotised. As always ready to try something new, my beloved immediately volunteered. Phil had no difficulty 'putting him under'.

He was soon in a deep trance. After asking him some personal questions, which he readily answered, he started screaming, 'Daddy, don't hit me! Daddy, don't hit me!'

We were all shocked by this, until he changed his mood. Transforming his attitude, he blurted out without any form of provocation but with the most intense passion, 'Thalia, I love you! I love you!'

He repeated these same words over and over again, many times before stopping. He then appeared to have fallen asleep. The intensity which he injected into his outburst, made him sound as though he was in pain whilst imploring his devotion to me.

Phil became worried at Harold's performance and tried to bring him out of his trance. This took quite some time, as he was very fast asleep.

I was strangely deeply moved by my darling's fierce demonstration of his avowed love. It was a genuine pronouncement, having been made in a definitely true state of hypnosis. No one could have doubted his condition at that moment, and his affirmation of devotion.

It reassured me that we were going to be happy now and for evermore, and the bad times were over, so convinced was I with his sincerity.

No one discussed the contents of Harold's performance. I think we had all been transfixed by it, and the evening continued as pleasantly as it had started.

Chapter 70

Harold resumed calling me to help in the office. We did not discuss my returning to work, but from time to time, every few days, as soon as he got to the office he rang me in his usual panic that I was needed immediately. I had to drop everything, whatever plans I had made and get there as soon as possible.

I had read in the paper about a close relative who had been appointed as a director to a well-known bank, and they were floating shares on the stock market. I had a good feeling about those shares, knowing of my cousin's reputation in business, and suggested to Harold that we should have a dabble and buy some. It was our first foray into the stock market, and I thought it wise to keep the amount low, probably just a couple of hundred shares to start with.

The shares immediately rocketed and we made a decent profit in a relatively short time. This gave us a taste for the stock market, but Harold left it to me to make the decisions about what we should buy. I scoured the *Financial Times* before making any decisions, generally plunging for new flotations as a rule. Over a few months we had made a reasonable profit.

One evening, at the end of May, we made one of our extremely rare visits to the theatre. Harold was now in a much happier frame of mind these days, so he went with me to the Grand Theatre.

At the interval, we made our way to the bar. Harold ordered some alcoholic refreshment for himself and a cup of tea for me. My husband then saw an acquaintance, as I thought. The gentleman, an Asian, then joined us. Harold introduced him to me as a client and policyholder. The gentleman, I was informed, was a Bangladeshi doctor, the PhD type, and lectured at the university in philosophy or some such related academic branch of learning.

The conversation soon turned to Indian food. We had become acquainted with both Chinese and Indian foods whilst living in Newcastle and enjoyed it as long as it was not too spicy. When we lived in Newcastle, Harold had become friendly with an inspector from one of the local insurance companies. This person told us that he had lived in India for a few years and invited us to his home on several occasion to savour his Indian cooking. We had always enjoyed ourselves on those occasions, so that when Harold's Bangladeshi friend suggested he make us an authentic Indian dinner we both jumped at the offer.

Harold then told me he would like to invite two doctor friends and their wives. The doctors, GPs with a practice in Wakefield, had recently invited us to their home. They were initially policyholders and Harold saw this as an ideal way of reciprocating their hospitality. I welcomed the suggestion. That would mean there would be ten for dinner including the girls, who had also shown a liking for curries, though only mild ones.

The dinner was arranged for the forthcoming Saturday evening. Our Asian friend, who I will now call Dr Singh for convenience, as his real name escapes me, told us that he would come over to our home at four o'clock in the afternoon and would Harold take him to the Indian shop, one of probably only two that we knew of in Leeds, in those days, and which was situated near the university, some distance away. There he could buy all the spices and food he needed to cook the meal. I said that I would provide the chicken. Dr Singh asked me to buy three medium-sized chickens. It looked as though we could all look forward to a gastronomique feast.

True to his word, Dr Singh arrived promptly at four o'clock on the designated day. However, he told us that on second thoughts, he needed to have four chickens. It seemed an extraordinarily large amount. Harold said he would buy another chicken whilst he was out

Once back from their shopping, the good doctor set about his task of preparing the meal with great enthusiasm. He asked to be left to it in the kitchen. The guests had been invited for eight o'clock. Whenever I held a dinner party, I always made a point of my not only having the meal prepared for the table for when the guests arrived, but I also liked to have the dining table laid out and the necessary china and cutlery prepared. More importantly, I had to have my kitchen restored to its pristine cleanliness. All the worktops from where the food was served had to be spotless.

At eight o'clock, I had the china and cutlery organised, but my kitchen was a scene of utter devastation. I was shattered. No way could I have my kitchen in this state, but I could do nothing about it at that late hour. The floor was entirely covered with what seemed a half-inch layer of bright yellow rice. The worktops were similarly coated. Everywhere I looked in my beautiful kitchen, I saw masses and

215

masses of yellow rice. My kitchen table in the middle of the kitchen was hidden from sight with all the rice and various spices and condiments that our cook had used, and looked a sickening mess. Dr Singh had bought a huge sack of rice and most of it appeared to be strewn about my kitchen.

My stomach lurched over at the sight of it all. I wanted to cry. I was so angry but I had to control and stifle myself. I could not say anything to Harold. I did not want to spoil his evening, yet to me it was already ruined. I sensed catastrophe everywhere. The tension had started to build up in me, but I had to keep it under control.

The guests arrived on time, and I hoped my husband had been able to show them into the lounge without them having to see the unseeable.

After a round of drinks, Harold invited everyone to sit at the dining table. Dr Singh then brought the food in. He had arranged three of my largest platters each with a pile of rice, and then placed portions of chicken in a curry sauce on top. I was waiting for some accompaniments, as probably the others were, but none were forthcoming.

We each put some food on our plates and took a mouthful. The look on everyone's face was astonishing. My mouth burnt, everyone's mouth burnt. The food was completely inedible. No one said a word, their mouths were too paralysed from the fiery spices to say anything. We were all in shock. The fiery heat caught the back of my throat. No one could eat another morsel. I was already incensed and distraught from the disaster in my kitchen. I could not have been more furious.

Four cooked chickens on rice lay on the table hardly touched, and all anyone could do was to look at them in disgust. Harold had always boasted that there was no curry too hot that he could not eat it. One of his usual boasts was that he could go one better than anyone else, but even he had to admit that he had now been beaten, not with words, but the look on his face told me all. Then Harold asked if there was a sweet. I struggled to answer that there was no sweet. I had left everything to our 'visiting chef' and was too distraught to be able to think clearly enough to cope adequately with the situation. Everyone was still hungry.

Harold asked me to entertain our guests at the piano as a distraction. I could sense my husband's anger at the situation, but I was in no state to be able to play, and very meekly told him I just could not play the way things were. My nerves were tingling and I was beginning to feel unwell.

216

We were still seated around the table, all very unsure of what to do next, when Harold stood up and announced that it was long past the girls' bedtime and I should take them upstairs. I obeyed immediately. Whilst I was getting the girls ready for bed, which in actuality they had been doing for themselves for some time now, I was able to hear the conversation downstairs. To my horror, I heard Harold's strong voice complaining as to how I was bringing up my children. He told them, the doctors in particular, I thought, that I had no idea how to bring the children up. I put them to bed far too late. It was as though he was thinking of the girls as little children when in fact Anne was then almost fifteen, and Pamela and Ruth were almost teenagers.

I could hear his anger boiling over as he spoke to them. I thought it was rich of him to make such wicked complaints after the way he had been dragged up. If anyone had no idea, it was his mother, as had been proved to me so many times now. I was seething at my husband's remarks. I could tell from the conversation that he was laying the blame for the disastrous evening on me, and as his anger was getting out of control, he was digging even deeper to find fault with me.

I heard him asking for the doctor's advice. So far, from what I could make out, as I listened more intently now, Harold had done all the talking and was working himself up into a ferocious rage. He got no response to his request. Instead, all our guests made their excuses and left. I did not get to say good-bye as they departed from what I would have thought must have been, for them, a particularly memorable evening.

It was to become an evening to remember for me, for more reasons than that meal.

As soon as the door closed, Harold charged up the stairs. He came at me, as I stood in the doorway of the girls' bedroom, and I could not avoid the now familiar look in his eyes, those luminous black pointed pupils that I could feel piercing through my body to my soul. As those eyes bored through my body, I could see the violence in them. They told me that he was now in an uncontrollable and terrible, vicious rage. He pulled me from the bedroom, dragging me by my arms along the landing, and started punching and kicking me with more ferocity than I had ever previously experienced from him. At the same time, he screamed accusations at me that I had showed him up, letting him down and ruining his evening. I realised that, even before that evening, he had hoped to show himself off to his elite friends, and was now blaming me and taking it out of me for turning the dinner party into a disaster.

I tried to push him off me but I was not strong enough. I had been knocked down as he continued to kick me. The girls, hearing the screaming, came out of their rooms. They were sobbing their hearts out and must have been terrified seeing their father attacking their mother again. Pamela tried to help me, yelling repeatedly at her father to stop hitting me. She tried to pull him off me. She made a grab at him, she was probably trying to get hold of his arm to pull him from me, but she was not strong enough. Harold's strength must have been reinforced by the strength of his fury, when he was in these violent rages, or so it seemed, as he knocked Pamela over and she fell to the bottom of the staircase.

This turn of events stopped Harold in his tracks. He marched down the stairs and without saying another word he walked out of the front door.

Thankfully, neither of us was badly injured, but we were both hurting from the heavy bruising. I felt sore all over my body, but my children needed me now more than ever.

There was no point in calling the police. I had already learnt that they were not interested in 'domestic violence', as they called it. It was an even more worrying situation as, if anything, they took the husband's side for the most part, and were quick to blame the wife, regardless.

I was alone again. I just wanted to go to bed, and so everything in the house was left as it was. I took the children into bed with me. I think we must have spent most of the night crying.

As I lay in bed, I made a determined decision that this was the last time my husband would ever harm me or my girls as, this time, I was never, never taking him back.

Chapter 71

The phone rang early next morning. It was my stalwart rock, Cynthia.

'He's been hitting you again! I can feel it'.

Her psychic qualities had been active again, and correctly so. She came round within minutes to comfort me. How I would have got through those terrible times without her does not bear thinking about. She was always there for me.

There were still two to three weeks up to the schools' summer holidays, so the girls had things to occupy their minds. But I was on my own for some of the time and had time to reflect on what had been happening to me.

I did not realise at the time how badly I was suffering from all the abuse I had had to put up with over the years. But I was emotionally drained, weakened from lack of sleep, and had chronic diarrhoea. Somehow, I managed to keep going. I had to protect and care for my precious children.

I had been blamed for the embarrassment and humiliation my husband had suffered with the catastrophic dinner party. I truly believe that it was only through my efforts throughout our marriage that my husband and I were able to lead the affluent lifestyle that we were living.

When we first met, Harold had been most emphatic that he wanted to break away from his impoverished upbringing and lack of education. I had done my best to help him in that direction. My thoughts frequently went back to that week in 1956, when he started with Sun Life of Canada, and he was so full of hope for the future, and then to the third day of his training, when he was so willing to pack it all in. Since then, I had spent what must have been hundreds of hours doing the work for him that he himself should have been able to do, just to make him successful. And successful he had become, just for him to turn on me with years of abuse.

As he became more and more successful, his initial insecurities shrank, and his self-worth increased. He developed a desire to cultivate friendships from amongst the elite of his clientele, professional people, doctors and solicitors, not just for business connections, but it seemed to me that it boosted his social confidence and self-esteem. It now seemed as though it also boosted his arrogance and his controlling and bullyboy characteristics. Now, because he felt his self-esteem had been dented, he had to lay the blame on me, and get his revenge.

I thought about his attitude towards my girls. They were still a hindrance to him. They were growing up and had acquired their own circle of friends, which for some of their time kept them busy away from school as well as in school. They were spending time with their friends at their homes as well as in their own home. Thus I was forever, so it seemed, fetching them back and forth to wherever they wanted to go. I took Pamela to her regular violin lessons, but as long as they were happy, that was all that mattered to me.

That their father still regarded them as a hindrance and believed that they should be in bed early at night to be out of his way was a hateful idea.

About a month prior to this last incident, I was in the kitchen with Ruth when he came in and without any advance discussion with me, asked her if she would like to go to Queen Ethelburga's School in Harrogate. I was very annoyed about this. The school was a private boarding school and I thought he was trying on his old tricks, only this time he was going directly to my daughter.

I stopped him in his tracks, and although we were in Ruthie's presence, I told him that no one was going to boarding school. He quick as a flash answered that he was not thinking of sending Ruth to boarding school, but she should attend as a day pupil. He went on to try to describe to my youngest offspring the wonderful benefits of attending such a special school as Queen Ethelburga's.

I remembered our previous discussions about the girls going to boarding school, and I was aghast that he should bring the subject up again. He responded by insisting that we should at least look into the possibility. Pamela and Ruth were doing very well at school. Pamela was progressing to Allerton High School and hopefully Ruth would follow. Something felt wrong about my husband's proposal, and in truth it came as such a surprise that I had had no time to digest the idea.

Harold then suggested to me that at least I should get the brochure and think about it. I could see that he had successfully played his sales techniques on Ruthie, and had built her hopes up.

As a good wife, I sent off for the literature, but said nothing more.

The requested material was received through the post the following week and when I gave it to Harold, he was delighted and responded by saying that he had been waiting for the brochure. It was really the brochure that he wanted. It contained the names of all the school staff whom he could now canvass for business. He had no intention of sending Ruthie to the school.

No words could describe my reaction. I thought what an evil, despicable way to get what he wanted. He had used Ruthie and myself unscrupulously. There had been no need to build my little girl's hopes up for such a purpose. All he had to do was to ask me to request the brochures in the usual way.

What I did not know at that time was that Anne had started going into the local Chained Bull pub and drinking, underage, and then going with her friends to the Skeleton Key, the local community's youth club. The Chained Bull was the popular meeting place for teenagers. Underage drinking was rife at the time.

On one of these occasions, Anne had been seen drinking in the pub by my brother, Monty. He rang me up to let me know, and told me he was bringing her home. This did not stop Anne. She ran true to form as a rebellious teenager, and had to be brought home on numerous occasions, the worse for wear through drink.

It was quite a bit later that one of her friends told me Anne had been informing her friends at both these places about how her dad had been hitting her mother. This information was being spread about the community.

These thoughts on my husband's behaviour, and especially on how they were affecting my children, brought me to the decision that I had to get a divorce. I discussed this with my parents. They had both been very supportive throughout my ordeals, and continued to give me all the help they could.

Dad rang Colin Frazer. He was originally articled to Uncle Charlie, and then became a junior partner. He took over the practice on Uncle Charlie's death. Since then, the practice had relocated to new offices in Albion Street and now practised under another name. Dad had nevertheless continued to use them as our family lawyers. An appointment was made for me.

When I kept the appointment, Colin told me that he was handing my case to Robert Collins, as the firm's divorce specialist.

At that time, seeking a divorce involved giving details of the reasons one wanted a divorce, which were then written into the petition as grounds for the divorce. After I had explained my reasons for my action, Mr Collins showed me a long list of undesirable behaviours of one's spouse, which amounted to grounds for a divorce. I had to pick out all those that applied to me. These included very intimate details of one's private life. I ended up with a long list.

These were all put into the petition that eventually found its way to my husband.

A couple of weeks later, I had an unexpected visitor. Cyril came to see me. I was informed that Harold had asked him to come and see me. Cyril was very concerned about what had happened between Harold and myself, and said he wanted to help. Harold wanted to come back, and Cyril, as a friend of both of us, had come to plead his case.

When I told him that Harold had beaten me up several times now, Cyril was dumbfounded. His friend had not told him the truth about the break-up and the news came as a great shock. I admitted to Cyril that I still loved my husband and missed him, but could not take him back under any circumstances. I could not stand any more torture.

A very dejected Cyril went back to his friend.

Whether it was Cyril's intervention that weakened me, or I was ready to be weakened, I cannot answer, but weakening I was. As always, the girls were missing their father, in spite of what they had seen. I kept having second thoughts. I loved my husband so much, but I tried to convince myself that the divorce had to go ahead.

I had had no reply to my divorce petition. I then had a second visit from Cyril, who with the greatest earnestness pleaded for Harold's return home. Cyril told me that he had confronted Harold about his abuse towards me, and that Harold was so full of remorse and shame. He swore that it would never, ever happen again. Cyril pleaded for Harold's forgiveness so strongly, that I agreed to think about it.

I suppose I dared to believe that as Cyril now knew the truth and would look out for me, Harold really meant what he promised, as he would have to answer to Cyril. He would never dare to attack me again.

I contacted Cyril and asked him to arrange a meeting to discuss reconciliation. The meeting was again held at the Griffin Hotel in Boar Lane. Cyril had once more booked a room, unknown to me, for an evening and had again asked his friend and business partner George to help mediate. Cyril saw the advantage of having more friends know about Harold, and believed it would help to make Harold feel more ashamed and ultimately behave himself permanently.

The meeting went ahead as arranged, and we all had an interesting but pleasant evening. Harold could not have been more apologetic, begging for forgiveness, swearing that he would never hit me again. I had heard it all before, but my feelings for him took over and I was happy to see him again, believing that things were going to go back to normal. I agreed to drop the divorce.

On the last occasion when Monty and Cyril had arranged a similar meeting, the room had been booked for the night. The boys were so positive that I would take my husband back, that the room had again been booked for the whole night. Our friends left us in our hotel room, happy in the knowledge that they had done a good job.

We had been separated for three months, but I was positive that everything was going to be all right from now on.

Chapter 72

'Why did you do it?' my husband asked. 'Why did you tell all those private, intimate details?'

It was only a few days since our reconciliation. Nothing more about my divorce action had been said, that is up until now. Now, he had brought the petition up, and he sounded very hurt. He went on to say that we had never discussed our private lives with anyone, and that we had long since agreed that what went on between husband and wife was sacredly private. I wondered about that. It seemed to me that much of our private life was common knowledge by then.

I tried to explain, as it had been explained to me, that it was divorce procedure, but he did not want to accept that. I had had no problems with him since his return home, though my health was still very precarious. He complained bitterly that he had had to pay my solicitor's fees, an unnecessary expense. He was now making me nervous again. I felt as though he was again trying to put the blame on me for everything that had happened. He was making out that I had provoked him in to attacking me. My fault!

My fault! No way would I take that. I tried to smooth things over. At least he was keeping his word and trying to be the caring, loving husband again.

He told me that he had tried a couple of investments on the stock markets, investments of his own choice, during our separation. Both had lost money. He strongly expressed his need for me. I had never yet lost any money through bad investments. I was not a gambler and only chose shares that I had studied and was convinced were worth buying. My husband now understood this. At least, that is what he made out to me. He poured out his appreciation of me, with his usual plausibility.

It was at that time that I had a particularly distressing visit from my husband's father. I had come to dislike him intensely. He was such a horrible person. I had tried to get on with him and his wife but it was very difficult, in fact virtually impossible. In fact, I knew I was not alone in my feelings. I do not think there were many people who did like him.

As soon as he came into the house he started shouting at me.

'I know what you have been up to!' He startled me. What was I supposed to have been up to?

'I know what you have been up to. I know how you have been carrying on!' He repeated. I thought he was going to hit me, but Harold put his arm out to restrain him and then the penny dropped.

I realised that Harold had been up to his dirty tricks, lying again. He had been living with his parents during our separation. The parents who, when we first met, he could not get away from quickly enough. It was obvious to me that he had made out to them his usual story that I had been having an affair to explain the problems in our marriage.

It soon dawned on me that his parents had been trying to convince their son that he could run his business without me. I had always felt that they had been jealous of the fact that their son's success was due to me, that without me Harold would most probably not have got anywhere. I firmly believed that Harold's school education was sadly lacking because of the absence of any parental interest. Now the Cohens were reacting, and Harold's lies were the ammunition with which they could try and make their case to get me out of the picture. They were never prepared to listen to me.

Harold managed to control his father and made him leave, but never contradicted his story. I felt mortified. My husband would not accept any blame for anything. He had to put all responsibility for our troubles on my shoulders. I felt the weight of my anxieties increase. Our social activities diminished. Harold refused to go to any more meetings of The Friends of Donisthorpe Group that we had only recently joined.

Anne had continued her teenage rebellious behaviour, even though her father was back home. Her father was blaming me for this and told me she was my responsibility. He refused to accept that Anne was just a normal teenager and criticised me for failing to keep Anne in check. He clearly knew nothing about teenagers and did not want to know. The feeling that I was walking on broken glass as far as my husband was concerned was as strong as ever.

He came home from work during all this hassle and tried to tell me that I was mentally ill. The reason I was not coping with my family was that I was mentally sick and he wanted me to see a doctor. I was not even aware that I was not coping. I thought I was doing especially well under the circumstances. He had arranged for me to see a GP

225

who came highly recommended in dealing with my type of illness! It was arranged that I would see him privately at his practice in Oakwood, near Foundry Lane.

I did not have the strength to argue, so I agreed to keep the appointment with Dr Shapiro. Harold took me as usual.

The consultation took about 20 minutes, after which Dr Shapiro told us both that he could find nothing wrong with me. This angered my husband very much.

It seemed that Harold was determined to have me declared insane, and went out on a campaign to do just that.

He then arranged for me to see privately Dr White, a consultant psychiatrist who worked at Stanley Royds psychiatric hospital at Wakefield. I was led to believe that he had been discussing my health with our GP Dr Feldman, as I did not know how Harold kept finding these doctors, but he was determined to have me declared mentally sick.

A couple of weeks later, Harold took me to Wakefield to Dr White's private consulting rooms. The consultation was with myself only. I told the psychiatrist my history but Dr White made no particular comments. I had to go back two weeks later.

At this second visit to Dr White, after more discussion about my health, nothing still was said or done except that Dr White told us he had consultation rooms in Leeds in Clarendon Road, where many consultants had private rooms. Would we prefer to see him there? A further appointment was made for two weeks later at his Leeds rooms.

At that appointment, the psychiatrist asked to see me on my own to start with. He began by telling me what I had expected, that there was nothing wrong with me. I was certainly overstressed and anxious. I was not mentally ill. He then pulled out all the stops. He was definitely a doctor who pulled no punches. I had to leave my husband. He continued by explaining that it was my husband who was mentally ill. He was mentally unstable and very unpredictable, and was the cause of all my health problems.

He then added that if I did not leave him, if I kept on living with him, his behaviour would continue. If anything, it would worsen. I would never be well, and in fact in the long term, my general health could only get worse and I would end up permanently ill.

Dr White reasoned that there was no point in me seeing him again. The cure was in my own hands. And if I did not leave him, the doctor said, there was no point in my continuing to see him. He would not see me again.

He then called Harold in to the room, and in front of me, repeated all that he had told me. That I was not mentally ill and that he, Harold, was responsible for the state of my poor health. When Dr White told Harold that he thought that Harold was the one who was mentally ill, I could feel my husband blowing up inside himself. He was struggling to control his temper, and could not get out of that room quick enough.

It is at this point that I wish to reveal that I was aware that there was a history of mental illness in Harold's family on his mother's side.

When I first knew Harold, I was told that his mother had three sisters. I never met the youngest sister and no one ever spoke of her. I met her husband, Sydney, a couple of times. The son Laurence, Harold's cousin, was a few years younger than Harold and lived and worked in London. He came to see us a couple of times when he was in Leeds. It was then that I learnt that his mother, Harold's aunty, lived permanently in a psychiatric hospital. I was never able to learn more about her.

Another of Harold's aunts, Sadie, also had mental problems. When I first met her she had just been divorced after a very short marriage and lived with another sister Minnie. I thought Minnie was the only sane person in the family. She was a lovely, homely person. I liked her very much.

Hearing Dr White tell us that my husband was the one who was mentally ill did not really come as a surprise. Many such remarks had been made to me about his behaviour over the past dreadful years. I did not think he would take this news kindly. It seemed that perhaps my husband had inherited his mental state. My mother frequently referred to his 'bad blood' when discussing his behaviour towards me. She knew there was something wrong in that direction.

Even though it was a relief to me in a way, I was now faced with the dilemma about what I should do. I still felt that I could not leave Harold in spite of the psychiatrist's strong words of advice.

Going back home was an ordeal. Harold was furious at the psychiatrist. He was not going to accept Dr White's advice. I started to fear that Harold would resume his aggressive attitude. I know that in itself should have told me what I had to do, but I had too much to consider in taking the psychiatrist's advice. The rules on separation and divorce, especially with regard to the children, were much more diffi-

227

cult in those days. I had tried it once before and had taken my husband back. I had nowhere else to go with three children, and I had to keep a roof over our heads.

In those days, there was no form of organised help for women with my problems, no aid agencies, telephone helplines, no refuges, nothing. My help came from my family and friends like Cynthia and Cyril, but they were not in a position to put a roof over the heads of my children and myself.

It was all very well Dr White giving me the wisdom of his knowledge and experience, but following it was not that easy. I was not able to make the drastic decision of leaving my husband for good. The bottom line was that I still loved him very deeply.

My husband was more determined than ever to prove himself right and all the previous doctors wrong. He was not going to let anyone make out that he was a mental case!!

During the last week in November, without any consultation with me and certainly without my express permission, I had a visit from Dr Chandler. Dr Chandler was an eminent physician, working in the Leeds General Infirmary. My caring husband must have asked our GP again without my permission, for a consultation at home with the physician. Goodness knows what more lies he must have plied Dr Feldman with.

Dr Chandler checked me out briefly and then suggested I be admitted to the infirmary for tests. The whole procedure was conducted as though I was deaf, dumb and blind. Harold happily agreed. No one listened to me, although I was aware that I was not well. Dr White had explained the reasons, but of course neither the physician nor my husband cared to listen to me. Husbands reigned supreme.

Arrangements were immediately made for me to be admitted to the Brotherton Wing of the infirmary. I was soon subjected to the most horrific tests. I had to have a series of enemas over several days. I was told that due to the colitis and constant diarrhoea, I had lost weight, which probably accounted for all my weakness. My medical records stated that I had lost three stone for no explicable reason. These and all the other tests made me feel much, much worse and I was now in a state of total shock and collapse.

At the end of the week, I was informed that Dr Chandler had found nothing physically wrong with me and therefore it must be mental illness. He was referring me to Dr Roberts, a consultant psychiatrist at St James's Hospital.

My beloved, darling had got his wish! I felt as though my husband had been up to more of his evil tricks and that this was another conspiracy. It may sound far-fetched, but I now knew that my husband was capable of anything, and it certainly looked that way. I had had no say in anything during that week. I was consulted on nothing. On 7th December I was transferred to the psychiatric wing of St James's Hospital.

During my time at the hospital I was apparently kept sedated. I was said to be suffering with nervous tension and anxiety. No mention was ever made, to me at least, that I was mentally ill. I just needed rest. My happy husband visited me constantly, bringing the girls from time to time. At the end of two weeks, I was allowed home over the Christmas period. On my return I asked to be discharged. I wanted to be back with my family. I was now given tranquillisers and stronger medication for sleeping. An outpatient appointment was made for me. It was never kept, as Harold would not allow it.

On reading my hospital records, some time later, I was curious to learn that an entry stated that the doctors sought my husband's consent to my discharge before allowing me home. There was also a statement to the effect that it was suspected that my husband was responsible for my ill-health. This was never put to me. Again, I feel that this was in accordance of the thinking of the times, that the husband had number–one say in all things, and the wife was just his possession. At least, that to me appeared to be the thinking at St James's Hospital in 1970.

Chapter 73

My husband's whole personality had now changed. He had become
even more arrogant and egocentric, which seemed to show in his dress
and appearance. He made repeated demonstrations of his love and
devotion, though these periods grew shorter and shorter, and he still
kept making his demands for wifely loyalty. What more I could do? I
had no idea. He had resumed his practice of phoning me from the
office as soon as he arrived there, demanding I drop everything and
get down to the office immediately as the place was in chaos. This was
usually after he had told me I was not wanted that day, and I could
get on with my personal activities. I never knew what to expect from
him. My hairdresser became more and more annoyed with cancelled
appointments. More frequently, I was not even allowed the time to
cancel. This applied to everything, including shopping. It became quite
embarrassing. I grew more and more dismayed at Harold's controlling
demands, but I was too fractured to disobey him.

Shortly after the commencement of the New Year, 1971, he did
another unexplained disappearing act. He failed to come home from
work, causing me more worry. Later that night, he phoned me to tell
me that he had had a heart attack and was in the Airedale General
Hospital. This hospital was a considerable distance away, at Steeton,
near Skipton, about an hour's drive away.

He then announced that a large insurance company had gone into
liquidation. He had an agency with this company and had done a
large amount of business with them. His many policyholders would
be frantic with worry about their money. I had to go into the office
first thing in the morning and deal with the situation. I heard the
news on the media, so I knew it meant panic amongst his clientele. I
was not to visit him as the hospital was too far away under the
circumstances, and it was more important that I looked after the
business.

I rang the hospital the next morning to be told that he had not had
a heart attack. It was just a bout of nerves. He was being kept in
under observation and he would be home in a day or two. This
incident propelled Harold in to a penchant for having 'heart attacks'

because it was to be the first of a long history of many so-called 'attacks' over the next 18 months or so.

He returned home after a couple of days and life continued its precarious path. He seemed even more unstable and the strain continued to affect me. In the middle of the night of the 29th January, when we were in bed, he started hitting me. Whether I was actually asleep then and he woke me up, I was never sure. All I remember was he was hitting me and thumping me in the back, demanding sex, shouting that he was entitled to his 'marital rights'. He tried to force himself onto me at the same time as his attack grew more vicious. He put any romantic thoughts right out of my head. I was too frightened to be able to cooperate and I was gradually being pushed out of bed.

As I fell on to the bedroom floor, he must have jumped out of bed after me and was kicking me as I lay on the floor. I heard the girls running into our room. They had heard my screams. Apparently the police had been called and it was not long before they arrived and I was hauled away. What my so-called darling husband told them can only be imagined, as they obviously listened to him, in spite of the already mentioned police policy of non-interference in 'domestic violence' situations.

Yet again, I was taken to St James's Hospital to the same psychiatric ward as in the previous month. I was said to be suffering from 'acute anxiety'. Harold admitted hitting me. He told the doctors that I had prostrated myself on the floor of our bedroom for no reason. I was hysterical, and as the children were watching, he hit me to restrain me!

Oh yes! My husband could weave a likely yarn!

After a very short stay, I asked to be allowed home. I was told that this was not advisable as I was not considered well enough to leave hospital. If I insisted on going home I would have to sign myself out, but even so I could leave only if my husband agreed to take me home. He was responsible for me and had to take care of me. He apparently agreed. Another outpatient appointment was made for me. Once again, my husband stopped me from keeping it. The medical staff realised what I had to put up with, and yet they returned me to that man. I was trapped by the attitudes of the times.

Within days my husband came up with one of his bright ideas, a skiing holiday. He said he had always wanted to ski, though I had never before heard him mention the word 'ski', ever. None of us, neither the girls nor myself, had any ambitions in that direction. We

231

were totally unprepared, having none of the necessary skiing clothing, nor any skiing equipment.

My other half was showing his belief yet again that one lesson made him an expert, and no way could I put him off. He said we would hire the necessary skiing equipment at the resort. He then took us all into town to a sports shop and bought us anoraks.

He had chosen Davos, one of the most exclusive skiing resorts in the Swiss Alps, and he himself made the bookings. We were to drive there, in the height of winter. This was not a holiday that I looked forward to.

The journey as far as Zurich was not too bad. The ferry crossing from Dover to Calais had been done before, but not in the winter. Still, we made it. There was very little snow on the Swiss roads as far as Zurich, and then the fun began. We still had to drive through narrow twisting lanes, climbing higher and ever higher as we progressed, with the snow getting deeper with each mile. This was not going to be an enjoyable week. I felt it in my blood, and I was right.

The hotel room accommodated the five of us, but it was very cramped. Tempers were poor from the time of our arrival. Harold was determined to get on the slopes and start skiing. I remarked that he would have to have some lessons first. He dismissed that idea. He would quickly pick up the technique, he insisted. The girls did not want to know. I suggested the junior slopes were a more suitable option for young learners. Harold went off to sort himself out with the skis and whatever else he needed and then had one lesson, as he told me. The girls stayed with me.

When my husband showed himself, he was in an awful mood. I was right, so it seemed, and that was something he could not stand. Learning to ski was not the walkover he anticipated. He suggested we should try the lower slopes with the girls the next day. I had no intention of trying anything. I was not well enough, and the strain of living with Harold when he was in that mood was too much. I was happy for him to take the girls and let them have a lesson. That was another mistake. The girls told me they did not enjoy that morning, so Harold was faced with the fact that nobody wanted to ski. As a compromise, I suggested we all go to the skating rink. The rest of the week was spent with the girls learning to skate on ice while I looked on. And Harold and myself were hardly talking to each other.

By the end of the week I was completely drained, and Harold's moods had worsened. The entire holiday was a dismal failure, and my dearest other half decided to show his feelings about this on the journey home. He insisted on taking the wheel from Davos. He was clearly in no state to drive, but I got no response when I asked to take over. Enveloped in a black mood, he drove like a madman down those treacherous mountain roads. Winding and twisting at high speeds on snow and ice, I was completely petrified.

The children cowered in the back of the car. We skidded several times. I thought every yard was to be our last. From time to time, Harold kept glowering at me with his piercing black eyes. I felt sure he was trying to kill us.

On the outskirts of Zurich we stopped at a café, but he would not let us go in. Instead he went to get us some drinks. I never in my wildest dreams thought I would live to see my husband behave as he had to us all on that day, even with all that had already happened to me.

We eventually made it to Calais. There was some time to wait for the crossing, so we decided it would make a change to take the Hovercraft across the channel. It was while we were waiting at the terminal, standing against a building wall, when for no apparent reason and without any warning, Harold exploded into a rage – throwing his arms about, he knocked me against the wall. I was stunned, paralysed with shock for a moment. Could it be that he was releasing all that tense ferocity, an accumulation of the tensions built up with his frenzied driving during that terrible and tortuous drive down from Davos to Zurich, and which continued all the way to the port of Calais?

I was really lost for words, struck dumb. I could not believe what he had done in full view of all the passengers waiting to cross the Channel. This was too much. I got on the boat with the girls and ignored my husband for the rest of the journey home as best as I could under the circumstances, feeling relieved, at least, that we were all still alive.

Unfortunately, the girls were all sick on the short journey. The motion from the winter seas affected the Hovercraft and many of its passengers. We were thrown all over the place and nearly everyone was seasick.

This was one occasion when I could not get home quickly enough.

Chapter 74

Harold was now unnerving me more and more with each passing day, but I could still not find the strength to leave him. Several times over the next few months, for no reason, to me at least, he lifted his arm as though he was going to strike me, but restrained himself, his arm poised above his head, statue-like, for several seconds. He would then apologise profusely, stating that he did not know why he was doing it, over and over again.

A couple of times, he phoned me during the evening to tell me he was in the Airedale General Hospital. He had had another heart attack, so he told me. Yet again he told me not to visit, as I had to keep the office running. Now each time I rang the hospital, I was told that no one knew anything about him. He was not there. I had no idea where he was. I began to wonder if he was up to his former trick, *à la* Wright. Was he with some woman again? He usually came home after a couple of days.

Another of his bright ideas came forth. He wanted a caravan. He tried to persuade me of all the fun we could have with one. We could go anywhere, especially on the Continent, stop anywhere, see places so far unknown to us. He certainly made a good effort at selling me the idea. It was something I had never thought about and I was not keen on the idea. Living in a confined space like a caravan as a holiday was not my idea of happiness. Nevertheless, he was so keen that I agreed to look at some, if only to keep him happy.

He took me to the caravan sales site at Yeadon, next to the Leeds/Bradford airport. As Harold rarely took no for an answer, I let him make his choice. This was a Sprite Major with four berths. He then told our sales lady that he required a five-berth. At this point, he had not even considered whether the girls would want to join us in a caravan. They were growing up quickly and wanted to do their own thing sometimes. I thought a five-berth would be very cramped.

The sales lady told us there would be no problem in adding a small extension. Harold had told her he wanted a tourer. Our salesperson checked the make and size of our car, that is the horsepower, to make

234

sure our Volvo was capable of touring with the enlarged caravan. She said it was fine. But it was clear that what Harold did not realise was that a large caravan would be much more difficult to tow and manoeuvre. I made it clear that I had no intention of driving with a caravan on my heels.

Now, Harold wanted all the luxury refinements. The bedrooms were to be separated into two, one at each end. A very up-to-date toilet cubicle and very expensive fittings were chosen. As to be expected from my beloved, everything had to be of the very best, money was no object.

We placed the order, and for the next couple of weeks we waited patiently until the caravan could be collected.

Harold drove the mammoth structure home. I sat next to him in the car. He now realised what he had bought. A caravan of that size was not easy to drive. There was also the speed restriction. I doubt whether he had thought about it. My husband was a very fast speed-merchant, and maximum speed allowed for such a vehicle was 50 miles an hour. The final straw came when he tried to park the caravan on our drive. My clever darling spent the best part of two hours trying to work the vehicle into a driveway that was only just wide enough, from a street that was not that wide, either. He did not say much, but I think he realised that maybe he had been a little hasty in his purchase.

Our daughters were not too happy about it, either. They also made it clear that they were not interested in a caravan holiday. All five of us in such a confined space, no way! Their father did explain that he could get a canopy to give an extra room, albeit outside the van, but I think the seeds of disappointment had been sown.

After much discussion, and some argument, Harold came to accept that his family were not interested in his hoped-for plans. The vehicle was too heavy to take anywhere, let alone to the continent. He decided the best plan was to find a permanent site for it. We eventually found a pretty site just outside Settle, in the Yorkshire Dales just beyond Skipton.

Taking the caravan to the site was an ordeal. First, pulling the thing out of the drive had its difficulties, as it was such a tight fit. Either the garden could be ruined or our neighbour's fence was in danger, at the slightest slip. The haul to the site, especially through Addingham, as it was then, climbing uphill with so many hairpin bends, was an experience. In fact, having the caravan at all was an experience.

235

Once in situ, no one wanted to use it. Harold persuaded me to spend a weekend with him there. The girls were happy to be left at home, with big sister Anne in charge. Mam promised she would keep an eye on them.

So that nice Spring Saturday, my love and I went to the caravan. I did not really look forward to it, but Mam said it would be an opportunity to be alone together and, hopefully, help our ailing marriage. It was not to be. The place was too cramped. Harold must have sensed my mood and was complaining at my attitude.

There was a pub about half a mile away where we thought we could get our evening meal. Suddenly, Harold jumped up and said he was off, before I was ready. I tried to stop him to ask him to wait, but he just ignored me and went off. I followed him, catching up with him at the pub, but he refused to talk to me. I remember wondering, just what was the matter with him.

He was not trying to help matters. We spent the evening in total silence, with one drink each. We did not have anything to eat. When he eventually left, I followed and got back to our site so very unhappy.

The next day we just sat by our van for a few hours. The weather was beautiful, and it was a pity to waste it, in spite of the fact that there was no change in our moods. I think my other half now realised that having a caravan did not come up to his expectations. I could think of no other explanation for his behaviour.

It was late afternoon when we made for home. On our arrival back, we had a wonderful surprise. Anne had made the most scrumptious tea to welcome us home. She had been working all day with a little help from her sisters, to give us this surprise. One thing she had learned from me, and was good at, was cooking and baking. The table was laden with salads and all sorts of delicatessen goodies, with apple pie, home-made (she knew that I never bought bakery goods), for dessert. The girls had missed us. It was the first time we had left them on their own. It was a wonderful feeling to have my children welcome us home like this, though I was not too happy at Anne spending all her time cooking, but the thought was very uplifting after the horrible weekend I had just spent with the man who was supposed to make me happy. However much I tried, there was nothing that I could have done to make him happy.

Harold had to accept that buying the caravan was the least successful of all his enterprises so far, and he decided to sell it. He went back to Yeadon to the caravan business from where we had bought it. He negotiated a trade-back, but had to let it go at considerably less than he would have liked. Losing so much money made my husband an angry man – and who was he likely to take it out on, when it came to the crunch?

Chapter 75

I was once more on my own. My beloved, in spite of all his promises to behave himself, had let his temper get the better of him, and after giving me another beating, he walked out. I no longer had to throw him out. He was now leaving immediately before I told him to go.

I promised myself that this was the last time this had happened, once and for all. Over recent months my investments had been doing well. I sold out as soon as a decent profit had been made. We had opened a joint account with a building society. Harold told me he had put the book in his bank for safety, but I had access whenever I wanted some money, and either of us could sign. I had made a tidy sum in a short time and now I was on my own, I felt entitled to it, to keep me going.

When I went to see the bank manager to retrieve the bankbook, he told me that my husband had already been and taken the book away. In any case, he could not let me have it. When I pointed out that it was a joint account where only one signature was required, he replied that I still needed my husband's permission to get the book, even though it was a joint account. I sensed collusion again, but I was sunk. The bank manager told me he could not discuss the matter any further.

This made me even more determined to break away from this person who was making my life so dreadful. Divorce was once more on my mind. The only thing was that I felt ashamed and humiliated with myself for taking that husband of mine back after my first attempt at divorce. I felt embarrassed at having to go back to my solicitor and go through the whole procedure again. I decided to think it all through for a little while. It was while rummaging through my mind how to go about another divorce action that I stumbled upon the very thing that determined that I had to go ahead.

I was cleaning out my daughters', Pam and Ruth's bedroom, and thought it time that I gave their wardrobe a good going over. These were fitted wardrobes that ran along one wall. I was on my hands and knees cleaning out the bottom of one of the sections when it seemed to me that the wooden base was loose. On closer inspection, I discovered

238

that it was a false bottom with little holes whereby one could put one's fingers in and lift the bottom out. This was something that I had never known existed in all the three years that I had lived in the house.

I lifted the false bottom out and was now immensely curious. I put my hand inside the newly found space, felt around and could feel two packages. When I drew the packages out I was struck dumb. I had found two bundles of cheques. Each one was held together with a couple of elastic bands. I removed the bands and looked closer. On examination, every cheque was made out to cash in denominations of either £10 or £20 each. In total there was £600-worth of cheques.

The signatures on the cheques were yet another staggering blow. They looked like mine, but I knew I had never made out these cheques. I became more and more troubled when the dates on the cheques revealed that they had all been cashed in the period between the date of the account being opened in my name only, when Courtney and Co. started business, and the account being closed with the sale of the business in Burley-in-Wharfedale. The majority of them were dated during that period when I had that latter business. The most revealing feature was that every cheque had the stamp of the bank's Merrion Centre branch, a branch that I had never been in. I never, ever, at any time had been in that branch of Barclay's Bank. The bank that the company and I dealt with was in Albion Street.

My signature had been forged. The culprit's name was obvious to me. He had had plenty of practice since becoming a life assurance salesman. Harold had been chastising me constantly and accusing me of frittering the money from my household account. It had been combined with the one for my shop in Burley-in-Wharfedale. My mind turned to those days when I was running the business. The accounts never added up. I knew something was wrong, but the statements were sent to Harold's office. I could never get to see them. No wonder he insisted on administering my business from his office. In those days, cheques were returned to the payer with the statement. He clearly did not want me to see them and had hidden the cheques.

This looked like more conspiracy to deliberately undermine my efforts. I concluded that the mistress, Wright, must have cashed the cheques in a branch where she would not be recognised.

There are no words that can describe the anger I felt at that discovery. The cheques had been hidden away. I presume I was not to know they existed, and it was a mere fluke that I had found them.

Now I knew what I had to do. I chose another solicitor, though how I came to choose him I cannot answer.

At the time I had arranged to see my new solicitor, the divorce laws had changed from those in practice at my earlier petition. The grounds for divorce were now 'irretrievable breakdown'. I had to explain my reasons, but I was not presented with a list of such details as on the previous occasion. I showed the cheques to my solicitor telling him that I knew them to be forgeries, and that the money had completely disappeared. He told me that he would send the cheques to the Police Fraud Squad for investigation and to see what action, if any, would be taken. At the same time, he emphasised that any action taken was dependent on my getting a divorce as a wife cannot sue her husband. I expect he was thinking of my earlier withdrawal.

I told him that there was definitely no way I would have my husband back. My solicitor then told me that he would require a list of all my assets and what I knew of my husband's. This I did, telling him that I had two life assurance policies with Sun Life of Canada. I guessed that their current value would be about £800 each. He asked me to find out the current surrender value.

I subsequently paid a visit to the Sun Life of Canada offices and met with my old friend Rose Hardy, who was now the office manager. That meeting was to be the enlightenment of a lifetime. I told her why I was there, and her reaction was that she had been wondering for some time when I was going to find out about Harold's affair with Wright. She said it was about time that I took action and left him. When I asked her for the surrender value of my two policies, she looked amazed, dumbfounded.

'But you've cashed them in,' she told me.

Now it was my turn to be dumbfounded. I told her that I had not cashed them in. Why would I have come now to ask to surrender them if I had already cashed them in? Her reply was a definite assertion that the policies had been surrendered. She then offered to show me the surrender documents with my signature on them. My heart sank. Not again. She went to find the documents and my heart was beating ten to the dozen. When she returned and showed me the documents, my stomach lurched. True enough, what looked like my signature was ascribed there. I noted that the signature had been witnessed by my one-time adversary, Wright. Again the date was significant. The document was dated at the time when I was in Leeds

General Infirmary suffering from nervous exhaustion. I knew that this was one more of my husband's dirty tricks.

He had been visiting me every day, behaving as the devoted, loving husband, and all the time he was double-crossing me behind my back.

Two cheques for a total of nearly £2,000 made payable to Thalia L. Courtney had been sent to me, as Rose believed. I had not only not received them, and knew nothing about the transactions, but the cheques had been cashed. It meant that whoever cashed the cheques must have forged my signature.

Rose got me photocopies of the two offending documents for my solicitor. This incident so enraged Rose that she was motivated to inform me about my husband's nefarious activities. She was amazed that I knew so little of his and Wright's activities after all this time and proceeded to fill me in and so complete the jigsaw that had troubled me all these years.

The whole company, all the members of the branch in Leeds as well as in Newcastle knew of Harold's affair more or less from the beginning. Harold and his secretary would go out drinking at lunchtime, mainly on a Thursday and Friday, and then go back to the office to have sex in the medical room. That explained my husband's outrageous phone call in 1964, telling me that he could not meet me as arranged, and more or less demanding I meet up with that awful representative, and his continuing abuse towards me.

Their liaison was eventually uncovered when the company's visiting auditor made one of his unannounced spot checks. He and the branch cashier, Ian Ferguson, walked in on the two of them in the medical room having their usual lunchtime sexual fling.

They had been caught in the act! Both were the worse for drink. They were reported to head office and both were asked to leave the company.

I now knew the truth as to why my husband decided to return to Leeds, and as to why he insisted with such determination on bringing his secretary with him.

He had been sacked! She had been sacked!

Other questions were answered in that meeting with Rose. So many missing pieces of the jigsaw fell into place. He had taken Wright to the Bournemouth conference. That month's stay in Scarborough was part of Harold's grand scheme of things, a planned manoeuvre so that Harold could have time with his inamorata. It occurred to me that he was most probably staying with her, which explained to me the mystery of his accommodation and the absence of phones during that month.

That hasty phone call he had been so desperate to make to Wright at eight o'clock in the morning following Mr Brown's abysmal party was also explained.

Dr Rose's and the other doctor's explanation as to why my husband tried to make out I was having an affair, indeed why he tried to coerce me into one, were now so very real.

My instincts had been faithful to me all along. Now I had to get on with my divorce action.

Rose Hardy suggested that if I wished to verify all she had told me I should speak to Ian Ferguson in Newcastle, also Jack Brindle, Sun Life of Canada's chief executive at the head office in London. She concluded by telling me that she would never have anything more to do with Harold. She had already been shocked by his treatment towards me. These latest revelations that day in her office were even more dreadful, and convinced her to rebuke more determinedly the person whom she had once thought of so highly.

I could not wait to phone Ian Ferguson and hear what he had to say. When I eventually managed to speak to him he confirmed everything Rose had told me. Mr Brindle was less forthcoming. I presumed his position put him in a delicate position, but nothing was denied. The truth about my husband's affair and his activities with his mistress was well and truly out.

The surrender documents for the two missing policies were handed over to my solicitor. I told him what had happened in the Sun Life offices. He told me that they would have to be passed on to the Fraud Squad with the forged cheques. My solicitor then repeated what he had told me at our previous meeting. As I was still married to Harold, no action could be taken unless I went ahead with my divorce action.

I, too, repeated that I had no intention of not going ahead. I left my solicitor's office knowing that my divorce petition was going ahead.

Harold had been absent for nearly four months, and had not shown any interest in his family since. I learned that he had bought a flat in Gledhow Valley Court, a small block of flats that were situated at the bottom of the same street where we had lived at the beginning of our marriage.

During this time, the girls kept asking questions as to their father's whereabouts and when he was coming home. They were missing him more and more. We had now been separated for almost five months and, in spite of all I had been put through, I, too, was now missing him. If only for the girls' sake, their happiness, I had to keep my family together.

Chapter 76

After a few days back home, I discussed with Pamela and her sisters their feelings about their father. They had seen so much, and yet they still loved their father. They were still young, and perhaps they were not really old enough to understand the severity of what he had been doing. Pamela missed her father dreadfully and wanted him to come home. So did her sisters.

My husband had now bought himself another place to live. This could complicate things. Pamela was adamant she needed her father and asked to phone him. She wanted to ask him to come home. The girls all wanted their father home and in spite of everything he had done, they still loved him. I remembered Dr White's warning that the violence could only get worse if I did not leave him. Things had gone from bad to worse since then, but I wanted to put my children's needs first and hoped everything would turn out all right.

Pamela did ring her father up, and told him he could come home. He seemed very happy about that when Pamela passed the phone to me. He repeated his previous remonstrations, how much he loved me and no way could he hurt me. He did not know why he did what he did, but it would never happen again. His apologies were so profuse. I had heard it all before. Yet I still loved him. We both agreed to discuss the situation, but he told me he wanted me to come down to his new abode to discuss it. He refused to come to our home in Gateland Drive.

Up to this point, nothing had been mentioned about my divorce petition. Whether he had received it or not was not disclosed at that point in time. Pamela's illness had put the matter out of my mind for the time being, but it was now something to be considered.

I agreed to meet him at his Valley Court flat. Harold was so very happy for us to be together again, but he made one condition. He would never take one step inside our house in Gateland Drive. He insisted that the house was unlucky. He had used that excuse about the house in Birney Edge, in Newcastle. Now he was using the same excuse again. It was if he was making our homes an excuse for his despicable behaviour. He did make all the usual apologies, and

244

repeated the same affirmations of remorse and shame for his behaviour. It would never happen again, he promised emphatically. I must leave Gateland Drive with our children and move into the Valley Court flat, for the time being at least.

He suggested that we find another house, but in the meantime, most of our furniture would have to go into store. The flat had only two bedrooms and he had furnished it throughout. There were fitted wardrobes in both bedrooms. The place had been furnished very tastefully, I thought. It would be cramped. The flat was not meant to house a family of five, but at least we would all be back together and no one would be happier than the girls. In spite of my trepidations, I still loved him so very much. I knew I could not refuse his suggestion. After our longest period of separation, five months, I moved with the girls into the flat.

Harold soon brought up the divorce petition, telling me how annoyed he had been at receiving it, but he did not mention the contents. He remarked on having to pay off my solicitor once again. It was proving a costly exercise.

By withdrawing my divorce petition, I had to acknowledge to my solicitor that the fraud charges would not go ahead. I was now glad about that. I wanted everything to be smooth and plain sailing. Our happiness, the family's happiness, came first. Sometime later, I was informed that the signatures had been found to be forgeries, but I did not care any more. We were making plans to find another house. I wondered if the forgeries had been put into my petition. Was that why my husband was so keen on reconciliation? I could never bring myself to ask him. It was something I was never to know. He did tell me that the insurance policies had been cashed, but the circumstances surrounding their encashment he refused to discuss, never admitting that he had forged my signature on so many items. Neither would he explain what had happened to all that money.

The house in Gateland Drive was sold without any problems. The bulk of the furniture had been put into store. All the valuables, the silver, antiques and Wedgwood, I took with me to Valley Court. Again, we had to consider the type of house we wanted to live in.

Having scrutinised several possibilities without finding anything suitable, Harold made one of his creative suggestions. We should buy a house with room for expansion. We had looked at an older house on a corner site, still in the same area. It was a semi-detached and had a large garden on all sides. There was plenty of room to build out. It

245

only had three bedrooms, but there was scope to do what we thought we wanted. It would mean a huge upheaval, and cost a considerable amount of money. Overall it seemed a good proposition. The deposit was paid with a date for completion early in the New Year. The Valley Court flat was also sold quite easily with similar arrangements for completion.

During the few weeks since we were back together, Harold had resumed his practice of phoning me each morning, panic-stricken, to come down to the office to work immediately. When I went back to work, I found a couple of changes.

We had a new firm of accountants. They were a private husband-and-wife team. The personal touch was much in evidence. I sensed that my husband had spun them his usual yarns to explain my absence and sudden return. Whenever they were in the office, which was frequently, I could feel them glaring at me, as if to say, What are you doing here? Why have you bothered to come back? They always made me feel uncomfortable and intimidated on those occasions. I made a point of getting on with my work and tried to be sociable with them.

The best change, to my mind, was Harold's secretary. Jean was a lovely person, with loads of personality. In about her late thirties, she knew her job. She was very efficient. Married to a French man, he was frequently in the office. She had brought a breath of fresh air to the business. She had the right attitude, to my way of thinking, and was certainly able to talk to people and make them feel comfortable. The atmosphere in the office was a pleasure.

I had said, mostly to myself, that with patience and perseverance, the right person would be found to help run the office. Jean proved herself to be an asset to the business.

By the time we had organised and arranged our proposed house move, it was now almost Christmas.

Chapter 77

Christmas Eve, 24th December 1971, was another one of those days that still haunts me, and it seems that it always will. I am sure it is going to continue to stay in my mind for always. Christmas-time was a time for celebration for lots of other people, but for me it had become a time I dreaded. It seemed as though my husband, whom I still loved dearly in spite of the horrors he had put me through, needed to liven up his festive spirit and use me to this purpose. That year was apparently going to be no different, just another nightmare to endure.

I had woken up at about my usual time and went about my normal morning routine with the children. They were on school holiday, so I busied myself with them. Harold had stayed in bed much later than usual, getting up just after eleven o'clock. He immediately reprimanded me and accused me of disturbing him when he wanted to sleep. He refused any breakfast and told me he was going into town, as he needed to get some last-minute presents. He added that he would only be an hour and would be back for lunch.

The hour passed. The girls and I had a light lunch and another hour later, Harold had still not returned home. I wanted to do some shopping myself. I would have to get to the shops pretty quickly if I was to catch them before they closed for the holiday. It was now after two o'clock, and with no sign of him, I decided I would have to go up to Moortown, to Fine Fare, the local supermarket of the time. Being only a few hundred yards up the road, it was my nearest and quickest option. I would have to be as quick as possible, knowing how much my husband objected to coming home and finding me not there, even though I left the girls at home and he would have no problem getting in. I forgot at the time that he had keys for the flat, since he had lived there alone.

I took the car and drove the couple of hundred yards up Harrogate Road. At Moortown Corner the lights were at red so I had to stop. On the opposite side of the road, having come from the opposite direction and also waiting at the lights, I saw Harold sitting in his Volvo. In the passenger seat beside him sat his mother. Seeing my husband, and believing he had seen me, I did what I assumed any loving wife would do in that situation, I decided to stop and let him know what I was doing and where I was going. As soon as the lights changed to green, I pulled round the corner left into Street Lane West and stopped immediately in front of the casino, only a couple of yards past the lights. It seemed the best place to stop. Harold also turned into Street Lane West and parked his car directly in front of mine. I waited in the car until he stopped his engine and then I got out of my car. I was still closing my car door as both Harold and his mother, with the speed of lightning, propelled themselves as though catapulted out of their car, and charged straight at me, arms frantically flailing.

I heard the old lady screaming, 'Hit her! Hit her! She's following us.' She repeated it several times.

Still standing at the side of my car, I was pelted with punch after punch to my face and chest with Harold's clenched fists. He was also kicking me, whilst his mother slapped me around the face. At the same time his mother kept screaming and urging him on. It all happened so quickly. The attack must have been thought up whilst they were waiting at the traffic lights.

Seeing no other way out, I gradually managed to manoeuvre my car door open as the blows kept coming. I slithered backwards into my car and managed to close the car door. Harold continued kicking and punching my side of the car. I put the gears into reverse and snail-like backed away from Harold's car. I was nervous of hitting him as he was still banging my bonnet with his fists. With some difficulty, as the bully was trying to stop me, I pulled away from the kerb, drove further down the road so I could turn round, and then drove back along Street Lane. Fortunately, this time, the lights were in my favour and I was able to drive straight to my parents' home.

The attack had only lasted a few minutes, though it seemed much longer, but I was terribly shaken and trembling as I drove the short distance to safety. My heart was pounding away, and my head felt as though it was made up of millions of little bubbles. I was in such pain that I did not know if I was light-headed or I had a dead weight on my head. During the whole time of the assault not one word had been said to me. I was never asked why I was there or what I was doing. Nor did I get the chance to say anything to them, so ferocious was the attack.

I rang my mother's doorbell. As soon as she opened the door and took one look at me, she blurted out, 'Oh no, not again!'

My bruises must have been clearly obvious. She helped me into the

248

kitchen, by which time Dad had joined us. He had been resting in the lounge. He sat down with me and Mam put the kettle on. I started to describe the incident. We were all trying to enjoy our cups of tea, and I was beginning to feel a little relaxed, when the phone rang. It stood on the kitchen worktop, so Dad picked it up and answered it. We could all hear my husband's voice bellowing down the line. Dad passed the phone to me.

'Don't you dare come home,' Harold screamed. 'If you do I'll kill you.'

He repeated his outburst a couple more times and then slammed the phone down. I jumped up.

'I must go home,' I cried, panic-stricken.

My immediate thoughts were for my children. I had left them in the flat, and now it seemed they were with this violent lunatic. My mother started crying hysterically, that I must not go. I said that I must, I had to get home to protect my girls. I was frightened for them as Harold was totally out of control. Both my mother and father pleaded with me not to go, telling me that they feared for my life. This was not the first time my husband had threatened to kill me, but all I could think of was my girls, and I had to get to them. I had to get home.

I must have driven like a lunatic. All my pain seemed to have been replaced by thoughts for the safety of my children. I parked outside the flat, and walked through the front entrance into the large hallway. The hallway housed the entrance doors to three ground-floor flats. One was immediately to the left of the front entrance, and a second door was placed at the end of the hallway on the right. The main door to our flat was situated at the very end of the hallway, about twenty feet from and directly facing the front entrance.

I walked through the hallway and as I approached my flat door I opened my bag to look for my key. As I delved into my handbag, the flat door opened, and for the second time within an hour or so, my husband and his mother charged at me and without a word, exploded, pelting me yet again with punch after vicious punch to my face, neck and chest. Harold again resorted to kicking me with all his strength, knocking me to the ground. He continued kicking me in my back for a few moments, as I lay curled up on the floor, unable to help myself. Then, just as quickly, the beatings stopped. I heard my flat door slammed shut, some whispered words, and footsteps down the hall. My husband, with his mother, had gone, leaving me lying on the floor.

The next thing I knew, my neighbour from the flat immediately next door, Mrs Benson, an elderly lady, was trying to comfort me. She helped me to my feet and practically carrying me, took me into her flat. As I stumbled into her lounge, I got the surprise of my life. My three darling girls were all sat there, looking very subdued, frightened and nervous. I was so relieved and delighted to find them with Mrs Benson. How or when they went into Mrs Benson's flat I never knew. I never saw them come out of my flat and go into the one next door. And I did not know if they had seen their father assaulting me. Being so stunned myself, I never thought to ask at the time. Sometime later it occurred to me that their father might have thrown them out. All I could think of was that he had gone off and left us, obviously not caring how the children or I were.

Mrs Benson must have phoned Dr Feldman, our family GP, as he arrived quite quickly.

His first remark as soon as he saw me was, 'You should be used to this by now!'

He gave me a very cursory examination and then announced that apart from some bruising, no serious damage had been done. He told me to take my Valium and go to bed. Mrs Benson said she would look after the children for the evening. I then very worriedly exclaimed that I had no means of getting into my flat. As soon as I was attacked, my handbag went flying and all the contents had gone sprawling on the floor inside the flat doorway. I still had my coat on, and put my hand into the pocket. There, as though by a miracle, I found my key, a Yale key. I do not remember finding the key in my bag, let alone putting it in a pocket, but there it was. I was saved and I could get back into my home. All I wanted to do was go to bed.

Dr Feldman and Mrs Benson helped me into my flat to ensure I could get in, then the doctor left us to it. My good neighbour helped me into bed and then returned to see to my girls.

I lay in bed, smarting from the battering I had been subjected to, in spite of being doped to the eyeballs. I tried to sleep but found it almost impossible. Then around about ten o'clock in the evening, or so I believed, the doorbell rang. I dragged myself out of bed and shuffled to the door still feeling very dazed, not at all with it. On opening the door I found myself facing four young men, two of whom looked very familiar. I realised they were friends of Anne's. As soon as they saw me they gasped.

'It's true, then!' they announced in unison.

I then recognised two of Anne's friends, frequent visitors to my home. The other two were unknown to me. They told me that Anne was in the Skeleton Key Club, the youth club they all frequented, and which was in the basement of the casino building at Moortown Corner, the very place where I had been set upon earlier in the day. They went on to tell me that she was in the most terrible state. She was drunk out of her mind, hysterical, crying and screaming that her father had beaten up her mother. They added that she was in such a bad way they could not do anything with her and could I go and bring her home

I pointed out that they could see the state I was in, and that I was also doped up with tranquillisers. I would most certainly come and get her, but I was in no fit state to drive and would they help me, to which they gladly consented. I took my car, and with all four lads in it, I drove very precariously the hundred yards or so up Harrogate Road to the club.

As we walked into the club, I could see it was packed to capacity with about a hundred young people dancing and having a good time. The lights were dimmed and the boys guided me to the back of the room where I could see Anne with some club members who were trying to make her sit down. She was clearly in a most terrible state, throwing her arms about and resisting all efforts to calm her down. Her make-up was smudged around her face from crying. She was wearing a full-length red flouncy gown. She must have gone into the flat to change when I was in bed but I had not heard her. Now she was in a very distressed state and had no idea what she was doing, in front of the many members of the club who watched, full of curiosity.

We realised that we would have to carry her out of the club to the car. The four boys, with my help, managed to manoeuvre her out of the club and once in the car, they escorted us back to my place so they could carry her into the flat. By then Anne was calming down.

Once in the flat, we laid her on the settee in the lounge where she immediately fell fast asleep. She slept there, still fully clothed until morning, as I did not want to disturb her. I also found Pamela and Ruth fast asleep in their beds.

I have never been able to thank those young men sufficiently for helping me to bring Anne home in such a state. The one thing I did learn from all this is that the girls did witness their father beating me up. I decided then that I would not allow that to happen again. I changed the locks straight after Christmas, and promised myself that this time I would definitely never take Harold back.

Chapter 78

It was the school Christmas holidays and yet again I was on my own. Only this time I was living in a property that I did not own. All our previous homes had been in joint names. This one belonged to my husband, although it had now been sold subject to contract. Completion was arranged for the middle of January 1972. I was caught in the middle. I do not think either of us gave a thought to the flat being in Harold's name only, as we intended moving out as soon as possible.

Nevertheless, I continued to get on with things. Two weeks later, I had a visit from Cyril. Harold had asked him to speak to me. He told me that Harold wanted to make things right with me. It was a recurrence of the past. I agreed, partly because I was in such a precarious situation, partly because I could not reconcile myself to the fact that I should leave him once and for all. We discussed our position with the flat.

Harold was angry with me for changing the locks, as the property was in the process of being sold, but he told me he still wanted us to get back together. It was the opportunity to make a new start. How many times had I heard that! The house we were buying was soon available for occupation, so I agreed to try and make a go of it once more. I did point out that this would be the very last time. Once more, I was given all the usual apologies and promises that everything was going to be better. He would never, ever hurt me again.

When we got the keys to our new home on completion, we went over to see it and got an awful surprise. Almost all the contents had been left in the house. It was in a terrible state, indescribably filthy. We had decided to leave our furniture from Gateland Drive in store for the time being which was as well. Our solicitor was contacted, and he told us that as the previous owner had emigrated, we could get rid of everything.

It was a terrible job. The bedroom cupboards and drawers were full of clothes which we threw out of the windows and sacked up outside. The furniture was put outside for the refuse department to collect. The worst job was the carpets. They were worn, rotten and decrepit, horrible. It took us the best part of a week to clear everything out.

Then we realised how dreadfully filthy the whole house was. I had to go through it from top to bottom, scrubbing and cleaning. It made us think whether we had done the right thing in buying it, it needed so much work doing.

Architects were called in to plan the extensions. When we got the costings, we realised that we had made a mistake.

Business still had to go on, and yet again, I went into the office to work on a part-time basis. Harold told me then that he had been discussing the property market with an estate agent friend, from the point of view of investment. He asked my opinion, and I replied that it was worth considering. There was a market for rental properties in the student area, in Headingley, near the university. I looked at some potential properties and chose one.

It was a through terrace house, suitable for converting into five bedsits. Harold had contacts in the building industry who could do the conversions. We decided to go ahead in the hope that the house would be ready in time for the new student year in September. There was plenty of time. Whilst looking, I came across a second property that was suitable for rental in Harehills. It required cleaning up but no major work was needed. I went ahead and bought it.

We had decided not to build the extension, and move into something more modern. A new development was going up in Shadwell. The beautiful detached homes that were being built in the Shadwell Park area were very attractive and we thought we would go for it. This was an opportunity for us to have a much better start, or so we thought. The house we picked was going to take several months to build. The one we were living in had proved to be a disaster and a big mistake, so we wanted to get out as quickly as possible. We thought up the idea of a temporary move, and then to rent that house when we moved in to the completed Shadwell house. We bought a town house in the Brookhill estate, on Shadwell Lane. With four bedrooms and a sizable through lounge, it was a much better proposition than the one we were in. It would make a good investment to add to our property portfolio.

The move into Brookhill went ahead about a month before Easter. The furniture in store was to remain there until we took possession of Shadwell Park Court. The usual 10 per cent deposit was paid. Then Harold had a change of heart. We had only been in the house a couple of weeks when he decided to sell Brookhill.

We had not been in Brookhill more than a couple of days, when my darling husband resumed his antics. He disappeared again. The usual phone call told me he had had a heart attack, and was in his favourite hospital. His penchant for heart attacks was increasing. His reappearance a few days later, well recovered, introduced me to his latest game. He would have his heart attacks at home. If he did not get his own way and sometimes for no reason at all, he ran speedily round the living room in circles, banging his chest with his clenched fist and screaming that he was having a heart attack.

The first time, I was very shocked and upset. I sat him down, and when I suggested calling the doctor he told me he did not want one. After that he would get up and continue with what he was doing as though nothing had happened. This incident was repeated many times over the following weeks and months. I soon came to realise that these so-called 'heart attacks' were play-acting. Since when can someone suffering such an attack run around repeatedly like a maniac and yell so loudly? These occurrences were clearly meant to be for my benefit. He was taunting me, playing mind games, but at least on those occasions he did not hit me. They did cause me more anxiety as I became frightened again as to what he would do next.

Two visits from the in-laws aggravated matters for me. The old man wanted to have a go at me. The usual wild accusations about my so-called affair flew from his mouth. It was obvious where my husband got his temper from. His father just would not give up. Harold made him stop shouting at me but made no attempt to counter the lies. The old lady hurled more abusive remarks at me. I was 'too big for my boots', a 'clever clot', and similar derogatory observations. There seemed no end to the torment. Even if my husband wanted to make things right between us, his parents would not let go. They made everything worse.

Already weakened from years of abuse, during Easter week I succumbed. I felt ill and exhausted, struggling to keep going. On Good Friday evening, I collapsed and my husband took me down to Casualty at St James's Hospital. He must have woven his usual lies as I found myself admitted to the psychiatric ward where I had been previously admitted.

I was under the care of the same consultant, but the doctor who attended me told me that he could find nothing wrong with me other than nervous exhaustion. He noticed I was losing weight. He let it be known that he thought that my husband could be responsible for my condition. I read in the notes, a long time later, that he had asked for my domestic situation to be investigated. This was not revealed to me.

On the Sunday, I was feeling much better. The rest had done me good and I asked to go home. As before, this was conditional on my husband accepting responsibility and looking after me. This was in spite of the fears that the doctor had about the source of my condition. But rules are rules. Harold took me home.

My husband's behaviour was becoming more and more erratic. He could be so loving and caring, the true devoted husband one minute, and then turn on me. He would usually have one of his 'heart attacks', only these became more and more dramatic.

Having run round the room, banging his chest with both his clenched fists, and yelling at the top of his voice that he was having a 'heart attack', when he got no response from me, he then threw himself on to the floor lying on his back. Up went his arms and legs, beetle-wise, and he would thrash then around, still screaming that he was having a heart attack. I refused to be intimidated by these dramatic displays and continued to ignore him. He, as always, got up when he realised he was getting no reaction from me and then continued as though nothing had happened. I knew his actions were fake. There was nothing wrong with him. Curiously, he always put these performances on when the children were not present. Nevertheless, I was quaking in my shoes. They would have been laughable if they had happened in other circumstances. I grew more and more terrified as his senseless behaviour continued to escalate.

Chapter 79

It was time for a holiday, if only to have a change of environment, a break. Yugoslavia, as it was known then, was suggested. Mam and Dad had been to the area, and it sounded lovely. It was one place we had not been to, and as it was on the Adriatic Coast, it sounded a pleasant proposition. The brochures recommended a small place called Cavtat, just a few miles south of Dubrovnik. It sounded just the spot. This was initially Harold's choice and we booked the holiday for two weeks.

On arrival, we found that Cavtat was more a village than a small town. The hotel there was situated in a small bay and was the only hotel in the area.

We soon learned that the easiest access to Cavtat itself was along an unmade path that ran along the edge of the sea from the bay. There was a steep 5-foot drop from the path to the sea, the side of which had been banked up with bricks. Trees were scattered along the sea edge, otherwise there was no protection from falling into the sea. No cars ran along it. The whole place had a primitive feel about it, but it made a change. The road from the hotel into the town meandered all over the countryside before arriving at its destination, so we usually walked into the town along the path.

There was little to do in Cavtat itself, after the first visit. The small beach by the hotel was pebbly and not really suitable for the children to play. We did sit out a few times, as the weather was ideal, but we tended to spend more time touring around and visiting some of Yugoslavia's historic sites.

One trip into Dubrovnik was unforgettable for me. The town itself was wonderful with all its old buildings, particularly the castle. On that day, we decided to take a boat trip across the bay. We had been told that the view from the sea was magnificent, which it was.

It was a very small motorboat. It did look rickety, but the boatman, an elderly looking 'son-o'-the-sea', tried to reassure us that the boat was registered as safe and seaworthy. I had my doubts, but I knew what my husband's reaction would be if I refused to go. He believed there was no danger. The girls were happy to go along. I did not want to spoil their enjoyment.

My fears were confirmed when, half an hour into our trip, sparks started to fly from the engine. Within moments, the engine was fully on fire. We were only a dozen passengers, and we were all terrified. The boat appeared to have no life-jackets either. The boatman spoke little English, but in any case, he was too absorbed in trying to quench the flames. He was blowing on the engine with all his strength. Ten minutes later the fire was out, to everyone's relief. The boatman seemed to wonder what all the fuss was about. Perhaps it was a regular occurrence. I, certainly, would never be taking any more boat trips in that part of the world.

A few days before the end of the holiday, we all went for dinner to a little family restaurant that we had found up in the hills. It was a good walk, and we had a very pleasant evening. The meal was typically local, just like Mama used to make.

When we got back to the hotel, I saw that my topaz ring was missing from my finger. I loved that ring. It was the first piece of jewellery Harold had bought me, after he had joined Sun Life. I had treasured it all those years, and now I had lost it. I had put it on specially before going out earlier.

I thought it must have come off my finger at the restaurant, but it was too late to go back and look. It would have to wait till morning. Our return to the restaurant the next day failed to produce the ring. The owner had not seen it. It looked as though I had lost it for good. I was heartbroken. We went to the police station to report it and were given the usual police letter for our insurance company. But the ring was gone forever. It was, however, going to be a great bone of contention in the near future.

Chapter 80

Our holiday in Yugoslavia had been planned so that we would be back home in time to get ready for a family celebration, my cousin's son's barmitzvah. New party dresses had already been bought for the girls. Ruth was to wear her first full-length dress. I had also been indulged by my husband and had a new evening gown. The function was a dinner and dance.

All the Kleiman family were present with all my nieces and nephews. It was a pleasure for us all to be together for such a special occasion. The girls were a delight to behold, dressed up with their glamorous hair dos. It was a truly lovely evening.

What I, or any of us, were not to know was that this would be the last affair when all my family were to be together.

I was required to work in the office again, so I immediately put in my claim to the insurance company for the lost ring. Everything in those days of that nature was done in writing, so I expected it would take a while before my claim was processed.

That same week, Harold told me that he thought it was time I changed my car. He was going to buy me something special. It would officially be a company car for tax purposes, but it would be registered in my name as sole owner. So he said.

My husband must have had in mind the type of car he wanted for me, as he took me down to Brown & White's showroom. He selected a Ford Capri, a very sporty-looking car, which was most appealing, and certainly more expensive than any previous car I had owned. What had brought my husband's generosity back into play, I was unable to understand. It seemed a very, long time since he had had one of these good moods.

The trial run was most satisfactory, and the deal was done. Arrangements were made for us to collect the car a few days later.

We kept the arrangements as planned and when the paperwork was completed and the car was officially mine, as we were about to drive off home from the garage, my business husband told me that he had a policy to deliver on the way home, and I was to follow him to the address. The call was in the Bentcliffe's, near Moortown corner, so it was not out of our way.

Arriving at the designated house, I parked immediately behind him. He got out of his car, walked up to me and speaking to me through the opened window, he asked me to move my car back and park lower down the street. I was to wait for him there. He said he did not want his client to see the two cars parked outside his house and get the wrong impression. His client would think he was 'loaded.' This was, to me, a most peculiar excuse. My husband had always been fond of showing off. He always boasted that any sign of affluence was a sign of success, and it was good for business. I did not question him and did as I was told. I reversed several yards down the street.

Harold told me that he would only be five minutes, but after twenty minutes I began to wonder why I was still sitting in the car doing nothing all this time when I had plenty to do at home. A few minutes later, my husband emerged from his meeting, and was about to get into his car, when he turned and walked up to me with a very profound scowl on his face. I recognised the signs, he was working himself up into a temper.

'Why was I waiting? Why wasn't I at home?' or words to that effect were hurled at me.

He made it sound as though I was stalking him. I replied that he had asked me to wait for him there. His answer appalled me. No, he did not ask me to wait. He expected me to have gone straight home. He was denying that he had told me to wait for him. I thought he must have forgotten that he had told me to wait. Later, I wondered if perhaps it was one of his mind games. I was never to know.

Once home, he started arguing with me again, making horrible accusations against me. Why was I wasting time sitting outside clients' houses? He was working himself up into one his violent lathers. He started to hit me, lashing out with his fists around my face. I dashed out of the house and ran into my next-door neighbour's.

Mary and Alan had lived next door for a few years and we had become good friends. They were slightly younger than Harold and I. By now, they knew something of what I had been going through. This was the first major attack on me since moving into the Brookhill house. Being townhouses, their front door was immediately next to mine, and I was able to make an easy escape. I had managed to get away from Harold before he had really hurt me so that I felt more battered mentally than physically. Mary comforted me and let me stay until we thought Harold had calmed down.

A couple of days later, Mary suggested that I have a break with Harold away from the girls. She thought it would do us both good. I did not really feel up to it. When the suggestion was put to my other half, he asked Mary and Alan if they would like to come with us. They soon agreed. I think they thought it would make me happier if they were there to keep an eye on me.

Arrangements were made for the four of us to go up to Scotland at the weekend. We travelled in Alan's car. I have no idea where we went in Scotland. The hotel had been booked for me. The truth was that I was feeling very depressed at my husband's continued abuse and I could not relax and get in a holiday mood.

We travelled on the Saturday morning, and I remembered little of the journey. I just went along with the others. By the evening, when we were in our hotel bedroom, my loving husband started complaining at my behaviour. He told me that I was morose and lethargic, and my laziness was spoiling the break. It was a repeat of similar earlier incidents, as were the slaps across my face that accompanied his verbal onslaught.

I was unable to do anything about it. I was in a hotel, unable to get away, as I had no transport. I was ill and helpless, and all my husband could do was hit me. A sleepless night resulted in me being unfortunately even more desultory and I was unable to enjoy the weekend. Mary and Alan never made any comments, but I felt that their presence probably made Harold temper (pardon the pun) his outbreaks of violence.

For me the weekend was a total disaster. Once home, later on Sunday, I did feel more relaxed and glad to be home with my girls.

I was preparing to go to bed, when I received what I thought at the time was a pleasant surprise. Harold was full of apologies and asking for my forgiveness, when he gave me a small package. He said it was a present to make up for his behaviour. I unwrapped it with wonder, and was so delighted to see that he had given me a cameo brooch. Harold had known for a long time that I had always wanted a genuine antique cameo brooch. He had promised he would do his best to find me one, and here it was. It was such a lovely surprise.

I placed it on my dressing table, thinking how much I would treasure that present, and went to bed. The next morning, after everyone was out of the house, I went to look at my cameo. It was not there. The cameo was missing. I knew I had left it on the dressing table and now it had gone. I never saw that brooch again. I had no one else

260

to blame for its disappearance, as no one else knew that I had it, and none of the girls had been in our bedroom that morning. I could never tell my husband, and he never mentioned it to me. Its disappearance remained a mystery.

Some time later, when it came to mind, I was also reminded once more of the play *Gaslight* in which the husband played these kind of mind games with his wife. Why would my husband want to do this to me? There was no other explanation for my missing cameo brooch.

My husband continued having his frantic 'heart attacks'. They occurred with ever-increasing frequency, but only when he was in the house. I continued to take no notice.

I was in the office during the week when Harold's accountant friend came in. They invited us to a cocktail party on the following Sunday. It was being held in someone's house in Harrogate. Nothing further was said about it during the week, so I mentioned it to my husband on the Sunday, the day of the party. His reply was that he was not taking me. He was going alone. I asked him why. He produced some harsh words in which he told me I was unfit to take anywhere. I was being so insulted by the man who kept professing his love for me. Eventually he relented, and we did go together.

I had a very uncomfortable evening. The hospitality was great, but my husband hardly spoke a word to me all evening. He was very distant, as were his accountant friends to me. They had obviously been told Harold's usual lies, that I had been carrying on with other men and acted accordingly, with some hostility towards me. In a way, I wished I had stayed at home.

The following morning, when I was in the office, Harold told me quite bluntly that he was having an affair with his secretary, Jean. He pulled no punches about it. I was so shocked, I was speechless. I ran out of the office in tears and went home heartbroken.

Once home, I was given more aggravation. Over the past few months, I had been trying to employ domestic help, to come in each weekday morning to make my life easier when I was working in the office. I interviewed a number of ladies from time to time. My dilemma was that none of them lasted more than two or three weeks. The three or so ladies I had engaged had left without a word. Harold had been making nasty remarks at my inability to keep my staff. It was something that had started to worry me.

I had returned home that morning earlier than usual because of the distress my other half had caused me. The latest cleaning lady was still working. She then asked me why I had asked her to leave. I did not have a clue as to what she was talking about. I asked her what she meant. She then explained that Mr Courtney had rung home and told her that she was no longer needed, and that she was to finish that morning. I had advised my ladies that they should answer any phone calls and take a message. I was perplexed. Did this explain why my ladies left without explanation after only a couple of weeks? Was this yet another example of my husband sabotaging whatever I did for myself? It certainly looked like it. There was no end to my husband's cunning and manipulation. I asked the lady not to leave, but the damage had been done. I was once more without domestic help.

I spent the afternoon in Mary's house. I was devastated and felt betrayed. It was too much learning that my husband was having an affair again, and then finding out that he was playing games with my home helps. I was petrified as to how he would behave when he got home. Mary came in with me for a brief time when I did go back in to the house.

The evening was uneventful, silent. The tension was stifling. I wondered whether Harold was actually telling me the truth, or playing another of his games. I had become so accustomed to his constant lying, that it preyed on my mind. I decided that I was going to have to speak to Jean. It may not have been the right thing to do at that time, but I had to have peace of mind. It was a risk I had to take.

The next morning I went to the office, and waited a while, seeking the right moment. I then went up to her. She was seated at her desk. I told her that my husband had admitted that they were having an affair. She looked up at me for a long moment, aghast. It was nonsense, absolute rubbish, she insisted. She became quite angry at the suggestion. She told me that she was a very happily married woman and would never contemplate such behaviour. I was satisfied, and that was the end of it as far as I was concerned.

It was not the end of it for my husband's secretary. She presumably went in to his office and confronted her boss with my announcement, as shortly after, my husband called me into his office and started hurling abuse at me, telling me that I had no business to talk to his secretary as I had. Wasn't this history repeating itself? I had no right to repeat to her what he had told me. He had confessed in confidence. Now I had upset her and she no longer wished to work with me and wanted me out. I had disrupted the office and I had to get out of the office for good.

I replied that he could not make me get out of the office. I was a partner and as such could not be sacked. I then tried to remind him of all the years of help and support I had given him. I asked him about the exams I had done for him at the very beginning of his career. Where were the files? He had always been so proud of my devoted loyalty and efforts to make him a success. His reply cut through me. He had thrown them away a long time ago. It was as if he was denying that I had had any part in his climb up the ladder to success.

My words aggravated him and he started slapping me around. At that moment, his accountant friends walked into his office. He stopped hitting me, but I still think they saw enough. He told them I had hit him. Having been fed a liberal meal of my husband's fabrications and never hearing my side of the story, they believed him and tried to back him up. During these altercations, someone had called the police as a police officer had arrived quickly on the premises.

Mr Courtney in his usual domineering manner was quick to explain to the police officer that I was causing a disturbance in the place and he had asked me to leave but I refused. I intervened, stating that he could not ask me to leave. I was a partner in the business as well as his wife. The policeman asked to see the business registration certificate. I was certain that this would resolve matters. I could not have been more wrong.

I had been asking my husband where the registration documents were for a long time, but could never get a proper answer. I was about to learn why. My husband produced the certificate and handed it to the officer, with a broad smirk across his face. He looked at me. I could never forget that smile of triumph he threw at me.

The certificate stated that Mr Courtney was the sole proprietor. I had been duped all this time. The certificate forms that I had signed had never been used, and my husband had continued to pile lie upon lie to me. I had been cheated and humiliated in front of all those in the office. How could my husband do all these things to me? The policeman told me that he had no option but to ask me to go. I left, feeling thoroughly defeated and worn out.

The evening at home was again passed in silence, but in the morning, Harold told me he was taking me straight down to the hospital. I was a 'nut case', and he was going to insist that I got the treatment I needed. I could not fight him. I was too tired and dejected to object.

He took me to the outpatients department of the psychiatric unit and demanded immediate attention. For all his barracking and blistering demands for attention, we still had a long wait till we were attended to. When I was eventually seen, the doctors insisted on seeing me on my own, in spite of my husband's aggressive remonstrance that he be with me, I was able to tell the doctor my story. They tried to reassure me that I was not mentally ill. I was overwrought and suffering from anxiety. They seemed to now realise and accept that my husband was causing my problems. They advised me that I needed a rest away from him. I was reminded of the advice I had received from Dr White, so long ago, that I should leave my husband, as the abuse would only escalate if I continued to live with him. It was suggested that I go into hospital, if only to get away from my husband and have a rest for a little while. I refused, telling them that I could not leave my girls, particularly at this time. The doctors then spoke to my husband, but not in my presence, so I could only go by his later reactions as to what he was told.

I was then told I could go home. This time no instructions as to my husband's care over me were given. Very reluctantly he took me home. When we got home, he told me that he had been advised to have a rest away from me, and he was going to stay at his mother's for a while. With that he left.

Chapter 81

It was now 1st July 1972. I had been alone with my girls for two days and was happily enjoying the peace. No intimidation, no harassment, and the tense atmosphere had lifted. I was feeling so much more relaxed.

I was preparing the evening meal. It was about five o'clock and the girls had just come home from school, when the front doorbell rang. When I answered it and opened the door I was confronted by a very tall, slim, grey-haired gentleman. He looked very elegant and aristocratic. He introduced himself as Dr Valentine, the principal psychiatrist of Menston High Royds Psychiatric Hospital. I knew this to be a long-term hospital, a few miles outside Leeds. He told me that he had been asked by Mr Courtney to come and see his wife, Mrs Courtney, as she was very ill. I told him that I was Mrs Courtney, and invited him in. He looked at me, amazed. He informed me that he was expecting to find a very sick person. Mr Courtney had called him to arrange for me to be sectioned, adding that my husband had asked that I be sectioned for three months!

I invited Dr Valentine to sit down. We sat at the dining table. He wondered where Mr Courtney was and whether I was on my own. My answer that my husband was away perplexed him. He later remarked that my husband had made a big mistake calling in a psychiatrist and then leaving me on my own if he thought I was so ill that I needed sectioning.

We spoke for twenty minutes or so, during which time I told him my situation and answered his questions. At the end of that time, he told me that he could not understand what Mr Courtney wanted as there was nothing wrong with me. He said he found me a very pleasant, capable person. He could see I had been busy with the girls, and there was no question of him putting me in hospital.

He closed our interview by telling me that he would report his findings to my husband, that there was no question of me being sectioned.

As soon as he left, I ran to the phone to speak to Harold. He answered. I asked him why he had sent Dr Valentine to see me

265

without consulting me. He repeated what the psychiatrist had told me, that he wanted me sectioning for three months. I relayed the gist of my meeting with Dr Valentine, telling him that the doctor had found no reason to section me. There was nothing wrong with me. He repeated himself, telling me that if I were sectioned for three months he would take me back! That was rich indeed! He would take me back!

My husband just could not take no for an answer. He had been told several times now that I was not mentally ill, but he was determined to prove all the doctors wrong and to continue until one gave him the answer he wanted. But he was never going to get that answer. He would phone me back after he had spoken with Dr Valentine.

Two hours later, in the evening, Harold rang back. He refused to tell me the contents of his conversation with the psychiatrist but I could tell he was not very happy with it. He repeated that he would take me back if I was sectioned for three months. Then he asked me to come down to his parents' house the next day so that we could talk about it and discuss reconciliation. It sounded to me that Harold had not got the result of his manipulating that he wanted from Dr Valentine. I agreed to meet him at his parents' home at seven o'clock the next evening.

As arranged, the next day, 2nd July 1972, all four of us, my three girls and I, walked down to Stainburn Drive. I knocked on the door. It was the back door, the only one that was accessible. Immediately it was opened, Harold's father flew at me without a word and started hitting me. I caught a glimpse of my husband. He came to the door, presumably to see who was there, and immediately disappeared back into the house. His mother then came out and charged at me like a demented animal. Both his parents were beating me with their fists, pummelling me and pushing me back down the path to the road. At the same time, they were shouting and screaming at me that I would never get their son back! They would never allow him to come back to me!

The girls were with me the whole time and saw their grandparents attacking me. I was forced back on to the pavement outside their house. Once in the road, the Cohens withdrew and went back into the house, leaving me dazed and hurting. In tears, I collected my children to me, and holding hands we walked away.

I was angry now. I had been asked to go to that house to speak to my husband, and I had not been allowed to. It was not my in-laws' business, and they had no right interfering like that, I kept thinking, as we went on our way home.

By the time we had walked a few yards up Harrogate Road, I had become so furious at what had just happened that I decided to go back and insist on speaking to Harold. No one could stop me from speaking to my husband!

Once again, I walked up the path to the back door and knocked. The door opened and all hell was let loose. His father, mother, then Harold came at me hell for leather, hitting me, punching me, kicking me. As before, I was forced along the path to the road. Only this time the assault became even more vicious.

In the midst of all the chaos, I suddenly saw Harold come at me with both of his hands aiming for my throat. At the same time, his father had produced a vase and the last thing I remember at that moment was the vase being held above my head.

When I came to, I was lying on the pavement's grass verge outside the in-laws' house. I was surrounded by some policemen, two or three, I never really knew how many. I was too badly hurt, in pain and probably confused to count. I had been concussed but did not know it at the time. A couple of neighbours came to help me, but the policemen insisting on dragging me to my feet. I could barely stand, let alone walk.

The policemen told me they were arresting me for attacking Harold's family. They could see I had been beaten up, and they were accusing me of attacking three people! I had to be picked up off the ground, traumatised, hurting all over my body, and yet the police insisted on arresting me. Jean and her husband, neighbours, told the policeman that I was in no state to be taken away, I needed help. She would make me a cup of tea first. The policeman allowed it. She and her husband practically carried me into her home, which faced the Cohen's house. The children stood watching all that was happening. The officers waited outside whilst Jean so very kindly made me a cup of tea and tried to comfort me. Harold's parents had a very bad reputation in the street for their shouting and fighting, and I doubt if Jean and her husband had been surprised by events that evening. They were keen to support me.

Twenty minutes later, the policemen insisted on taking me in the car. Battered and bruised, and very dazed, I was pushed into the police car. The children were still standing outside their grandparents' house. As I got into the car, I cried out that the girls were being left on their own. I could never leave them. The old lady shouted back that I was not to worry, she would look after them. They would be all right. Nothing could be worse than for those violent maniacs to be looking after my children. I do not know of any words that could describe how terribly wretched and terrified I was. As I was being driven away, I saw the wretched look of bewilderment on my children's faces. I kept looking at them and would not take my eyes off them until they were out of sight.

Every bone in my body screamed with pain as I was driven down to the police station in the Bridewell under the Leeds Town Hall. I was shown in to some sort of indescribably antiquarian and filthy premises that served as a police station. A number of policemen in open shirts appeared to be working behind a long counter. Terror mounted in me. They were so rough-looking. I was ignored for some considerable time.

There was nowhere to sit down. All the terrible things that one hears about, about police brutality, came into my mind. I began to realise it must all be true. I cried to some of the men that I did not know why I was there. I insisted that I had done nothing wrong. I was the one who had been attacked. I was answered by loud guffaws of raucous laughter.

'You're not in here for nothing. We know your type.' Other such words were also hurled at me.

It was if they were telling me that no one is brought in to that prison hell unless they have definitely done something wrong. One is automatically guilty.

The whole time the attitude of all the police personnel was totally belligerent and intimidating.

I asked to use the phone and at first I was ignored. I then demanded more strongly to use the phone. I told the men I had a right to use the phone. They just laughed even more, and told me I had been watching too much television and that I shouldn't believe all I see on television. My fear was all-consuming. All the pain I was enduring was nothing to the terror that I suffered that night. Now I believed that no one knew where I was. Anything could happen to me, and there was no one to protect me. I would be there for ever. In spite of feeling so weak and ill, I had to keep fighting for my rights. G-d only knew where I found the energy from to keep me going!

I kept on demanding to use the phone. Someone had to know where I was. Then I warned the policemen that I had relatives who were lawyers, and they would have something to say when they heard how I had been treated. The police officers still took no notice of me until I mentioned names, two barristers, and then a solicitor, all of whom were cousins. Whether that name-dropping influenced them or they got fed up of hearing my demands, I could not tell, but I was handed the phone. At least I could let Mam know where I was and hopefully get help.

It was nearly two o'clock in the morning on the station clock. Now it was my mother's turn to get an horrific shock when I phoned her, but there was nothing else I could do. I was so happy to hear her voice and in spite of her being shattered in the middle of the night on hearing of my plight, she remained calm and ordered in her mind. She would get everything sorted out and not to worry. My mother was always so unemotional and practical in a crisis.

I was shown to a cell. I was told there was no hope of me getting out that night. There was no furniture at all in the cell, other than a very narrow wooden bench, the type I used to see in school gymnasiums. There was no other place to sleep. The floors were filthy. I tried to lie down on the bench, but it was hopeless. I could never have slept if there had been a decent bed in the place. I thought how right Dr White and the other doctors had been when they advised me to leave my husband. I had been warned that if I stayed with Harold, things would only get worse. His behaviour and the assaults would get worse, and my health would get worse. They had been so right.

Nothing could get any worse than being put in a prison cell for the night for being assaulted.

They had beaten me!

They had attacked me!

I had been terrorised over and over again!

My mind rambled on, and on, and on, all through the night.

First thing in the morning I was given a revolting-looking enamel mug. It was badly chipped, especially around the rim. I was told it contained tea. I could not drink it, even though I had had nothing to eat or drink since leaving home the previous early evening.

At no time whilst I was in the station were the charges mentioned. I was never questioned. From my experiences at the time of my arrest, and when in custody in the police station, it seemed to me that police procedures and practices were haphazard and disorganised. I was treated without any rights or respect. To the best of my knowledge, I believed that this situation continued to be so until the Police And Criminal Evidence Act (PACE) 1984 was introduced. This Act of

Parliament introduced codes of practice, a legislative framework for the powers of the police, the aim of which was to establish a balance between the powers of the British police and the rights of the members of the public. Sadly, police attitudes towards domestic violence have been less amenable to change until quite recently.

It was at eight-thirty that I eventually received help. My mother had arranged with Colin Frazer for one of his junior solicitors to come to my aid. I knew she would come up trumps. He told me he had to take me up to the courts to see what they were going to do.

He held my arm as he took me up the stairs to the main floor of the Town Hall. He could see the dreadful state I was in. As we reached the top of the stairs, an important-looking police inspector came up to me. He told me that I should really be in hospital. I had strangle marks round my neck. He called it a 'strangle bracelet'. That was the last I remembered until I woke up in hospital.

I do not know how long I was unconscious. I do not think it was very long, but I woke up in the Leeds General Infirmary. I was in a ward of the Martin Wing. As soon as I felt able, I asked for a mirror. The nurse brought one straight away. When I looked at it, I knew that what the police officer in the Town Hall had told me was correct. I had been strangled. My husband had tried to kill me. I then learned that as well as all the bruises, I had a fractured skull and had been suffering from concussion.

A couple of hours later, I heard a disturbance in the ward. My husband was running in, demanding to see me. He was yelling his apologies at me, telling me how sorry he was. He then made a revealing declaration.

'I never intended it to go this far!'

He had never intended for things to go so far and he was so very sorry. It was as I had suspected. I had been ambushed. The attack on myself had all been planned. This had been another of my husband's devious and scheming machinations to get back at me because he had not got his own way with Dr Valentine. I was certain of that.

I did not want to hear him. I screamed back at him as best I could as I could hardly speak at all, for him to get out. My throat now hurt. I yelled at him several times until some nurses came and asked him to leave. He had brought another gentleman, unknown to me, with him. When I asked a nurse who he was, I was told that the gentleman was a doctor. I suppose Harold had hoped to make his own diagnosis, which would be to his advantage. No way would I have anything more to do with that evil being.

I was in hospital for nearly three weeks, during which time my girls visited me regularly. They told me early on that it was Nana who had called the police and had told them that I had attacked my husband's family. I never wanted to have anything more to do with Harold or any of his family ever again.

Chapter 82

It was good to get back home after my last ordeal. I was more or less recovered from my physical wounds, but I was not to know that it was going to take a long time to recover from the mental and emotional wounds I had suffered. The frequent nightmares and panic attacks would last well into the future, in spite of all the psychotherapy and help I was to receive at St James's Hospital for many years to come. I often saw my husband's arms outstretched aiming for my throat, or that vase in my father-in-law's hands as it was about to be smashed on my head, and then I would wake up. There was no more sleep to be had on those nights.

I would never forget what my husband had put me through. Nor could I ever forgive him for causing me to spend a night in a prison cell. It was some time much later that I began to wonder why my husband had not been charged with attempted murder. He had tried to strangle me. It was obvious to all who saw me at that time, including the police, and nothing was ever done about it.

But now, I had to get on with my life as best as I could. I had been away from home for a while and things had to be dealt with.

The house had been sold subject to contract some weeks earlier. The intended purchaser was a neighbour and friend from our previous home in Shadwell. At that time, when she was told that we were building a house and could not give a definite completion date for some time, she said she was happy to wait. Now I had to go back on my word. I was going to stay put for the time being at least. The future was an unknown quantity, but I was certain that I would not be living with my husband again.

The lady was very disappointed at losing the house. The sale would have given us a profit of over £2,000 in the short time I had lived there, but I had to keep a roof over our heads for my children's sake.

Another matter concerned my daughter Pamela. Some months previously, she had brought home from school details of an exchange scheme organised by the Anglo-Austria Society. A child of a similar age and sex from somewhere in Austria would come and stay with a pupil and her (or his) family for a week during the school's summer

272

holidays. The host pupil then travelled back with the guest to stay in their home in Austria for a week. Pamela was eager to take part in the scheme, so I filled in the application forms and paid the deposit.

I now found among the correspondence awaiting me, a letter from the Anglo-Austrian Society. The remainder of the fee was due as the trip was almost upon us. The problem was that I did not have the money to pay the remaining amount. Harold had cut off my bank account and I had no access to cash.

I once again went to see our bank manager, to ask him to let me have our bankbook. As before, he refused me. His excuse this time was that the book had been signed over to the bank as security for the business. My husband was making sure that I had no access to money.

I discussed this with Mam and Dad and they said they would phone Harold and ask him for the money. They thought, as I did, that it was very wrong that Pamela should suffer for what we had done, and Dad said he would tell Harold just that. Dad then told me after he had spoken to my husband that Harold was willing to pay the money but he would send it direct to the Anglo-Austrian Society. Dad told Mam and myself that Harold had had the audacity to tell him that I was making up an excuse to get money out of him. I had no intention of letting Pamela take part in the scheme and wanted the money for myself! Harold wanted the details of where to send the money.

Dad told me he was furious with Harold that he could make such terrible allegations against me, but he said that it was not worth arguing about as long as Pamela could go on the trip. I gave him the details to give to Harold.

The Society then sent me a letter saying that as they had been informed that I was a single-parent family, the proposed child guest could not stay with me. Pamela could still go to Austria and stay with the proposed visitor and her family, but the scheme was really only intended for regular two-parent families. The proposed guest came from Vienna and would be placed with another Leeds family.

My husband had told them our situation when he sent the money. Pamela was very disappointed, but she could at least take a trip to Vienna. Her travelling details were given. She had to join the travelling party at a numbered platform at Victoria Station, in London, at 11.15 a.m. on that particular date in August.

I now had a few days to get her ready and pack. I would have to take her down to the station. It would mean travelling down the night before. I at least had a credit card. It was still viable, I hoped.

The day before we were due to travel to London, I went out shopping to get some last-minute items. After tea, Pamela and I started packing. I collected all the things Pamela wanted to take with her and laid them out in the lounge. The case was on the floor. I had packed about half the items into the case, with Pamela's help, when at around seven o'clock, my husband drew up in his car outside the house. My mother was sitting in the front passenger seat.

My husband got out of the car and ran down the drive into my house. My mother remained in the car. The door was unfortunately unlocked so he was able to come into the house. He grabbed Pamela by the arm and told her that her grandma wanted her in the car, so she ran out and climbed into the car. Harold picked up the suitcase, as it was, half-packed, leaving the rest of Pamela's things behind. I watched him trying to close the case as he ran out to the car. In a flash, he had driven off with Pamela, leaving me bewildered, perplexed. I could not understand what had happened.

I must have stood around dazed, and then wandered around the lounge for several minutes trying to make sense of what had happened. Then I rang Mam, thinking that Harold had taken Pamela there. Mam had just got in. She told me that Harold had just dropped her off, and had then driven away with Pamela. She sounded as bewildered as I was at what had happened and the speed of it all. I told her I was coming down, and drove like a lunatic to my mother's. Anne and Ruth were upstairs in their bedrooms, so I left them there.

Mam told me that Harold had come to tell her that I was refusing to let Pamela go on the trip, and he wanted her to help. If Pamela saw her in the car, she would go to her and then he could take her away. I explained that nothing was further from the truth. I was actually packing and getting Pamela ready to go. My mother then realised that she had been used, had been duped. She was terribly angry. We had become used to my husband's lies, but this was outrageous. We believed even more so that he really was insane. I had no idea where my darling daughter was.

I told Mam that I would go to London all the same, the next day. It was the only way I could be sure as to whether Pamela was going to be on the boat train to Vienna. If not, then I knew what the next step would have to be. I would have to call in the police. Mam said she would look after my other two girls. I still had the credit card. I hoped fervently that it was still valid, and had not been cancelled. Mam gave me a few pounds cash.

I travelled down by train the next day, having booked into a hotel in Bloomsbury for the one night. Once I had checked into the hotel, I spent most of the day on the phone. I knew Harold had a friend in the London area, an insurance colleague, and I had his phone number. I hoped he might know where Harold and Pamela were. None of my phone calls were answered. This made me even more despondent.

Immediately after breakfast, I made my way by Tube to Victoria Station, to the departure platform and waited. It was then half past ten. I sat with my eyes watching for Pamela, and any sign of the group. Around eleven o'clock, I saw what looked like the group I was waiting for start to congregate. I was starting to get agitated, when at quarter past eleven, I saw Pamela approaching with her father. They were accompanied by the gentleman friend whom I had been trying to contact the previous day.

I ran up to them, delighted and very relieved. I told Harold I had been trying to get in touch with him. He replied that he and Pamela had stayed overnight with this friend, but denied hearing the phone ring. He introduced his friend to me, though very reluctantly. I think he was too surprised by my unexpected appearance. The point was that Pamela was safe and was going to get on the boat train to go to Vienna and have a lovely time after all.

After checking in with the party organisers, and after lots of hugs and kisses, I watched Pamela get on the train with everyone in the party. I waited as the train drew out of the station. Harold waited with me. He agreed to accompany me back to Leeds. The train journey was most uncomfortable, with little conversation, and I was glad to get back home, in view of my husband's surliness. We parted at the end of the train journey in Leeds station.

One week later exactly, Anne asked me if she could take Ruth swimming to the Westgate baths in town. It was the school holidays, and I was happy for them to do so. They went out during the morning. The day was passing and it was not until late afternoon that Anne returned home, accompanied by a lady I had never met. Ruth was not with them. Anne was clearly frightened and agitated.

The lady then introduced herself as Mrs Crooke. She went on to explain that she was a social worker who had been called in to look after my children. Anne had gone to her for help as Ruth had disappeared, and Anne was frightened to come home and face me with the news. I was growing more and more afraid as the story went on. My girls had already met the social worker and I was puzzled as to what was going on. But Mrs Crooke suggested that I listen to what Anne had to tell me first.

Anne's story was that she had arranged to meet her cousin at the Ceylon Tea House in the Headrow, after swimming. She and Ruth were walking up the Headrow from the swimming pool and as they were approaching the Tea House, Daddy stopped in his car and told Ruth to get in. Anne then told us that her father had said that he was taking Ruth shopping and would be back in half an hour. He would bring Ruth back to the Tea House. Anne said she waited two hours but no one came back and she did not know what to do. She was too frightened to face me and so went to Mrs Crooke for help.

Mrs Crooke then told me that my husband had reported me to the Social Services for being an unfit mother, that I was negligent and ill-treated my children. Now that the social worker had met me and saw my home, she realised that she had been fed a pack of lies. She added that she had already met my girls, all behind my back. I told her a little about the way my husband had been ill-treating me. She had already spoken to my mother and knew that Mr Courtney was violent. Now, Mrs Crooke went on that the circumstances warranted I needed her support, and that she keep an eye on my girls and me.

There was nothing she could do for the moment about Ruth. Her father had a right to take his daughter shopping if that was what he was doing, so I was informed. I would just have to wait and see what happened. I was now out of my mind with worry.

Ruth never came home that day. Then the following day, late in the afternoon I received a phone call. It was from Ruth. She told me she was with her daddy but could not tell me any more as Daddy had made her promise not to tell me anything. When I asked her where she was, she repeated that she had not to say. I then got an even more earth-moving shock. I recognised Pamela's voice. Pamela was with Ruth and her father. It was a very brief conversation, just to tell me they would ring again tomorrow.

I was devastated. I had no idea how Pamela came to be with Ruth. I had seen her off on the boat train to Vienna. She was not due home for several days and yet she was with her father. Not only that, but they had been sworn to secrecy as to their whereabouts. I was so dreadfully worried, I really feared for their safety. That to me meant they were missing and in danger, and I decided to call the police.

Two police officers, one a woman, came, and were most sympathetic when they heard my story. They then said they would go and talk to the father's parents and see if they knew anything. They returned a little while later and reported that they had been told by my in-laws, that my husband had taken the girls on holiday. As there was no legal separation and no court order to the contrary, the girls' father was entitled to take them where he liked, with or without my permission. I explained his violent character, but was told that none of us could do anything about it for the moment. They suggested I made the children Wards of Court to prevent this sort of thing recurring.

I was left to wait around and go out of my mind. I heeded the police officers' advice and rang my original solicitors, but could not get an appointment for a couple of weeks. I urged them to reconsider under the circumstances, but I had to be disappointed. I was demented with worry, and Anne was no better.

The next day, I received a second phone call from the girls. They repeated that they had been instructed not to tell me anything other than that they were in the south of England. They were going to be there for another ten days and they would not be able to ring me any more until they were ready to come home. They would ring me and tell me when to expect them. I thought I would die from the anxiety. I just could not think how I was going to cope, how I was going to get through the next week or so. The pain was excruciating, unbearable. I could not bear to be in the house not knowing where my children were or what they were doing. I was helpless. Of all the terrible things I had already been through to me it was the worst form of torture I had ever had to endure.

I remembered Mam and Dad had gone to Blackpool, and decided there and then to join them. I told Anne to help me pack our bags as we were going away for the week. I told her why. At least I had Anne with me. The whole situation was so unbearable. And I still had my credit card.

I drove as far as Preston and then I had second thoughts. How could I explain to my parents what had happened to their grandchildren? It would tear them apart, like it was doing to me. They had come to hate Harold and were continually worried for their grandchildren. I did not want to spoil their holiday, so I changed my mind and decided to go to Southport.

I was able to get accommodation in one of the resort's larger hotels for a week for Anne and myself. How I ever got through that week, I never knew, even being away from home. Every day was like a year.

The whole seven days were a total blur, the children occupied my mind the whole time. There are no words sufficient to describe the torment and horrendous despair I was going through. I began to wonder if I would really ever see Pamela and Ruth again.

I had to get back home at the end of the week, and just prayed and prayed. I did not even bother with the post that was waiting for me. One day back, and the phone rang. The girls could tell me they would be home in two days. Two more days! Two more weeks! Two more years! It was all the same to me. The time seemed never-ending.

Two more days and they did come home. Their father dropped them off outside the house. No one could have been happier or more relieved to see her children than me on that day.

Mrs Crooke came round. She had been kept up to date with the turn of events and felt that we all needed her continued support. Once the children had settled down, I started to hear Pamela's version of what happened. She was at first reluctant to give any details, but with Mrs Crooke's compassionate assistance, she let us have her story in dribs and drabs.

She had been very unhappy from the start. She was introduced to her Austrian hostess on the train, but the girl would not speak to her, only when she had to. Pamela said she tried to be friendly towards her, but the girl did not want to know. She could speak some English, sufficient to get by. Once the two girls reached the hostess's home the hostility escalated. Pamela told us that the girl's family were lovely and tried to make her feel welcome, but the daughter kept up her campaign to make Pamela miserable. The girl was angry that she had been unable to stay with us in England, and was taking it out on Pamela. Pamela said she could not stand it.

She told us that her father found out about it, although she had not contacted him, and he made arrangements for her to go home. I could not get any answers for a while as to how her father knew. The day he had met the girls in town and disappeared with Ruth, he was actually on his way to meet Pamela off the boat train at London's Victoria Station. He did not have the decency to inform any of us about Pamela's troubles and his plans on that score.

He had taken both girls from London to Bournemouth, and they had stayed at the Royal Baths Hotel, a five-star hotel in the centre of the town. I knew why he had chosen that hotel and asked the girls if their dad went to the casino there. They told me he was on the tables there all the time. His gambling on the roulette wheel had become more frequent and time-consuming since coming back to Leeds from Sunderland.

I was more and more convinced now that the whole escapade was a means of getting back at and hurting me. It was a lucky coincidence for him that had enabled him to disappear with the girls at that time.

Mrs Crooke now asked me to call her by her first name, Merlynne. Then she related to me how my husband learned of Pamela's plight. Anne told her that when she and Ruth told me they were going to the swimming pool, they had already arranged to meet their father. A couple of days before, Anne had seen a letter arrive at our home. It was addressed to me, and was from Pamela in Vienna. Anne took it to her father instead of handing it to me. In the letter, Pamela had described her unhappiness, saying she wanted to come home. Harold had then arranged with the Anglo-Austrian Society to have Pamela brought home immediately. No wonder Anne was frightened to come home that day, and could not tell me the truth. Her betrayal in taking a letter addressed to me to her father resulted in all of us having to endure untold suffering with her father taking advantage of the situation. Thankfully, I was reunited with my girls and we were all glad to be back safe together.

Even though I was now separated from my husband, his scheming never stopped. I felt as though, over the past few years, I had been dragged through a constant series of emotional quagmires, to which there was no end. There was, it seemed, only one way to end it all. In fact, in trying to stop him, I was yet to learn just how bad his cunning and deception was to get.

Chapter 83

It was now time I dealt with the mail that had been accumulating since I had been away from home, and I was to face up to my husband's trickery at its worst.

Opening an envelope, I could see that the correspondence was from my husband's solicitor. I had been sent an injunction, the purpose of which, I deduced from its contents, was to prevent me from having anything to do with Courtney & Co. I surmised that my husband was worried that I might poach business from him, or go into business for myself. I was ordered not to contact, in any way, all policy-holders, insurance companies, solicitors, accountants, or anyone to do with the company at 12, East Parade, Leeds, under penalty of imprisonment.

The whole document seemed ludicrous to me. Many of my family and friends, including my parents and both brothers, were policy-holders. Did my husband really think he could stop me from seeing, or phoning them? I could think of no way in which the injunction was going to affect my life. Neither was I in any position to go into business for myself. I dismissed that injunction as an irrelevance and chose to ignore it. I was never advised that I could contest it, at least not until many years later. It never occurred to me that I should contest it. It was never enforced.

A second letter from Mr Courtney's solicitor was more important and did require me taking action on it. It was my husband's divorce petition against me. It had, as far as I could tell, been drawn up whilst I was in hospital. Thoughts of starting divorce proceedings for the third time had crossed my mind, but being in hospital and then the problems over my girls had of necessity delayed my intentions to see a solicitor about a divorce.

My husband must have realised that he had gone too far this time and there was never going to be another reconciliation, so he had seized his opportunity to get his petition in first. Not only was he to get his petition in first, but he was to try and make sure that he was going to delay any response from me for as long as possible.

His grounds for divorce were the same as my previous, second application, namely 'irretrievable breakdown'. Two reasons were given.

The first stated that I objected to his friendship with three ladies: Barbara Wright, his secretary Jean, and Rose Hardy. I found this ludicrous. Of course I objected to his friendship with Miss Wright. The reasons have been well documented in this autobiography. I had never objected to Jean. In fact, I think we would have been good friends in other circumstances, away from my spouse.

When I told Rose Hardy that Harold had mentioned her in his divorce petition, she responded, as I expected, that she was no longer a friend of his, in view of his behaviour to me, and was too disgusted to want anything more to do with him. She added that she was very disappointed in him. In fact we became even closer friends, meeting from time to time until her early demise two years later.

The second reason given I found exceedingly laughable: whenever he had a heart attack, I always ignored him and left him lying on the floor.

It seemed a stupid reason on the face of it. I wondered if my husband had described his 'heart attacks' to his solicitor, or told him how very numerous and farcical they were. His attempts at acting would have fooled no one, but his solicitor had used these, all the same.

My next move would be to take this petition up with a solicitor. I thought I would go back to my original solicitor at Fox, Hayes & Co. An appointment for a couple of days later was made.

Anne came with me and on our arrival at the office we were met by Colin Frazer, the principal. I showed him my husband's divorce papers. He produced yet another bolt out of the blue. Neither he nor anyone in the practice could act for me. When I asked why, he answered as though I should know why. He put it to me that I had sent a letter of complaint as to the manner in which his company had carried out my earlier divorce action.

I was baffled. I knew nothing about this and told Colin this. He refused to believe me, and then produced the offending letter. One glance, and I knew where that had come from. The complaint had been written on Courtney & Co letterheaded paper, and bore what appeared to be my signature. I repeated that I had nothing to do with the letter and had never written it. It was obvious to me that this was my husband's doing. Colin Frazer still refused to accept my denial, and insisted that he could not act for me. I begged him to reconsider as I had this petition to deal with. He answered that there was no more to be said. I would have to go elsewhere. Anne had watched and heard all that was said.

I went home feeling very angry and dejected. I had been subjected to more of my husband's trickery, producing a document bearing another forged signature. Over the next week or so, I phoned solicitors whose names were familiar. The reply from all was that they did business with my husband and could not take on my case.

I did eventually get an appointment with one solicitor, who will have to remain anonymous. The interview started from the very beginning with a demand for £3,000 cash up-front as a deposit. And that was just for starters, I was informed. I did not have such a sum, but I had never been asked for a deposit by any solicitor, ever. This was outrageous and I told him so and walked away. The solicitor was not long afterwards struck off. This meant more delay to add to my anguish.

But I was still without any legal representation. In desperation, and without an appointment, I went back to see Colin Frazer. He did speak to me, and enlightened me that he had since received a second letter of complaint, written in the same manner. No way could he take me on. I protested that I could never have written any such letters. I had not been in my husband's office for some time, and certainly not at the times when those two letters were sent. I argued that I would be a fool to send such letters and still expect Mr Frazer to act for me. He then told me that he did now believe me, but he still could not act for me. Instead, he would refer me to a solicitor friend. He then phoned this solicitor and arranged an appointment for me, much to my relief.

I had used a different solicitor for each of my two previous divorce actions, and had now decided to return to the first solicitor, our family solicitor, for this latest petition. I wondered why my husband had sent his letter of complaint to the very solicitor whom I had now decided to have act for me.

My new solicitor proved very helpful. He told me that I did not need to present my own petition if I was not going to defend Harold's, that is if I was going ahead with the divorce. I did not have to go to court. I still had feelings for my husband, I am now ashamed to admit, but I could never go back to him, not this time, after all the terrible things he had done to me, and was still trying to do. He was a Dr Jekyll and a Mr Hyde, a bullying control freak, and I had to end our marriage.

We discussed the last horrendous attack on me, and I told my solicitor that I wanted to sue all the attackers, my husband and his family. The solicitor sympathised very strongly with me but he thought that it was an unwise step to take in light of my poor health. From what he knew of my husband and his family, they would try every dirty deed possible in court. It would become a long protracted affair, and although he knew I was an innocent victim, my health in its very fragile state would not stand up to a long arduous court case. It would be suicide. I had to agree with this advice. I was still in a very nervous and anxious state and I needed to avoid any more aggravation. At least I would not have to go to court for the time being. This was to become the story of my life for a long time. My poor health was to prevent me doing many things, which was to be regretted, but I had no choice.

The divorce proceedings now went full steam ahead.

Chapter 84

Now that it was official that the divorce was going ahead, other problems arose. I had had forms to claim for my ring lost in Yugoslavia. The insurance company wanted the receipts for the ring to process my claim. Harold had taken all receipts and put them in the safe in his office. I phoned him to ask him to let me have them. He refused. I asked the insurance company if they could make the claim without the receipt. I explained the circumstances, but they insisted on having a receipt. It was to be many months before I was to get my receipt.

Ruth was very friendly with a school chum, Geoff. They would go cycling together round the block on an evening after school, and sometimes at the weekend. They were very happy children and enjoyed each other's company. Geoff came to see Ruth at that time and told her that his parents, who were well known to me, had told him that he could not play with Ruth any more as her parents were separated and getting a divorce. He told Ruth that he was going on holiday for two weeks and would still come and see her when he came home.

He did come and see Ruth two weeks later, when he got back, but it was to tell her that his parents had demanded that he could not play with her any more. They never did.

I could not have been more angry. I thought what cruel people his parents were to hurt two eleven-year-olds because the friend's parents were getting a divorce. Needless to say, I could have nothing more to do with such people.

Now the worst problem that I had to face had happened. My credit card was stopped. I had no access to any money at all. I phoned Harold to ask why. I needed money for the children at least. He did not want to know.

I had made arrangements for Ruth to go to Habonim camp for a week in the middle of August. Habonim is a Jewish youth organisation. The campsite was near Eccleshall, in Staffordshire, and the group from Leeds travelled together, so I had no problems in seeing her leave with the others from Moortown Corner. I was troubled that there would be a repetition of my husband's recent behaviour with my girls, and he would take her away again. My solicitor had tried to reassure me that Harold would not attempt that again, as it could prejudice any application for access to the girls that he might make, but I could not get the idea out of my head.

The following afternoon, he turned up at my parents' home. I happened to be at their house. He told my folks that the reason he wanted a divorce was because his mother had been onto him to prove to us and to me especially that he could run his business without me. He could manage well enough on his own. His mother had been onto him! It was laughable, but it did confirm what I had always believed, that she, in particular, had been perpetually jealous of the fact that I was responsible for her son's success. Mrs Cohen could not accept the fact that she had done very little for her son, and that he would never have got anywhere on his own. I knew in my heart that my husband could not have got anywhere on his own, without me, because of certain features that he lacked, particularly in his upbringing, which has been described elsewhere in this history.

My father then challenged Harold on his behaviour towards me and in particular his affair with White. My husband categorically denied any such affair. Dad produced a *Sidur*, a prayer book, and asked him to swear on the *Sidur* that there had been no affair. Dad passed the prayer book to Harold. In front of my mother, myself and my father, this man, whom I, myself, had seen in bed with the woman, as well as everything else we knew to be true, got down on one knee, and in true Harold Courtney dramatic style swore on the *Sidur*, saying that he had never had any affair with that woman.

We were all disgusted with him. We all knew the truth, and the fact that he could go on lying on the prayer book put him well beneath all our contempt. The man just could not help himself. As the doctors had told me so many times, I had married a pathological liar. Dad asked him to repeat himself on the *Sidur* as we knew he was lying. Harold did so in the same dramatic way.

This episode so upset me that I became distraught with worry that he would go to Ruth's camp and do something silly. So I decided I had to go and make sure she was all right. I drove down to the campsite the next day and was happy to find that Ruth was safe. I spoke to the camp's leaders and advised them of the situation and that Ruth should not be allowed to leave the camp. She should come home with the entire group. We spoke to Ruth and advised her that she had not to leave the camp under any circumstances, and to come home with the group. She said she was enjoying herself and would not leave.

I may sound paranoid, but my children had to be protected at all costs. They were the most precious things on this earth and had been put through so much trauma already. I had to try and prevent any more.

My husband did go to the camp to see Ruth. He later told me that she was enjoying herself so much, he could not disturb her.

Still my problems continued to grow. I was now completely penniless, with three children to feed. Harold refused to let me have any money at all. Mam and Dad phoned him several times to ask him for money. He showed no feelings even for his children. I had always felt that he had very little feeling for his children, and used them whenever it suited him, to hit back at me. I had to resort to desperate tactics.

There were a number of grocery and greengrocery shops in the locality. I placed an order at each of these shops, one a week over the next few weeks, for food and supplies to be delivered to my home, sufficient to keep us going for the time being. I asked for the accounts to be sent to my husband. One by one, as he received the bills, he cancelled the accounts. By mid-October, there were no more shops in my area from where I could make an order. All this time I had no money for other things, clothes, school requirements and other normal everyday living expenses.

Dad repeatedly asked my husband to let me have some money, and still Harold refused.

Now I had no option but to go to Social Security and ask for help. I took Anne with me to their offices at Hume House in Leeds. When we both walked into the premises, we were both shocked at the decrepit state the place was in. I asked at the counter for attention and was asked to wait. The clerk disappeared. We waited and waited, sitting on rickety, uncomfortable chairs. I felt like a tramp. I was being treated like one.

Anne then turned to me and cried, 'Is this what Dad has made us come down to? How could he do this to us?'

My darling daughter was distraught. My heart went out to her. I felt the same way, but tried to hide it from her. She could not believe that her father could let us have to resort to this, wait in a filthy office for money to keep body and soul together.

We were eventually seen and interviewed. I was then told I would get some money through the post. When it did eventually arrive, I found I had been awarded about £7 a week for my three children and myself. Not long after that, on the Thursday, I found a parcel on my doorstep. It turned out to be half a chicken. My husband must have had his conscience pricked, or so I thought at the time, and had come to some arrangements with a local poulterer to send me some of his cheap leftover chicken, because that was how the chicken looked and smelt. It was horrible.

For the next month or so, every Thursday I found a parcel with a half a chicken on my doorstep. And on most weeks it was so rotten, it was unfit for cooking. I had to throw it out.

I learnt at a later date that the Social Security had contacted my husband and asked him to repay the money that was sent to me. He maintained that he had been giving me money, and to prove how good he was to me, he had ordered the chickens to be sent to me.

In the middle of November, I received my Decree Nisi. The court had also made an interim maintenance order for £120 per month, the final settlement to be sorted out in early 1973.

My Decree Absolute was delivered to me six weeks later, on 29th December 1972.

Chapter 85

Certain issues had now to be settled. The first one to be dealt with was the matter of custody and access concerning the girls. When I told my mother that I had an appointment to see my solicitor to discuss these arrangements for the girls, she insisted on coming with me. She vowed that she would do anything to prevent that now ex-husband getting his hands on my girls. I went along with that, sure enough.

At the meeting, my solicitor explained that arrangements would be decided for my two younger girls, Pamela and Ruth, at a court hearing. Anne was no longer a minor as she was 17, and was free to live with whomsoever she chose.

He put it to us that in order to avoid unnecessary trauma for the girls in them having to appear in court, he would take a sworn affidavit from them in which they would tell us their wishes, who they wanted to live with, and whether they wished any contact with the other parent. Anything to avoid my girls going to court was extremely welcome to us all. A further meeting was arranged when I would bring the girls and they could tell the solicitor what they wanted.

Mam came to this meeting as well. Both Pam and Ruth said they wanted to live with me, but still wished to see their father. This was all sworn in an affidavit which my solicitor was to present to the court.

Mrs Crooke, the social worker would also give her report at the custody and access hearing.

Merlynne Crooke had been in frequent contact with both my mother and myself. She had become a good friend to us both. A few days before the court hearing, which was to be held in the middle of January, 1973, Merlynne came to see me to reassure me that I had nothing to worry about. She told me that she was going to tell the court that she thought I was a wonderful mother, and how in spite of all that I had suffered, I was the most loving and caring mother she had ever had to work with. My two younger daughters, who were at the centre of the custody hearing, were very stable. I knew that Mam had put her fully in the picture as to how my former husband had ill-treated me, as at that time I found it very difficult to talk to strangers about all the violence I had had to suffer. The court hearing was held in closed court, which meant that Mam could not be present, very much to her displeasure. It started off as I had been advised. My solicitor read out the affidavit. Mrs Crooke read her report. She told the court exactly what she had told me, that I was a wonderful, loving and caring mother. She then added, in some detail, that she had found Mr Courtney to be a very mentally unstable person, totally unfit to be a father. The bombshell for me was that Merlynne then told the court that in fact Mr Courtney had asked for the girls to be put into care. She asked the court that custody be given to me, as she feared for the girls if their father was granted custody. He would have them put into care, and that was totally unwarranted.

At that, Mr Courtney jumped up in a temper, shouting abuse, and had to be restrained. His solicitor responded by telling the court that his client believed that Pamela and Ruth had been coerced into saying they wanted to live with their mother when Mr Courtney knew differently and wished to hear the girls tell him themselves in private with whom they wished to live. It was strongly pointed out to the court by my solicitor that he had produced the affidavit to avoid the girls being put under unnecessary stress, which is what would happen if they had to come to court. It also meant another hearing.

The judge was most sympathetic, stating that Mr Courtney could not speak to the girls himself, but he did order them to be brought to court and he, the judge, would speak to Pam and Ruth privately in his chambers.

I walked out of court feeling drained and exhausted. I had severe pains in my chest. A few moments later, I collapsed and found myself once more in Leeds General Infirmary. All the trauma of past events had again caught up with me. I still had colitis and learned that I had now lost another 3 stone, making a total of 6 stone, with no effort from me.

More tests revealed that I had gallstones, which would require an operation. Two days later I was allowed home, having been told I had been put on the waiting list for a gall bladder operation, an operation which had to be undergone a couple of months later as an emergency when I collapsed once more.

A date in the middle of February was arranged for the girl to be brought into court. Then the judge spoke to my two girls in private whilst the rest of us anxiously waited in the courtroom. Twenty minutes later, the judge came back into court to report that having

289

spoken to both Pamela and Ruth, he was satisfied that they wanted to live with their mother. They did still want to see their father.

The judge added that as the girls were old enough to know their own minds, it was in their best interests that the court order was made in my favour. Anne also chose to remain with me, so I had my girls safe home with me. Certain weekend visits were specified, but as far as I was concerned the girls were always free to see their father whenever they wanted. Nonetheless, my former husband persisted in lying and telling the girls that I was always trying to prevent them from seeing their father.

The court also decided my maintenance settlement now that the girls' future had been sorted out. For the three girls, who were all still at school, and myself, Harold was ordered to pay me a more reasonable, though still far from satisfactory, monthly sum. The final matter to be sorted was the property settlement. A meeting had been held earlier in the month between my ex-husband, our legal advisors, and myself to decide how the properties were to be allocated.

In my absence, Harold had been looking after the two properties that I had bought earlier in the year as investment properties. The house in Headingley had now been converted into five bedsits, but had not been let. Harold had not dealt with that side of the deal. The house in Harehills was all ready for occupation. A tenant had been found, but not given the go-ahead to move in. Harold was clearly reluctant to let the properties go.

At the court hearing, I was told I could keep the house I was living in, in the Brookhills, together with all its contents. The contents included a quantity of valuable items: ornaments, silver, antiques and other such objets d'art. During our several separations, my husband had been dabbling in antiques, especially clocks, which he had brought home, intending to sell at some time. These still remained in my home. All these were to be mine now and were all itemised in the court order.

Both investment properties were given to me. The Harehills house had to be given to me as an existing business, which meant it had to have a tenant when I took over. All these properties were to be conveyed to me as sole owner, free of all debts ('encumbrances') and mortgages. I was asked to choose the solicitor to do the conveyancing, there and then.

Harold could have the house that was being built at Shadwell Park, and all the furniture that was still in store, except for my grand piano, the Steinway. My piano was to be delivered back to me. I also asked for all the receipts for my jewellery and property that were in Harold's office to be given back to me. I hoped to be able to complete the claim for my lost topaz ring.

In spite of Harold being ordered to give the latter two groups of items to me, he ignored the court order and my subsequent repeated requests for them for a long time, until some eight months later my solicitor had to write to him threatening him with further action. He returned me the receipt for my ring, but continued to refuse to let me have my piano. Only then was I able to complete my claim and the insurance money for my ring was finally paid out to me. It was nearly a year before my piano was returned to me. Harold had kept it in store the whole time.

Although my now former husband managed to get his petition in first, I was partially vindicated when he was ordered to pay all costs of the case, including mine.

People automatically believe that a divorce is, and should be, the end to a couple's bad marriage and the couple's relationship. I learned that that is not possible where children are involved. And even more so with a control freak as was my former husband.

I resolved from the end of my marriage that I would never have anything more to do with my ex-husband except under exceptional circumstances where my girls were concerned. He was a pathological and very plausible liar, and I could never, ever believe a word he said. So the further away he kept from me, the better. It was this very point, his dreadful fabrications and subterfuges, together with his desire to keep control, that were to be unending, and which brought me perpetual aggravation and prolonged ill-health for more years to come than I wish to remember.

Even to the last, when he was dying, he still persisted in lying to his children, my daughters with his denial of all the violence and abuse he had inflicted on me.

Much of my now ex-husband's continued harassment, I believed, was motivated by his deep dissatisfaction with all the court order settlements.

Throughout all these ordeals the girls and I still had the love and loyalty of our dear beautiful Labrador dog, Troy, who had had a very happy 'dog's life'. This was to remain so until he was fourteen years old. But all that is for another time, and perhaps, another book.

The wonderful, caring and generous man I had married had ceased to exist a long time ago.